THINKING THROUGH FAIRBAIRN

THINKING THROUGH FAIRBAIRN
Exploring the Object Relations Model of Mind

Graham S. Clarke

LONDON AND NEW YORK

First published 2018
by Routledge
2 Park Square, Milton Park, Abingdon, Oxon OX14 4RN

and by Routledge
711 Third Avenue, New York, NY 10017

Routledge is an imprint of the Taylor & Francis Group, an informa business

Copyright © 2018 by Graham S. Clarke

The right of Graham S. Clarke to be identified as author of this work has been asserted by him in accordance with sections 77 and 78 of the Copyright, Designs and Patents Act 1988.

All rights reserved. No part of this book may be reprinted or reproduced or utilised in any form or by any electronic, mechanical, or other means, now known or hereafter invented, including photocopying and recording, or in any information storage or retrieval system, without permission in writing from the publishers.

Trademark notice: Product or corporate names may be trademarks or registered trademarks, and are used only for identification and explanation without intent to infringe.

British Library Cataloguing-in-Publication Data
A catalogue record for this book is available from the British Library

Library of Congress Cataloging-in-Publication Data
A catalog record has been requested for this book

ISBN: 978-1-78220-570-8 (hbk)

Typeset in Palatino LT Std
by Medlar Publishing Solutions Pvt Ltd, India

CONTENTS

LIST OF FIGURES AND TABLES   ix

ACKNOWLEDGEMENTS   xi

ABOUT THE AUTHOR   xiii

PREFACE   xv

INTRODUCTION
A new interpretation of Fairbairn's "psychology of dynamic structure"   xxv

PART I: SCOTTISH CONTEMPORARIES

CHAPTER ONE
Suttie's influence on Fairbairn's object relations theory   3

CHAPTER TWO
Fairbairn and Glover: object relationships and ego-nuclei   23

PART II: MULTIPLE PERSONALITY DISORDER

CHAPTER THREE
Fairbairn's thinking on dissociative identity disorder
and the development of his mature theory — 51

CHAPTER FOUR
Evelyn's PhD in Wellness—a Fairbairnian understanding of
the therapeutic relationship with a woman with dissociative
identity disorder — 73

PART III: FILM

CHAPTER FIVE
Failures of the "moral defence" in the films *Shutter Island*
(Scorsese, 2010), *Inception* (Nolan, 2010), and *Memento*
(Nolan, 2000): narcissism or schizoid personality disorder? — 97

CHAPTER SIX
Trauma, dissociation, and time distortion in some
"puzzle" films — 119

PART IV: RELATIONAL PSYCHOANALYSIS

CHAPTER SEVEN
A modest proposal: Fairbairn's psychology of
dynamic structure is not "between paradigms" but
already a synthesis of classical and relational thinking — 147

CHAPTER EIGHT
Fairbairn's object-relations-based psychology of dynamic
structure, as a synthesis of the classical (thesis) and
the relational (antithesis) in psychoanalytic theory — 165

PART V: INSTINCT, AFFECT, AND NEUROPSYCHOANALYSIS

CHAPTER NINE
The place of instincts and affects in Fairbairn's psychology
of dynamic structures — 183

CODA

CHAPTER TEN
Thinking through Fairbairn redux   209

REFERENCES   213

INDEX   225

LIST OF FIGURES AND TABLES

Figures

Figure 2.1.	Fairbairn's model incorporating the topographical categories	34
Figure 2.2.	Glover's diagram of libidinal primacies and ego-nuclei (redrawn)	35
Figure 2.3.	Glover's classification of mental disorders (redrawn)	41
Figure 2.4.	Representation of an object relationship for Fairbairn	44
Figure 2.5.	Early splitting of the ego and object for Fairbairn	44
Figure 2.6.	Development of basic endopsychic structure for Fairbairn	45
Figure 2.7.	The developed model of inner reality based on Fairbairn	46
Figure 3.1.	Fairbairn's original diagram (1944) (redrawn)	64
Figure 3.2.	Fairbairn's endopsychic structure and Freud's topographic categories	67
Figure 3.3.	Trauma-induced vertical splitting of dynamic structures (1)	70

Figure 3.4. Trauma-induced vertical splitting and duplication of endopsychic structure (1)	71
Figure 4.1. Trauma-induced vertical splitting of dynamic structures (2)	82
Figure 4.2. Trauma-induced vertical splitting and duplication of endopsychic structure (2)	86
Figure 6.1. Fairbairn's original diagram (1944) (redrawn)	122
Figure 9.1. Panksepp's diagram	203

Tables

Table 2.1. Comparison of Fairbairn and Glover's developmental schemas	33
Table 2.2. Key to Figure 2.2	36
Table 2.3. Key to Figure 2.3	42
Table 2.4. Expansion of Figure 2.3	43

ACKNOWLEDGEMENTS

I would like to thank my friend, Paul Finnegan, the co-author of the papers from which Chapters Three and Four were derived, for his generous help in the preparation of this book.

I would also like to thank my wife Sandra for her support and encouragement throughout the process of developing this book and beyond.

I would like to thank the *Journal of the American Psychoanalytic Association* for allowing me to reproduce my paper on Fairbairn and Suttie (2011) as Chapter One of the present volume.

I would like to thank Karnac for allowing me to reproduce two papers co-authored with Paul Finnegan that appeared in *Attachment* (2011, 2012) as Chapters Three and Four of this volume.

I would like to thank the *International Journal of Psychoanalysis* for allowing me to reproduce my paper on failures of the "moral defence" in some films (2012) as Chapter Five of this volume.

Permissions

Journal of the American Psychoanalytic Association—Suttie chapter (Chapter One) (*Journal of the American Psychoanalytic Association, 58*: 5, Oct 2011, pp. 939–960.)

International Journal of Psychoanalysis—For permission to quote extensively from Fairbairn (1941) IJPA, 22 (3, 4) in Chapter Two.

Attachment—MPD/DID chapters (Chapters Three and Four) (*Attachment: New Directions in Psychotherapy and Relational Psychoanalysis, 5*: 2 (2011) (*Attachment: New Directions in Psychotherapy and Relational Psychoanalysis, 6*: 1 (2012) London: Karnac.)

International Journal of Psychoanalysis Film (Chapter Five)—Clarke, G. S. (2012) Failures of the "moral defence" in the films *Shutter Island, Inception and Memento*: Narcissism or schizoid personality disorder? *The International Journal of Psychoanalysis, 93*: 203–218. (Copyright 2011 Institute of Psychoanalysis. Int J Psychoanal (2012) 93.)

ABOUT THE AUTHOR

Graham S. Clarke, PhD, is Visiting Fellow at the Centre for Psychoanalytic Studies, University of Essex, and author of *Personal Relations Theory: Fairbairn, Macmurray and Suttie* (Routledge, 2006). Translated and published in German by Psychosozial-Verlag as *Theorie persönlicher Beziehungen* (2017). He was the lead editor (with co-editor David Scharff) for the 'Lines of Development' series entitled *Fairbairn and the Object Relations Tradition* (Karnac, 2014).

PREFACE

The title, "Thinking through Fairbairn", is meant to evoke at least two possible approaches to the work of Ronald Fairbairn that have been part of my own project since I first read about him and encountered his theory. At root, it means trying to think Fairbairn's theory through in its entirety. His theory was always under development to some degree, unfinished despite his best efforts. During this process of "thinking it through" I hope to offer some clarifications of the theory and explore its logical consequences. The title also means to make use of Fairbairn's theory, to understand the ways in which we come to be who we are, and the consequences for our understanding of how we might be better than we are, and how the theory might be applicable to wider issues, in particular the application of Fairbairn's theory to an object relations understanding of psychoanalysis, a new metapsychology.

I have been aware of Fairbairn and engaged with his work for nearly thirty years now. My introduction to Fairbairn's theory came through Neville Symington's *Introductory Lectures to the Tavistock* (1986). Following the advice of John Padel (1991), one of Fairbairn's most sympathetic interpreters, I subsequently read Fairbairn's oeuvre including his only book, *Psychoanalytic Studies of the Personality* (1952). What struck me most about Fairbairn's work was the dynamic system of persons in relation that underpinned his endopsychic hypothesis, which resonated with both my own experience and my previous reading of R. D. Laing (1965) and Gregory Bateson (1972). I subsequently spent a considerable period in trying to understand his model of endopsychic structure and in trying to develop it, in the direction that it seemed to be heading; that of a properly systems-based understanding of the dynamics of inner and outer reality and their interrelationship. One part of this process was to think through Fairbairn's model, which in his original diagram included the Freudian topographical features, and to find a way of integrating Fairbairn's dynamic structure approach (model) with Freud's topographical approach (model). I did this by suggesting the existence of preconscious libidinal and antilibidinal dyadic structures alongside the preconscious, ideal, dyadic structure that Fairbairn included in his original model (Clarke, 2005).

My earlier education in Architecture and later in Computing suited my predilection for visual and dynamic structural representations of those systems that I was engaged in studying, modelling or developing— indeed, in seeing the world as a whole as a hierarchy of nested systems and structures. This was also consistent with my interest in dialectical materialism, which later became an interest in critical realism (Bhaskar, 1978). This interest in a systems approach to all problems was developed in part by my exposure to the work of Buckminster Fuller while studying Architecture at University College London between 1961 and 1964 and his noble aim of helping to develop a "Comprehensive Anticipatory Design Science" as an extension of the architect's calling.

As I struggled to get a clear understanding of Fairbairn's thinking through his book *Psychoanalytic Studies of the Personality* I had a sense of excitement, wonder, and perplexity. And it struck me as I read Fairbairn that a favourite quotation of mine, from Nietzsche, was totally apposite to Fairbairn's work whatever his own intentions were.

> ... my ambition to say in ten sentences what everyone else says in a book—what every one else *does not* say in a book ... (Nietzsche, 1968)

My first attempts to use Fairbairn's theory were in trying to develop an object relations approach to cinema (Clarke, 1994) an enterprise that I am still engaged in, which is complex and not at all intuitive. At the time I wrote that paper I was thinking of training to become a clinician, a psychodynamic psychotherapist, and went into analysis with Ken Wright anticipating the development of a suitable training course at the University of Essex. However, the psychodynamic psychotherapy training at Essex was not developed until several years later and I entered the M.A. in Psychoanalytic Studies programme of the Tavistock Clinic run jointly with the University of East London in 1994 under the leadership of Meira Liekermann and Barry Richards, one of the many new courses on psychoanalytic studies developed in British universities during the 1990s.

I had been interested in how Fairbairn's theory might be able to throw light on the ways that dramatic narrative in any medium might work. This led to my taking Fairbairn's theory of art (Fairbairn, 1938a, 1938b)—developed before his paradigm changing work of the 1940s, and, in particular, the application of his theory of dreams as short films of the dynamics of inner reality (Fairbairn 1944, p. 77)—into account for an understanding of film (Clarke, 1994, 2003a, 2012).

While studying at the Tavistock in 1994 and 1995 I tried to develop my understanding of Fairbairn in relation to both Freud and other object relations thinkers like Klein and Winnicott. I focused on using Fairbairn to understand dramatic narrative as an extension to my work on understanding film and produced Fairbairn-inspired analyses of *The Little Mermaid* and, more substantially, *The Singing Detective*. It was during this period that I became more aware of the important and distinctive differences between Fairbairn's object relations theory and that of Melanie Klein and had the opportunity to discuss these differences in detail.

While doing my PhD in Psychoanalytic Studies at the University of Essex between 1997 and 2002, I became aware that Fairbairn's work had emerged from a Scottish milieu, and of the influence on him of important Scottish thinkers like Ian D. Suttie and John Macmurray (Clarke, 2006). In my doctoral research I was trying to provide a synthesis of Fairbairn's theory, including parts of his work that had never been updated in the light of his developed object relations theory, which is based upon a complex endopsychic structure. I was also keen to provide a comprehensive introduction to his model based upon his major works and including his one page account of his theory in *International Journal of Psychoanalysis* (IJPA) (1963). There is no doubt that this complex and dynamic personal system, which is never at rest and continues to mediate between the outer social world and the inner world of affects, is difficult to make sense of and to internalise. I did for a long time toy with the idea of producing an animation of the located dynamics of the inner world, which would still be useful pedagogically, but I satisfied myself with a number of diagrammatic attempts to capture the important stages of growth of the endopsychic structure and its subsequent behaviour. This was itself a novel approach to Fairbairn's theory and, given the "multiple intelligences" that people use (Gardner, 1983), an alternative to verbal descriptions of the same processes. As far as I am concerned, there is, in general, a lack of diagrammatic or visual material in most papers on metapsychology and psychoanalysis. I would like to add that during my doctoral research I was greatly encouraged and helped by Fairbairn's daughter Ellinor Fairbairn Birtles and by my supervisor Joan Raphael-Leff.

I edited my PhD dissertation to produce a book-length introduction to Fairbairn within a Scottish context—that is, read along with his relationship to Suttie and Macmurray, which I called *Personal Relations Theory*, the title being based upon a comment made by Fairbairn. I subsequently made an attempt to draw out the full complexity of the endopsychic structure diagram as the description of a universal system applicable to everyone, since I had discovered during my research that there were a lot of people who thought of the model as being generated anew every time one met a new person. The idea of a systems approach, of there being one complex multi-agent system of persons-in-relation at the heart of all of our selves, seemed both unfamiliar and difficult to understand for many people. It was my perception of this difficulty and the feedback I got from students to whom I introduced Fairbairn that led me to look in greater detail at Fairbairn's diagram and in particular his use of Freudian topographical terms, and to try to find a new synthesis of these two approaches (Clarke, 2005).

Ellinor Fairbairn did warn me against such an endeavour when she read my paper, since Freud's understanding of the ego, the id and the super-ego were not consistent with Fairbairn's dynamic structures, precisely because of Freud's Helmholzian understanding of energy and structure that had been so roundly criticised by Fairbairn (Fairbairn, 1952, p. 126). Nevertheless I persisted in investigating the sort of modifications to Fairbairn's diagram that would be necessary if the topographical categories were included explicitly. A number of other interpreters of Fairbairn, including James Grotstein and David and

Jill Scharff, had mentioned the possibility of a preconscious libidinal and antilibidinal self (ego-object dyad) and this led to my redrawing the model to include these preconscious elements. This new model of Fairbairn's endopsychic structure became the basis of all of my further thinking about his theory.

Soon after the publication of my 2005 paper in IJPA I was contacted by Paul Finnegan, a Canadian analyst who specialised in treating cases of multiple personality disorder (MPD). Paul had read my paper and thought that the modified version of Fairbairn's endopsychic structure I had developed fitted his clinical experience of multiplicity well, and invited me to collaborate with him in investigating the application of this model to MPD. This resulted in the publication of two co-authored papers, one on the degree to which Fairbairn's work was clearly directed towards understanding multiplicity consistently throughout his career (Clarke & Finnegan, 2011, see Chapter Three), and the other on applying the version of Fairbairn's model I had developed to a clinical understanding of multiplicity (Finnegan & Clarke, 2012, see Chapter Four).

In 2012 I was invited by Joan Raphael-Leff and Norka T. Malberg to consider the possibility of editing a book on Fairbairn in their *Lines of Development* series for Karnac. I thought about this briefly and then suggested that I ask David Scharff, who is one of the foremost contemporary interpreters of Fairbairn, to work with me on this and sent him an outline of the people I wanted to invite to contribute. David generously agreed to co-edit the book and made suggestions as to additional people to invite. This was an ambitious list and neither of us thought that we would get the response we did, but, happily, most of the people we asked responded favourably and we managed to edit together a wide and representative sample of contributions to Fairbairn scholarship (Clarke & Scharff, 2014). Our intention was to allow for as catholic a range of contributions as possible.

It was during this process that I became aware of some of the unresolved issues between different groups of scholars and analysts concerning their understanding of Fairbairn's theory, his model, and its relationship to other traditions—for example, the relational. With the considerable help of Ivan Ward and David Scharff a conference at the Freud Museum was run in 2014 to launch the book. The conference was successful, but it was clear that there was no unanimity about aspects of Fairbairn's theory. For instance, the whole question of the origin and development of the good object, a question that had been rumbling around since Fairbairn first published his book, remained a source of disagreement and tension. Similarly, the degree to which his fully developed model of endopsychic structure, which had been famously criticised by Stephen Mitchell—one of Fairbairn's greatest supporters otherwise—was also subject to different and, in my view, generally mistaken interpretations. Furthermore, there was a long-established difference between Fairbairn scholars regarding the process of psychic growth and change, with Rubens and Mitchell representing one side and John Padel the other. There is also a division between those supporters of Fairbairn who think his connection to Christianity is of primary significance and those who, like myself, think that this was an important influence but not the crux of his work, despite his deep connections with both Suttie and Macmurray. All of this was further complicated by the complex theorising based in extensive clinical work of the Argentinian "Espacio Fairbairn", represented by Rubens Basili and Mercedes Campo, who were trying to link Fairbairn's theory to other clinical theories and build a new theoretical and therapeutic understanding of psychoanalysis. It was while editing one of their contributions to the book on Fairbairn that I first encountered a reference to the work of Edward Glover and his idea of ego-nuclei.

Later on I discovered that Edward Glover, who had been both a friend of Fairbairn and an important influence on his work, had a direct influence on Fairbairn's thinking, although neither man acknowledged the importance of this connection.

I knew that Glover had presented Fairbairn's crucially significant, but generally ignored, contribution to the Controversial Discussions (Fairbairn, 1943b) at the time when the whole question of unconscious phantasy and its understanding was being introduced for the first time by Susan Isaacs in the context of developing a Kleinian object relations theory (Hinshelwood in Palmer, 2015). I tried to access Glover's 1932 paper on the classification of mental disorders but was initially unable to find a copy. I remembered that Fairbairn had mentioned Glover in his 1941 paper and reread with interest his acceptance of Glover's theory, a point no mention of which found its way into Fairbairn's book when it was published in 1952. This seemed a little puzzling until I looked a bit more into aspects of the Controversial Discussions where Glover, who had been highly influential in the British Psychoanalytic Society (BPaS) for several years, was implacably opposed to aspects of Klein's theory building and resigned from the BPaS in 1944 over differences in the approach to the training of analysts. Both Glover and Fairbairn were singled out for special mention by Klein in her most widely read paper on schizoid mechanisms (Klein, 1946) where she explicitly rejects both Glover's ego-nuclei hypothesis and Fairbairn's psychology of dynamic structure, despite accepting Fairbairn's suggestion regarding the fundamental importance of the schizoid, which she used to modify her account of the earliest "position" to become the paranoid-*schizoid*. Her suggestion in this paper introducing projective identification as a major defensive technique can be seen as a modified version of Fairbairn's suggestion for understanding neuroses as involving certain transitional techniques (Fairbairn, 1941) based upon characteristic projections and introjections of internal objects.

I studied Glover's paper on the classification of mental disorders, in which he first put forward the ego-nuclei hypothesis, and discovered that he had published two books including detailed discussion of this hypothesis. One was of collected papers (Glover, 1956) and the other was an attempt to re-present his idea of ego-nuclei (Glover, 1968), both of which include his 1932 paper and the diagrams he used there. When I looked in detail at the diagrams that he used in the 1932 paper it struck me that there were strong resonances with Fairbairn's endopsychic structure diagram and I looked for any critical or analytic references to the two men's models in the scholarly journals to no avail. Eric Rayner (1990) in his book on the Independents noted some similarities between the two models but went no further. As I read parts of Glover's *The Birth of the Ego* it seemed to me that Glover's viewpoint was very close to Fairbairn's, so I turned to making a detailed comparison of their diagrams. As I became more familiar with Glover's diagram and its dynamics, it began to be clear that this was indeed very similar to Fairbairn's diagram, and in particular to my development of it to include preconscious libidinal and antilibidinal structures. But Glover's diagram was based upon component instincts rather than object relationships. I decided to overlay Fairbairn's model of endopsychic structure, in the version of it that I had developed to include the topographic categories, onto Glover's own developmental model. To do this accurately required that I turn Glover's model, as represented in his books, upside down, at which point its isomorphism with Fairbairn's model became clear. It seemed to me that Klein's rejection of both Glover and Fairbairn was not just political, it was also based upon the fact that they were putting forward a model of development and internal reality that was essentially the same and represented a direct alternative to her own theory at the very origins of this new object relations approach to psychoanalysis. It is this model that gives the lie to the relational theorists' abandonment of a biological base to the self as a multi-agent system in the name of an overextension of the Fairbairnian notion of object relatedness as relatedness per se.

As mentioned above, during the Controversial Discussions, at a crucial time in the development of the object relations paradigm, Fairbairn, influenced by his understanding of Klein's theories, suggested that the conception of unconscious phantasy being developed by Susan Isaacs should be replaced by the idea of an inner reality consistent with his own theory of endopsychic structure.

> In my opinion the time is now ripe for us to replace the concept of "phantasy" by a concept of an "inner reality" peopled by the Ego and its internal objects. These internal objects should be regarded as having an organised structure, an identity of their own, an endopsychic existence and an activity as real within the inner world as those of any objects in the outer world. (Fairbairn, 1943b)

This suggestion was rejected at the time by Isaacs on behalf of the Kleinians but recent work by Ogden on Susan Isaacs's theory (2011) suggests that this rejection was based upon the internal politics of the British Psychoanalytic Society at the time. Crucial in this regard may have been Fairbairn's closeness to Edward Glover, who was virulently opposed to the direction that Klein's theories were taking the training of future psychoanalysts. In response to Ogden's paper on reading Fairbairn (Ogden, 2010a) Paul Finnegan and I sent a letter to the IJPA (Clarke & Finnegan, 2010) citing Fairbairn's suggestion for replacing unconscious phantasy with inner reality. Ogden's reply (2010b), which welcomed our intervention, agreed that "for Isaacs and Klein, internal objects are thoughts and impulses, not thinkers; while, for Fairbairn, internal objects are thinkers with impulses" (pp. 1002–1003). I believe that the substitution of inner reality, as understood by Fairbairn, for unconscious phantasy, as understood by Freud and Klein, is necessary for the full importance of Fairbairn's extended theory and its parallels with Glover's model to become apparent.

One significant development of Fairbairn's approach was his suggestion in his 1944 paper that dreams are like short films of the dynamics of endopsychic structures. As I continued to try to use Fairbairn's theory to interpret film I became aware that his theory of art, in particular the ideas of over and under symbolisation, along with the idea of an optimal symbolisation that satisfied both the need to pay respect to the demands of the ego-ideal on the one hand, whilst acknowledging the antilibidinal and destructive aspects of the film on the other, could be used to locate a film comparatively within a social milieu characterised by a conventional level of symbolisation. This reinterpretation of Fairbairn's theory of art, based in part upon his own later commentaries on other artists and analysts thinking about art, opened the way to an alternative interpretation of Fairbairn's theory as a whole and I built upon the conclusions that I drew in my earlier understanding of his theory of art and creativity to incorporate the dynamics of endopsychic structures as he conceived them into his theory of art (Clarke, 2006, Chapter 5).

I have introduced a number of novel ways of viewing Fairbairn's model of endopsychic structure all of which are grounded in a deep involvement with his work and many of which I would argue are implicit in the work itself. I think that my one omission is Fairbairn's understanding of the social dimension. I have written about the social in connection with critical realism (2003b, 2008a) and Fairbairn's thinking and its connection with the Scottish Enlightenment (2008b). I feel that critical realism is the political/philosophical approach closest to Fairbairn's theory but this is certainly not the last word about this subject by any means and I anticipate that I will have to return to this topic in the future in order to sustain the idea of a psychoanalysis that is based upon a bio-psycho-social understanding of persons.

In a talk that Zizek (56th minute to 62nd minute, 2015) gave at NYU he makes some comments on psychoanalysis through reference to an interview with Adam Philips. I think his conclusions are totally consistent with Fairbairn's understanding of mature dependence. These concern what he calls "stupid clichés about psychoanalysis". One is the idea that psychoanalysis is a form of self-knowledge and the second is that the aim of psychoanalysis is to diminish suffering. Zizek argues that Philips rejects both these common understandings of the psychoanalytic project. He argues that the goal of psychoanalysis is to be able to work productively for a cause in the real world, the point being to move away from concerns about the degree to which you are suffering or not, and to go beyond your own feelings to be able to devote yourself wholeheartedly to a noble cause. This seems to me to chime with Fairbairn's Aristotelean and Scottish sense that one can only flourish in a real engagement with the external world and the "polis" in which you live.

In an earlier book (Clarke, 2006) I suggested that personal relations theory, as an object relations paradigm, might constitute what Raymond Williams called a "structure of feeling" and it now seems to me that this concept might need to be supplemented by ideas of "embodied affect" (Rutherford, 2003). Thanks to Eleanore Armstrong-Perlman (personal communication) I have recently discovered that in 2000 Bernard Burgoyne edited a collection entitled *Drawing the Soul: Schemas and Models in Psychoanalysis*, which seems to have resonances with the approach adopted throughout this book. Unfortunately, I have not had time here to compare these approaches to my own, so this too is work for the future.

INTRODUCTION

A new interpretation of Fairbairn's "psychology of dynamic structure"

Fairbairn was widely recognised as being one of the foremost thinkers within psychoanalysis after his papers were published in the 1940s (1940, 1941, 1943, 1944, 1946, 1949), papers which later became core chapters of his book (1952). His critique of Freud's libido theory and the reorientation of the major motivational factor from a pleasure principle to object relatedness were paradigm shifting approaches to psychoanalytic theory and practice consistent with other thinkers in the field who had turned their attention to the mother-child relationship. In particular, these included Sandor Ferenczi and Ian Suttie but also included Fairbairn's contemporaries Melanie Klein, Donald Winnicott, and John Bowlby (Bowlby, 1988).

Trained philosophically, Fairbairn applied his considerable intellect in trying to make contemporary sense of Freudian metapsychology and was much helped by the Scottish thinkers by whom he was surrounded. It has become increasingly obvious to me that his work has to be read alongside the work of Suttie (1935), Macmurray (1957, 1961) and belatedly, on my part, Glover (1932)—all Scots, all inheritors of an Aristotelean conviction that we are social creatures from the very beginning, and that our flourishing is dependent upon and developed through our social relations and experience. I later wrote briefly about some significant Scottish Enlightenment precursors to the object relations tradition (Clarke, 2008b).

Using Fairbairn's own theory as a guide, it is possible to see his flourishing during the 1940s as a consequence of his antilibidinal self being reduced in its power by his being accepted as a full member of the British Psychoanalytical Society in 1939 and the death of Freud that same year. This might be seen to resonate with the death of his father in 1924 after which he changed from his father's church to his mother's church and began his training as a psychoanalyst (Sutherland, 1998, p. 9). These events can also be seen as helping to promote the development of his libidinal self, as he allowed himself to play with his developing ideas on metapsychology that he had been actively thinking about since the early 1930s. Through a number of papers written in the early 1940s this progressively developed into the fully fledged object relations theory that was a direct challenge to Freud, while it owed much to Freud. The idea of dissociated internal selves was there from the beginning in his M.D. thesis on Dissociation and Repression (1929b) and in his early clinical work where personifications were identified and their dynamics noted (1931). His work on art, the presentation of which resulted in his full membership of the British Psychoanalytic Society in 1939, uses Freudian language within what would become a Fairbairnian endopsychic structural approach. As I argue in Chapter Two, the development of Fairbairn's own revised psychopathology (1941) was based upon a reworking of Glover's (1932) classification of mental disorders. Fairbairn's idea that unconscious phantasy could be replaced by inner reality, delivered by Glover in 1943 during the Controversial Discussions, was paralleled by the refinement of his endopsychic model through his analysis of a dream of one of his patients and linked art-work and dream-work in new ways (Fairbairn, 1944). Nevertheless, this development of his theory, from the early nineteen forties into the late nineteen fifties, while it constituted his mature theory, was never completely worked through in all of its implications. Subsequent use of his theory, by relational thinkers in particular, while it preserved an interest in Fairbairn, did him a disservice, in my opinion, by trying to make his theory exclusively relational.

Process thinking is not recognised as widely as it might be within psychoanalysis, although Winnicott does on several occasions use diagrams to describe and clarify the processes he is trying to understand. Fairbairn's theory is a process theory, and it is a pity that he and Marjorie

Brierley (1944) did not cooperate to develop their understanding of the nature and advantages of process theory and make it more widely understood; the Second World War and the Controversial Discussions interrupting that, probably remote, possibility.

Scottish contemporaries

It was 2009 when I first visited the University of Edinburgh's (Fairbairn Project) archives to look at Fairbairn's library, which had been donated by his son Nicholas, that I found some heavily underlined books, one of which was *The Origins of Love and Hate* by Ian D. Suttie. I subsequently wrote a detailed paper commenting on the influence that Suttie had on Fairbairn, which was published in 2011 by the *Journal of the American Psychoanalytic Association* (Chapter One). In 2015, when I began looking in detail at Glover's account of a developmentally based model of his ego-nuclei-based approach (1932, 1956, 1968), having already been aware of the friendship between Glover and Fairbairn, I decided to attempt a detailed comparison of Glover's ego-nuclei model and Fairbairn's endopsychic structure model. The two models having been linked, and rejected, in Klein's paper on schizoid mechanisms (Klein, 1946) (Chapter Two).

Multiple personality disorder

In 2005 I had suggested that careful attention to Fairbairn's original diagram (1944) with its inclusion of classical topographic terms could lead to a modified version of that model and suggest that there is a powerful complex preconscious layer to our inner reality. Paul Finnegan, an analyst from Canada treating people with multiple personality disorder, contacted me about this paper, which he believed offered an insight into the sorts of dissociation he found in the multiple personality patients that he was treating. This led on to our trying to apply this modified version of Fairbairn's theory to understanding Fairbairn's attitude to both dissociation and multiple personality disorder and to trying to understand the clinical realities of multiple personality disorder (MPD). In collaboration with Paul (Clarke & Finnegan, 2011), I used this model to show the degree to which Fairbairn was explicitly interested in and supportive of the view that his model captured our essential multiplicity (Chapter Three). Paul and I (Finnegan & Clarke, 2012) also used this model to look at Paul's clinical work with people suffering from MPD and to suggest that dissociated aspects of preconscious ideal, libidinal and antilibidinal egos and objects might all be candidates as alter personalities (Chapter Four).

Film

My approach to film has been influenced by Fairbairn's theory of dreams developed in his 1944 paper on endopsychic structure and his argument that unconscious phantasy should be replaced by a theory of an inner reality peopled by the ego and its objects (Fairbairn, 1943b). In 2012 the *International Journal of Psychoanalysis* published a paper I had written about three films that seemed to me to be involved with a particularly important aspect of our development as we move into what Fairbairn calls the transitional stage. The development of our ego-ideal and the ability to internalise good object relationships forms part of what Fairbairn calls the moral defence and it was, what seemed to me to be, conspicuous failures of that process that were the key to understanding the films *Memento*, *Shutter Island*, and *Inception*. The place of the good object within Fairbairn's theory has been widely discussed and I was interested in clarifying what I think Fairbairn was arguing regarding the good object, which remains externally available during the early experience of the child when bad object relationships are internalised, and becomes available for introjection via relationships with others only after the basic endopsychic structure is developed with the ideal ego/ideal object in the preconscious (Chapter Five).

In 2015 I wrote about an approach to some "puzzle" films, which led me to revisit my earlier attempts to understand film and dramatic narrative from a Fairbairnian perspective. This led on to my combining aspects of Fairbairn's theory of art and creativity with the idea that a full recognition of the social function of art and the relative assessment of the value of art might depend upon the level of symbolisation achieved by the work of art. Where the symbolisation can be carried through to a degree that the meaning is more or less completely hidden, or, where the meaning of the symbol is so obvious as to appear crude and unsophisticated, then there is a failure to engage the viewer. It follows that the optimal work of art is symbolised in such a way that the amount of work required to interpret the work is proportionate. It satisfies libidinal, antilibidinal and ideal demands in a new synthesis. There is neither too much censorship nor too little censorship and the underlying content is sufficiently lively to peak interest, leading to the judgement that the art object is beautiful (Chapter Six).

Relationality

In 2014 I had the opportunity to edit a book on Fairbairn in the Karnac Books *Lines of Development* series with David Scharff (Clarke & Scharff, 2014) and became even more aware of the underlying and continuing differences between Fairbairn supporters, analysts and scholars across the world. One difference is the degree to which Fairbairn is regarded as a significant contributor to the so-called relational turn within psychoanalysis, as argued by Greenberg and Mitchell (1983). In my view this does some violence to Fairbairn's developed theory, which is particularly relevant because of the degree to which the underlying affective motivational processes (love and aggression) and Fairbairn's theory of endopsychic structure, in all its complexity, are criticised and ignored by later relational thinkers.

Psychoanalysis is a biological-psychological-sociological theory at its best, linking our biological endowments to the social order through a psychology of object relationships. This is the way I interpret Fairbairn's object relations theory. Based on ego-nuclei, which are the earliest integrated object relationships and at least one level of complexity above simple instinctive behaviour, endopsychic structures are integrated ensembles of ego-nuclei and form the building blocks of the personality, based upon the actual experiences of the child. This interpretation of Fairbairn provides us with an underlying model at a similar level to that of Freud's later structural model with which to analyse and theorise human behaviour. This is a paradigm shift that has still to be developed across the range of activity to which it is applicable. There are Fairbairnian therapists and theorists who have explored some of the range of possible applications that Fairbairn's theory might be gainfully employed to explain, but in general Fairbairn's account of early development of the endopsychic structure has been contested, by Kleinians in particular, which has meant that the project of using endopsychic structure as the embodiment of unconscious phantasy has never been seriously explored by any of Fairbairn's supporters. Relational psychoanalysis is the quarter from which Fairbairn garnered most support latterly, but it has developed what I believe to be a flawed and incorrect interpretation of Fairbairn's model, rejecting its affective core and the complexities of endopsychic structure and the psychology of dynamic structure to settle for a simplistic concentration on the phenomenology of relationships, disregarding the ontology of object relationships. It is the rejection of our multiplicity, our inner reality as a multi-agent system of persons-in-relation, that has been one of the greatest obstacles to the development and application of this theory within psychoanalytic discourse.

At about the same time, influenced by the parallels I had discovered between Fairbairn and Glover, I wrote two linked papers developing the idea that Fairbairn's theory is a synthesis of classical and relational ideas. The first paper attempts to explore the possibility that the relational turn had done a disservice to Fairbairn, despite the key role he played in its inspiration and development. In this paper (Chapter Seven) I consider the work of Stephen Mitchell to be a double-edged sword when it comes to an accurate portrayal of Fairbairn's theory, in particular the place of the good object in Fairbairn and the importance of both the motivational underpinnings (love/aggression) and a nuanced understanding of the endopsychic structure model. In the second of these papers (Chapter Eight) I look at the significant contribution that relational thinking has had in moving the area of debate away from the classical towards certain pre-classical thinkers, like Janet, about whom Fairbairn wrote and from whom he took the importance of the idea of dissociation. Jody Messler Davies' paper (1996) linking the pre-classical and the relational is certainly influenced by Fairbairn's oeuvre, though less specifically than it might have been. I look at the clinical work she describes in this paper and suggest that a Fairbairn-based approach to therapy that has room for relationality and affect, for repression and for dissociation, could be used to develop the analysis of the clinical facts in ways that could be of benefit to both therapist and patient. The consequences of ignoring the underlying motivations—ideal, libidinal, and antilibidinal—and rejecting Fairbairn's psychology of dynamic structure is based upon a misunderstanding of Fairbairn's theory and leaves the relational analyst somewhat disarmed in their approach to their clients. I suggest that other, Fairbairnian, interpretations of the clinical data, which include affective and endopsychic factors, are possible and that these are potentially useful.

Instinct, affect, and neuropsychoanalysis

In Chapter Nine I address the inevitable consequence of trying to combine my understanding of Fairbairn's model of endopsychic structure with Glover's model of ego-nuclei and the question of instincts and/ or affects in Fairbairn's theory. Since the relational interpretation of Fairbairn stressed the relational to the exclusion of the energetic, this question is to be expected, but if we look again at what Fairbairn wrote about the importance of the instinctual we find that he saw it as a "signpost to the object" (Fairbairn, p. 33). If we unpack this a little in relation to our understanding of an object relationship then we can argue that initially, although object directed, the instincts or affects are the most powerful motivators, but for Fairbairn they are always in the service of object relationships. This suggests that Freud's primary and secondary processes are mainly concerned with affects and objects, where the primary process is dominated by affective motivations and the secondary process is dominated by object related motivations and constraints. The continued existence of unconscious, repressed affect-driven object relations versus conscious object relations motivated by the search for the ideal object can account for what are considered fundamental differences in Freudian metapsychology, but, they can be seen to be intrinsic to the lack of readiness of the neonate and the relative promiscuity of an affect in search of an object, like the sucking response in latching onto anything that can be sucked, in the absence of an appropriate natural object (Fairbairn, 1952, p. 33).

This is also consistent with a developmental approach to human growth, where primitive affect-driven searches for adequate objects become replaced by sophisticated searches for relationships with appropriate objects for affective completeness and satisfaction. The primitive nature of the early introjects that form deeper aspects of the unconscious object-relations-based dynamic structures and ego-nuclei is accounted for by their being dominated to some degree by the early and more primitive affects, while the sophistication of the more civilised aspects of inner reality are all object related. Chief among these but with a different charge, positive or negative, are the ego-ideal—internalised, idealised (good) object relations—versus the internalised, antilibidinal (bad) punitive object relationships. Consequently, Fairbairn's comment concerning the pleasure principle as the deterioration product of failed object relationships (Fairbairn, 1952, p. 139) is related to the triumph of the affective over the object related aspect of ego-nuclei and object relationships in early development. For Fairbairn, maturity is the replacement of primitive affect-driven object relations choices by object related choices that contain and shape affect. Containment here being the replacement of affect-driven activity in search of an object, by object relations dominated channelling of affect.

In these papers I wanted to draw out the implications of Fairbairn's mature theory in the context of its being developed alongside other theories grounded in the work of Scottish thinkers, like Suttie, Macmurray and Glover, given that Fairbairn never replaced the energetic by the relational in its entirety, even if it was the implicit goal of mature dependence. I think that, for Fairbairn, the relational was always a container for the energetic and that had he been able to work on this now he would be keen to draw out the implications for the primary and secondary processes and to give them a properly object relations interpretation. In the model developed here it seems to me that the triangular object relationship—subject, object, affective relationship—starts initially with the affective relationship between the child and the world being contained by the relationship with mother or mother substitute and ends with internalised object relationships containing and completing (refining) affective relationships in general.

PART I

SCOTTISH CONTEMPORARIES

CHAPTER ONE

Suttie's influence on Fairbairn's object relations theory

Introduction

Within Fairbairn scholarship there is a consensus that Fairbairn made a creative breakthrough in the early 1940s when his psychology of dynamic structure—a consistent object relations approach to psychoanalytic theory—was developed in a number of papers (1940, 1941, 1943a, 1944). However, explanatory accounts of this "creative step" (Sutherland, 1989) are less clear and on this matter there is no general consensus.

The relationship between the work of Fairbairn and that of his fellow Scot, Ian D. Suttie, is generally recognised to be significant where Suttie is regarded as having "anticipated" (Grotstein 1998; Guntrip 1971; Harrow 1998; Kirkwood 2005; Robbins 1994) and influenced Fairbairn. However, there is little objective evidence for this, since nowhere in his work does Fairbairn mention Suttie, or his only book *The Origins of Love and Hate* (OLH), which was first published in 1935. This might have been thought remarkable in itself, given these two men's Scottish origins and the nature of their theories but, perhaps more importantly, there is no mention of the relationship between Suttie and Fairbairn in Pereira and Scharff's *Fairbairn and Relational Theory* (1989) or in Birtles and Scharff's invaluable two volume *From Instinct to Self* (1994). Nor is there any mention of Suttie in either of two books that deal exclusively with the Independents within the British Psychoanalytic Society (BPS)—Gregory Kohon's *The British School of Psychoanalysis: The Independent Tradition* (1986), and Eric Rayner's *The Independent Mind in British Psychoanalysis* (1991). This may be accurate in the sense that Suttie, a psychiatrist, was not a member of the BPS but it is nevertheless surprising given the influence he has been said to have on many of the Independents—Fairbairn, Winnicott, Bowlby, and others (see below).

I believe I have found a significant clue as to Suttie's influence on Fairbairn's object relations theory in Fairbairn's heavily underlined copy of a 1939 edition of Suttie's book.

While researching aspects of Fairbairn's theory I approached the University of Edinburgh Library (UEL) concerning an archive of Fairbairn's papers. In the course of this enquiry I asked about Fairbairn's library, which I had been told by Fairbairn's daughter, Ellinor (personal communication), was also held in Scotland. Ann Henderson, a librarian at UEL found that there was a collection of books, believed to be Fairbairn's library, held by UEL and I was directed to the Special Collections where Joseph Marshall and Tricia Boyd were very helpful in helping me locate the, at that time, uncatalogued, collection of books and provided access to them on a visit I made to Edinburgh in October 2009. According to the printed plate inside the front cover of each of these approximately two hundred and eighty books, they were from the library of W. R. D. Fairbairn "A Pioneer of Psychoanalysis" and had been donated by his son, the late Nicholas Fairbairn M.P. (1933–1995).

I suggest that it was Fairbairn's study of this copy of Suttie's book that helped to prompt the "creative step" that led to Fairbairn's groundbreaking papers of the 1940s. When one compares the underlined parts of Suttie's text with Fairbairn's development of his psychology of dynamic structure the influence is obvious, as I illustrate below. However, to be clear, this is only one root of Fairbairn's thinking and does not account for the *structural* aspects of his mature theory, which Fairbairn had been developing since the late 1920s (1927, 1931).

Many passages in Suttie's book are underlined in the characteristic way that Fairbairn marked the books he studied. There are several other books in the collection underlined in exactly the same way. In Suttie's book the underlinings include parts of (a) J. A. Hadfield's introduction, (b) the actual introduction and (c) the first four chapters of the book plus (d) two other later sections. These appear to be quite deliberate (see below for an example) and concern ideas that provide an armature for Fairbairn's developed object relations theory. I think that Fairbairn's close study of this book was instrumental in his making the "creative step" in his papers of the 1940s. The existence of this link back through the Independent grouping of the BPS to Suttie and before him to Rank and Ferenczi (1925) and back to the object relations based work of Freud provides an alternative "tradition" of object relations thinking to that traced back through Klein. Padel (1985, 1991) noted that one root of object relations thinking can be found in Freud's paper on narcissism, where the infant is described as internalising the nursing couple and subsequently identifying with one or other side of that relationship in making a choice of object. This, combined with the fact that both Klein and Fairbairn take the super-ego, of Freud's structural theory, to be the exemplar of an internal object, suggests that the full description of the development of object relations thinking goes back at least as far as Freud himself, whose Group Psychology is regarded by Padel (1985) as a good example of object relations thinking—in particular, in the case of group formation, where "a number of individuals ... have put one and the same object in the place of their ego-ideal and have consequently identified themselves with one another in their ego" (Padel, 1985 quoting Freud). Ogden (2002) also argues that Freud was developing an object relations approach in his paper on the origins of object relations thinking (Mourning and Melancholia), which he explicitly associates with Fairbairn.

A brief example

The following (complete) paragraph from page three of Suttie's book shows a typical marking that Fairbairn makes to Suttie's text. Fairbairn's underlinings are reproduced.

> When I began my studies of social behaviour twenty years ago, however, I never imagined that I would come to attempt to put the conception of altruistic (non-appetitive) love on a scientific footing. Rejecting the "ad hoc" and therefore sterile hypothesis of a "herd instinct" both on biological and methodological grounds, (A) I was nevertheless early compelled to recognise that the psychoses are essentially disorders of the social disposition; (B) and that all our theories of the construction of the social group are seriously inadequate.

(G) Five years ago, however, I realised that the infant differs more from our primitive ancestors than we adults do, in spite of Recapitulation Theories (C, D, E) and that this adaptation to infancy (as I called it) implies an innate disposition towards the social habit though not towards a "Herd Instinct". (F) Nurture of the young and "the social habit" appeared to me associated with each other, and with the replacement of blind instinct by intelligence, in their actual distribution throughout the Animal Kingdom (G). (Suttie, 1935, p. 3)

Suttie and Fairbairn: an overview

Before proceeding to a detailed comparison of Fairbairn's markings of Suttie's text with Fairbairn's mature theory I want to try to contextualise the relationship between Suttie and Fairbairn as it appears today.

Ian Dishart Suttie's book *The Origins of Love and Hate* has been widely influential among the British Object Relations group (the Middle Group or Independents) and explicitly acknowledged as such by Winnicott and Bowlby. Commentators have drawn attention to the importance of Suttie's work for this group (Akhtar, 1999; Beattie, 2003; Bowlby, 1960; Hoffman, 2004; Skolnick, 2006; Tolmacz, 2006; Wallerstein, 1988) and Bacal in particular:

> I would like to begin this survey of object-relations theorists with Ian Suttie, who was a central figure in the early Tavistock group … and whose ideas significantly anticipated the work of Fairbairn, Guntrip, Balint and Winnicott … (Bacal, 1987, p. 82)

Rudnytsky (1992) also has a very clear view of Suttie's, mostly unacknowledged, importance.

> In assessing both the historical unfolding and the theoretical achievement of object relations thought, special mention must be made of Ian Suttie's *Origins of Love and Hate* (1935). This book, largely neglected at the time of its publication, has increasingly been hailed as a classic and indeed contains the kernel of virtually every idea elaborated by subsequent analysts. (Rudnytsky, 1992, p. 294)

The importance of Suttie's work is becoming recognised and discussed in a wider context where some of the most interesting work on British object relations thinking is taking place (Gerson 2004, 2009; Miller 2007, 2008a, 2008b) but unfortunately Suttie remains outside the psychoanalytic mainstream. For instance *The Origins of Love and Hate* is not among the books in the PEPWeb database, and where Suttie does appear in the journal papers in PEPWeb there is little substantive discussion of his work and his influence is stated briefly rather than argued in any depth.

While Fairbairn is regarded by synoptic reviewers of object relations thinking as the most thoroughgoing developer of that mode of thinking, it is significant that neither Mitchell and Greenberg (1983) nor Judith Hughes (1989) have any indexed references to Suttie, or any discussion of his work or influence. This lack of reference to Suttie is also true of Frank Summers' *Object Relations Theories and Psychopathology* (1994) and of Otto Kernberg's *Object Relations and Clinical Psychoanalysis* (1981) and *Internal World and External Reality* (1984). In the latter there is a full chapter on Fairbairn but no mention of Suttie.

Scharff and Birtles (1997) have argued for the widespread but generally unacknowledged influence that Fairbairn's theory has had on psychoanalytic theory in the U.K. and the U.S.A. and Migone also makes the point that object relations theory has had a wide and generally unacknowledged influence.

> But the developments of Self Psychology are not an isolated phenomenon. They belong to a wider transformation of contemporary psychoanalysis: the latter is increasingly influenced by the so called "object relation theory" [sic]. Today this is probably the most fashionable psychoanalytic school on both continents. Its principal characteristic is an emphasis on environment and on the development of early interpersonal relationships. This school in Great Britain was anticipated by the pioneering work of Suttie. Later it was developed by Fairbairn, Guntrip, and Winnicott's "middle group". Then it was exported to the United States where it was "grafted" on to Ego Psychology and as such was spread by Kernberg and other authors who had been exposed to Kleinian theory. (Migone, 1994, p. 90)

Sutherland argues in his biography that Fairbairn's Freudian views on aggression in 1938 (Sutherland, 1989, p. 58), which are in marked contrast to his views a few year later, are due to internecine struggles over metapsychology in Edinburgh, but it would seem simpler to conclude that, after studying Suttie, Fairbairn changed his mind and made some of Suttie's approach his own. Sutherland did comment on Suttie's book and Fairbairn's relationship to it although this comment is not referenced in the index of his biography of Fairbairn.

> Fairbairn's views in some measure were anticipated by Suttie in his book *The Origins of Love and Hate* (1935). This book was known to him, and he thought it important. For Fairbairn, however, Suttie's arguments were apparently couched too much as a general protest without the carefully assembled clinical data and *structural theory* required—a view that was shared by Ernest Jones and Edward Glover, who did not dismiss it lightly. (Sutherland, 1989, p. 118, emphasis added)

I think that the most significant comment here concerns the development of a *structural* theory. When Fairbairn, towards the end of his life in 1963, produced his own synopsis of his theory it was a structural theory that he described and I believe that this structural theory can only be understood fully by taking into consideration the ideas Fairbairn adopted from Suttie. It is Fairbairn's structural theory, intended to rationally reconstruct Freud's own structural theory, which Fairbairn had already been developing in the late twenties and early thirties, which forms the independent line of thinking that he was developing, which then became so influential. I think that it is important here to recognise that Fairbairn's interest in a general psychology that is capable of grounding psychoanalytic theory as a whole is of deep significance.

I suggest elsewhere (Clarke, 2003b) that there is a strong "family" resemblance between thinkers of Scottish origin on object relations—Suttie, Fairbairn, and Macmurray—a viewpoint that I think has its roots in Scottish thinking on the Social from the Scottish Enlightenment (Clarke, 2008b). The connections between Bowlby and Suttie are well documented by Bowlby himself, who also acknowledges Fairbairn as important in his developing attachment theory, and Macmurray's debt to Suttie is also made clear by Macmurray himself (1961). Macmurray developed his own understanding of the alternative responses to disillusion that a child might make and their consequences for the child's ability to encourage fellowship and community. In an earlier paper (Clarke, 2003b) I have presented a detailed discussion of the relationship between Macmurray's understanding of this process and Fairbairn's psychology of dynamic structure. This theme is returned to below in the section entitled "Transitional techniques".

Initial comparison of Suttie's theory with Fairbairn's post-1940 theory

I think that the underlinings Fairbairn made to *The Origins of Love and Hate* represent his acceptance of a point of view that grounds his psychology of dynamic structure and that his mature theory contains ideas on libido theory, aggression, the oedipal situation, separation anxiety and the death instinct that reflect Suttie's own views. I will also look at Suttie's influence on Fairbairn regarding the relationship between mother and baby and the importance of that first relationship in sections entitled "The moral defence", "Transitional techniques", and the "Environment mother". In a section entitled "Further markings" I briefly consider Suttie's overall approaches to theory and therapy as underlined by Fairbairn, which is consistent with Fairbairn's own approach to these matters in later papers (Fairbairn, 1954, 1958).

Libido theory

Turning to Hadfield's introduction to OLH we find that Fairbairn has underlined the following:

> Love is protective as well as sexual, and the sense of security is more important to the child than feelings of pleasure (sensual). This love relationship and not sex is the basis upon which social life is formed: and it is in the disturbances of this love life that we find the origins of psychoneurosis. Mental development begins in a social relationship. (Suttie, 1935, p. xv)

Meanwhile on page 6 of OLH, again underlined by Fairbairn, Suttie writes:

> the tentative theory I have formed ... differs fundamentally from psycho-analysis in introducing the conception of an innate need-for-companionship which is the infant's only way of self-preservation. This need ... I put in the place of the Freudian Libido ... (Suttie, 1935, p. 6)

Again on page 15 Fairbairn underlines the following:

> We need ... only suppose the child is born with a mind and instincts *adapted to infancy*; or ... so disposed as to profit by parental nurture. This ... implies the conclusion that the child mind is *less* like that of primitive animals than is the adult mind. (Suttie, 1935, p. 15, emphasis in original)

Perhaps the most famous and the most important basis of Fairbairn's mature object relations theory is that libido is object-seeking not pleasure-seeking.

> In a previous paper (1941) I attempted to formulate a new version of the libido theory ... The basic conception which I advanced on that occasion, and to which I still adhere, is to the effect that libido is primarily object-seeking (rather than pleasure-seeking, as in the classic theory) and that it is to disturbances in the object-relationships of the developing ego that we must look for the ultimate origin of all psychopathological conditions. (Fairbairn, 1952, Chapter IV [1944], p. 82)

Fairbairn had spent considerable time and effort looking at and criticising Freud's libido theory as witness his long paper "Libido Theory Re-evaluated" (Birtles & Scharff, 1994, pp. 115–158, [1930]), but his 1941 restatement of the libido theory in terms of it being object-seeking rather than pleasure-seeking takes place after he read Suttie circa 1939.

Aggression

In Chapter III of Suttie's book Fairbairn has underlined the following passage concerning the child's early experience:

> In this ideal state anxiety is at a minimum and resentments are only transient. There is no abiding sense of insecurity or of grievance. But the exigencies of life itself—(for example the advent of a second baby), or of culture (e.g. cleanliness-training), or of civilization (e.g. the working mother who must leave her babies), interrupt this happy symbiotic relationship (Suttie, 1935, p. 39)

And in the next paragraph:

> The infant now appears to feel for the mother a mixture of love-longing, apprehension and anger that is called *ambivalence*. It is extremely uncomfortable because obviously none of these emotions can get free expression ... (Suttie, 1935, p. 39, emphasis in original)

Fairbairn's mature position on aggression is as follows:

> I regard aggression as a primary dynamic factor in that it does not appear capable of being resolved into libido ... at the same time I regard it as ultimately subordinate to libido ... Thus I do not consider that the infant directs aggression spontaneously towards his libidinal object in the absence of some kind of frustration ... (Fairbairn, 1952, p. 109)

But given the frustrations of civilised living:

> It is the experience of libidinal frustration that calls forth the infant's aggression in relation to his libidinal object and thus gives rise to a state of ambivalence. (Fairbairn, 1952, p. 110)

The Oedipus situation

The Oedipus Complex is a central concept of Freudian psychoanalysis but it is regarded by Suttie as contingent upon social and cultural factors. After the passage quoted above concerning the innate need for companionship, Fairbairn underlined the following:

> ... this conception ... lessens the importance attached to *individual sense gratification* as motive and increases the significance of *social* desires and interests ... It denies the sexual basis of culture-sublimation and it relegates the Oedipus Wish and Sexual Jealousy to third place ... as disturbers of social development and harmony ... no one seems to recognise ... *that the Oedipus Complex, being largely contingent on particular modes of rearing and forms of family structure, culture and racial character must vary within wide limits* ... (Suttie, 1935, pp. 6–7, emphasis in the original)

Fairbairn too rejects the Oedipus situation as primary:

> I have dispensed with the Oedipus situation as an explanatory concept not only in my account of the origin of repression, but also in my account of the basic endopsychic situation and in my account of the differentiation of endopsychic structure. These accounts have been formulated exclusively in terms of the measures adopted by the child in an attempt to cope with the difficulties inherent in the ambivalent situation which develops during his infancy in his relationship with his mother as his original object. (Fairbairn, 1952, p. 120)

It is clear from this that Fairbairn's thoughts on the importance of ambivalence towards mother (or primary caregiver) for the generation of endopsychic structure follow on directly from Suttie's view of ambivalence.

> So far from furnishing an explanatory concept ... the Oedipus situation is rather a phenomena to be explained in terms of an endopsychic situation which has already developed. (Fairbairn, 1952, p. 121)

Fairbairn uses his object relations theory of dynamic structure and inner reality to argue that the development of the basic endopsychic structure occurs pre-oedipally and that the "Oedipus situation", as he calls it, is essentially a social situation in which the child has to determine for itself the gender identity that it is going to adopt based upon its relations with mother and father. This view, which acknowledges the social but is not exclusively based upon social and anthropological evidence, provides an object relations explanation for the possibility of many different ways in which the Oedipus situation might be resolved. It is therefore possible that Suttie's view of the Oedipus situation although influential on Fairbairn was developed further by Fairbairn in terms of object relations and family structure and relationships. Importantly, Fairbairn's later view of the Oedipus complex was that it was "central for treatment, though not for theory" (Padel, 1991, p. 599).

Separation anxiety

The term separation anxiety does not appear in Fairbairn's work until after 1940 when it appears in his paper on a revised psychopathology of the psychoses and the psychoneuroses (1941), and in his paper on the war neuroses (1943a). Two quotations from Suttie, underlined by Fairbairn, indicate the degree to which Fairbairn's thinking in these papers is along lines already indicated, if not explored in depth, by Suttie.

> ... separation-anxiety is merely the felt discomfort at an inadequate social adaptation ... supposed phases of libidinal development would then appear to be merely means of adjusting to the mother's demands in regard respectively to sucking and weaning, to excretory pleasures and prohibitions and finally to the growing prominence of genital feelings. The supposed "phases of libido development" on this view would *no longer* appear as stages determined by inborn forces ... They would rather appear as *responses* on the child's part to a changing relationship between itself and the mother; and this relationship in turn is largely determined by the rearing customs imposed by culture and civilization. Character and mental disease would then [appear] ... as responses on the part of the mind to the social situation in which it finds itself. (Suttie, 1935, p. 47, emphasis in the original)

This passage could have prompted the discussion in Fairbairn's 1941 paper concerning an alternative to phases of libido development based upon erotogenic zones and related to forms of dependence—infantile dependence, transitional techniques, and mature dependence. If this was the case then it seems to lead to the development of an object relations view of the "transitional techniques" along lines indicated by Suttie but never pursued or developed by him (see below). The following links separation anxiety and aggression.

> ... love of mother is primal in so far as it is the *first formed and directed* emotional relationship. Hate, I regard not as a primal independent instinct ... but as a development or intensification of separation-anxiety which in turn is *roused* by a threat against love. It is the maximal ultimate appeal in the child's power ... Its purpose is not death-seeking or death-dealing, but the preservation of the self from the isolation which is death, and the restoration of the love relationship. (Suttie, 1935, p. 31, emphasis in original)

Fairbairn's paper on the war neuroses places separation anxiety at its heart and focuses on the serviceman's wishes to be reunited with his loved ones as a central feature of the complaint.

> ... the term "homesick" could quite appropriately be applied to the neurotic soldier in view of the outstanding part played by separation-anxiety amongst his symptoms and the compulsive nature of his urge to return home at all costs. (Fairbairn, 1952, p. 266 [1943a])

Death instinct

Following on from his account of ambivalence coming from the early mother-child relationship, Suttie puts a social interpretation upon a number of Freudian conceptions, which relate to a one-person psychology.

> They wish to account for the whole process of mental development in terms of what goes on within the individual mind itself, with a minimum of reference to any stresses of adjustment between one mind and another ... I, on the contrary, would say that "mastering anxiety" and "overcoming hate with love" refer to the *situation* between the child and the mother and later to its substitute relationships with its whole social environment. The child's attempt is *primarily not* to secure an endopsychic adjustment of conflicting feelings, but to remove the *cause* of the anxiety and hate by restoring harmonious social relationships. When the social disagreement is removed the feeling rapport can *change back from anxiety and hate into love and security.* (Suttie, 1935, p. 40, emphasis in original)

And:

> Thus I put a social interpretation upon these three processes, "mastery of anxiety", "overcoming hate with love" and "release of impulse", which Freudians regard as characteristic master-motives of human mind. By so doing I not only overcome the inconsistencies between these formulae themselves, showing how they are but different aspects of the same purpose (the love quest) but I avoid two fallacies ... The first of these is ... that anxiety is nothing but frustrated sexual desire. The second—the theory of Death-aggressive Instinct—is admittedly a very unsatisfactory explanation of sadism and masochism ... (Suttie, 1935, pp. 40–41)

Fairbairn, in addressing the question of an alternative to libido as pleasure-seeking motivation, offers an alternative account of the "death instinct" and the "repetition compulsion" and he argues that:

> If ... libido is regarded as primarily object seeking there is no need to resort to this expedient [the repetition compulsion] ... the tendency to cling to painful experiences may be explained in terms of relationships with bad objects ... [and] difficulties involved in the conception of primary "death instincts" (in contrast to the conception of a primary aggressive tendency) may be avoided if all the implications of libidinal relationships with bad objects are taken into account. (Fairbairn, 1952, p. 84)

The moral defence

In Chapter III of Suttie's book *Benevolence, Altruism and Hedonism*, Suttie discusses what Winnicott would later call "disillusion" in ways that seem to prefigure some of Fairbairn's later thinking. For instance, Fairbairn has underlined Suttie's account of the possible responses that the child might make to disillusion:

> Automatically ... the child's frustrated social love turns to anxiety ... and then to hate if the frustration is sufficiently severe. But hate of a loved object (ambivalence) ... is intolerable; the love relationship must be preserved as a matter of life or death, and there are various means of doing this. First it may be done by the preservation of the lovability of the first loved object—the mother ... An alternative is to abandon the mother, *as she now appears in reality*, for the mother as she once appeared and as she is remembered. This involves the technique of *taking refuge from reality in phantasy* ... the child may seek a "good" substitute for the "bad" mother in the nurse or in the father; but towards this substitute the same demands will be put forward and the same struggle renewed.... to the progressive transference of dependency to others than the mother, the normal person owes much of his success. A fourth alternative is found in the Adlerian technique of power (or in possession) ... [which involves aggression, coercion, anger and love-protests on the part of the child.] (Suttie, 1935, pp. 42–43, emphasis in original)

Fairbairn was a Medical Psychologist at the Edinburgh University Psychological Clinic for Children between 1927 and 1935 (Birtles & Scharff, 1994, pp. 463–464). Drawing on this experience he asserts that a delinquent child is usually reluctant to admit that his parents are bad and would rather be seen to be bad himself than "to have bad objects".

> In becoming bad he is really taking upon himself the burden of badness, which appears to reside in his objects … he seeks to purge them of their badness; and in proportion as he succeeds in doing so, he is rewarded by that sense of security, which an environment of good objects so characteristically confers. (Fairbairn, 1952, p. 65)

Fairbairn argues that there is a defence, which supports the work of repression, which he calls "the moral defence" or "the defence of guilt" or "the defence of the super-ego". Fairbairn introduces a modification to the idea of "badness" that he has been using in relation to objects. He says that unconditional badness is bad from a libidinal point of view and that conditional badness is bad from a moral point of view. He then suggests that in order to ameliorate the situation of internalised unconditionally bad objects the child internalises his good objects into the preconscious and that they then assume a super-ego role (he later used the older term ego-ideal) and that once this happens we have a situation in which internal objects are both conditionally bad and conditionally good.

> Insofar as the child leans towards his internalised bad objects, he becomes conditionally (i.e. morally) bad *vis-à-vis* his internalised good objects (i.e. his super-ego); and, in so far as he resists the appeal of his internalised bad objects, he becomes conditionally (i.e. morally) good *vis-à-vis* his super-ego. (Fairbairn, 1952, p. 66)

Fairbairn suggests that the appeal of this sort of defence might be most readily understood if couched in religious terms and suggests that a sinner in a world ruled by God may be bad but there is a sense of security in having God ruling the world; whereas a sinner in a world ruled by the Devil may escape the badness of being a sinner but there is no hope of redemption.

Transitional techniques

Fairbairn has underlined much of Suttie's discussion of the different responses to mother's attempts to disillusion the child and his having linked them with different forms of mental disturbance. *"The Preservation of the lovableness of the mother. Mother is good and kind; if she does not love me that is because I am bad'"*, which is like Fairbairn's moral defence, and can lead to an "inferiority complex" and, in the extreme, to "melancholia". On the other hand it can be the stimulus to becoming "what mother loves", which directly parallels a super-ego form of defence consistent with Fairbairn's thinking on the moral defence.

The second response to mother's attempts to disillusion the child results in a *"regression"* or turning away from reality leading to "Dementia Praecox" or "hysterical invalidism". In the third response to the attempted disillusion Suttie identifies a "paranoiac" response—*"I am good and you are bad"*. And in the fourth response he sees "Delinquency" or "Paranoia". Suttie also mentions "One other mechanism that operates at this early … phase of life is … 'phobic substitution'" (Suttie, 1935, p. 45).

From Fairbairn's perspective the sense of security such defences provide is purchased at a price, since the child has internalised bad objects against which defences have to be erected. Fairbairn argues that the first level of defence against these internalised bad objects is repression, but when repression fails the four transitional defences are called into operation—the phobic, the obsessional, the hysterical, and the paranoid. Fairbairn discusses the details of the working of each of these transitional defences with reference to the disposition by projection and introjection of acceptable (good) and rejected (bad) objects in his 1941 paper "A Revised Psychopathology of the Psychoses and Psychoneuroses".

Fairbairn's understanding of these different defensive processes moves from the description at a psychoneurotic level to a discussion of and explanation couched in terms of both object relationships and the characteristic distribution of internal objects that make sense of each of the defences. So the Obsessional characteristically internalises their accepted and rejected objects while the Phobic characteristically projects their accepted and rejected objects. The Paranoid internalises their accepted object and externalises their rejected objects while the Hysteric externalises their accepted object and internalises their rejected objects.

We have here an example of the way in which Fairbairn's thought may have been triggered by his reading of Suttie's work, but his explanation in object relations terms goes beyond Suttie in important ways.

Environment mother

It is worth pointing out here that the idea of the child starting out from a situation in which the mother is more or less its world and then gradually moving farther away from mother and finding substitute relationships with others and the world and moving on towards a position where the adult is independent in action but still dependent in a social sense is an overall pattern that both Fairbairn and Winnicott inherit and use. The process of becoming separate and independent without losing community is designated "transitional" by both of them, with Fairbairn using the term earlier than Winnicott as Winnicott acknowledges in his paper on transitional phenomena (1953). The following passage from Suttie, underlined by Fairbairn, makes this whole argument in brief.

> ... a need for company, moral encouragement, attention, protectiveness, leadership, etc., remains after all the sensory gratifications connected with the mother's body have become superfluous ... In my view this is a direct development of the primal attachment-to-mother, and, further, I think that play, co-operation, competition and culture-interests generally are substitutes for the mutually caressing relationship of child and mother. *By these substitutes we put the whole social environment in the place once occupied by mother—* ... A joint interest in *things* has replaced the reciprocal interest in *persons*; friendship has developed out of love. True, the personal love and sympathy is preserved in *friendship*; but this differs from love in so far as it comes about by the *direction of attention upon the same things* (rather than upon each other) ... or by the pursuit of *the same activities* ... (Suttie, 1935, p. 16, emphasis in original)

Rudnytsky in an exactly similar vein says that:

> Suttie prefigures Winnicott's (1967) entire thesis concerning "the location of cultural experience" when he writes that "play ... and culture-interests generally are substitutes for the mutually

> caressing relationship of child and mother. By these substitutes we put the whole social environment in the place once occupied by the mother" (Suttie, p. 16). Suttie likewise anticipates Bowlby in seeking "to put the conception of altruistic (non-appetitive) love on a scientific footing" (Suttie, p. 3) by drawing on research in animal behaviour, and he explicitly makes the methodological claim that these facts are important because they "are objective and can be checked by several observers, unlike evidence derived from the analysis of patients" (Suttie, p. 8). (Rudnytsky, 1992, p. 294)

This last comment seems to raise doubts concerning Sutherland's report of Fairbairn's view that Suttie was insufficiently scientific.

Further markings

Fairbairn also marks two sections much later in Suttie's book from Chapter XIII "Freudian Theory is Itself a Disease" and from Chapter XIV "Freudian Practice is a 'Cure' by Love". While I do not have room to consider all of Suttie's underlined arguments in detail it is clear that these two separate sections describe attitudes and ideas that inform Fairbairn's post-1939 work in general and his later papers on theory and therapy (1954, 1958) in particular. From Chapter XIII:

> I intend to maintain that the *theory* of Psycho-analysis has sprung from an entirely different interest from that which inspired the development of its *practice*. In fact, the metapsychology appears to me an expression of unconscious hate and anxiety while the practice of psycho-analysis represents a struggle to express love in spite of various inhibitions ... (Suttie, 1935, p. 218, emphasis in original)

And:

> ... the failure of theory seems to be due to its denial of the existence of love and to its depreciation of the social significance of the mother ... I will attempt to show that the successful developments of treatment and that of the *theory of treatment* have been in the direction of a covert employment and recognition of love in a strictly non-sexual sense ... (Suttie, 1935, pp. 218–219, emphasis in the original)

This is consistent with Fairbairn's critique of Freud and with his theory of the development of the basic endopsychic structure from the early relationship with mother or primary caregiver.

From Chapter XIV concerning the practice of psychoanalysis and with an explicit reference back to Ferenczi:

> When it appeared, however, that the essence of cure consisted in the *removal of resistances*, a much more social conception of mind was implied. Resistances were *against* the physician … while repression appeared very largely as a function of the *social instance in early childhood* … A further development in the recognition of the social factor occurred when it was realised that cure was effected only by an actual reconstitution of the loves and hates of the past with the person of the physician as their objective. This theory of treatment by "transference neurosis" recognises at least tacitly that … nothing is of psychopathological significance—which does not concern the love, hate and anxiety relationships of the subject to other people. (Suttie, 1935, pp. 246–247, emphasis in the original)

And:

> The overcoming of anxiety and hate appear as the assurance *that there is no occasion for them.* Reductive analysis itself in the negative transference acts by displaying the essential lovingness of others and their need for his love, i.e. his own lovability. Finding confidence in himself and trust in others, he finds thereby the interests whereby mental intercourse … is developed … The love-interest—rapport between himself and the social environment—lost in childhood—is restored because the forgotten quarrels have been explored and forgiven—threshed out to such an extent that the patient sees there never was anything to forgive—never any lack of love on either side. But this is a very un-Freudian interpretation of therapy … My account would not square with the abstract idea of mitigating the severity of the Super-Ego, or of acquiring a tolerance of Id impulses. Yet it squares very well with Ferenczi's dictum "The physician's love heals the patient" … (Suttie, 1935, pp. 247–248, emphasis in the original)

This is consistent with Fairbairn's insistence that within therapy it is the overall personal relationship between the patient and the therapist that is important.

Conclusion

I have suggested that the detailed comparison of Fairbairn's underlined copy of Suttie's book and Fairbairn's own post-1939 mature theory is sufficient to illustrate and support the probability of Suttie's influence on Fairbairn. Fairbairn's development of a thoroughgoing object-relations-based structural theory founded on the idea of object seeking and an underlying innate social need for object relationship, attachment or companionship, is an independently developed contribution of deep significance to psychoanalytic theory. That the development of Fairbairn's object relations theory had significant roots in the rich material that Suttie had produced in his only published book should be more widely recognised.

Although Fairbairn never acknowledged the influence of Suttie's work upon his own, Suttie's rejection of aspects of Freudian theory and his focus on the primacy of the relationship between the mother and child, through Fairbairn, have been widely influential on the development of the Independents' viewpoint within the BPS. Suttie's pioneering work, the history of his influence, and his role as perhaps the originator of an alternative strand of object relations thinking, all merit our further attention.

CHAPTER TWO

Fairbairn and Glover: object relationships and ego-nuclei

Introduction

In this chapter I continue a process of investigating the origins and significance of Fairbairn's theory by looking at the often-undisclosed influence of his contemporaries upon his ideas. This process began with an exploration of Fairbairn's work on the preconscious and psychic change (Clarke, 2005), which was followed by a consideration of the relationship between Fairbairn and his Scottish contemporaries, Macmurray and Suttie (Clarke, 2006). This work was then followed by a more detailed inquiry into Suttie's influence on Fairbairn (see Chapter One).

I will examine the relationship between Fairbairn and another of his Scottish contemporaries, Edward Glover, and I will attempt to reconcile Glover's theory of ego-nuclei and Fairbairn's theory of object relations. I shall seek to show that Glover's classification of mental disorders (1932) and his theory of ego-nuclei, and Fairbairn's revision of the libido theory (1941) and his theory of endopsychic structure and internal objects (1944), are closely related. Fairbairn's critique of the libido theory allows him to both rationally reconstruct Freud's structural theory and, using Glover's work on the classification of mental disorders, to rationally reconstruct a system of classification, based upon component instincts and ego-nuclei, as one based upon object relations and the primary need for objects. In summary, Fairbairn's model of endopsychic structure can be seen as a(n object-relations based) reworking of Glover's (component-instinct based) model of ego-nuclei first published in his 1932 paper on the classification of mental disorders.

I will also attempt to make clear that Fairbairn's theory is an integration of classical and relational ideas. This perspective is in stark contrast to that of Mitchell (1994) and Davies (1996) where Fairbairn is seen as being simply a precursor to relational thinking proper. In my view, their perspectives ignore what I consider to be crucial aspects of Fairbairn's fully developed model of endopsychic structure and they do not use the affective underpinning of that structure in any meaningful way. It is this issue that underpins Jon Mills' (2005) criticism of purely relational thinkers as ignoring the biological basis of the mind—embodiment.

The model developed at the end of this chapter goes beyond the model of MPD/DID used by Paul Finnegan and myself in earlier papers (see Chapters Three and Four) in that it takes an additional step in strongly suggesting that all alters can better be understood as ego-nuclei or object relationships that have not been integrated into some higher level structure like the libidinal, antilibidinal or ideal—egos and objects of Fairbairn's endopsychic structure—and are operating independently.

An introduction to Fairbairn and Glover

Fairbairn's object relations theory did not arise ex nihilo and nor was it born fully formed. As he says of the first section in his only book *Psychoanalytic Studies of the Personality* (1952), a collection of papers originally written between 1940 and 1951, these represent "the evolution of a point of view which derives its distinctive features from the explicit formulation of (a) an object-relations theory of the personality, and (b) a psychology of dynamic structure" (p. ix).

Fairbairn's fundamental assumption is that the child is object seeking and object relating, even as a "pristine ego". This contrasts with Glover's own ideas of a "primary functional phase", which he describes metapsychologically as:

> a central psychic path of excitation between the sensory and the motor boundaries of the apparatus, along which first unbound

> instinctual charges advance or regress according to the pleasure principle activating and reactivating in their passage primordial memory traces. (Glover, 1968, p. 72)

Fairbairn's fundamental assumption allows him to make object relationships the building blocks of his revised theory of psychopathology—a framework that is very close to Glover's classification of mental disorders.

By relating Fairbairn's object relations approach to Glover's Freudian, component-instinct based approach, it becomes possible to argue that Fairbairn produces a synthesis of Freud's structural- and instinct-based theories in a relational form that does not dispense with instinct, since instinct is now seen to be both intrinsic to, but also subordinate to, object relationships. As such I would maintain that this interpretation of Fairbairn's theory makes it a true synthesis of the classical and the relational.

Glover is less well known now than Fairbairn, but as Walsh in his paper "The Scientific Works of Edward Glover" (1973) says:

> Edward Glover, one of the great patriarchs of modern psychoanalysis ... He was a scientist, trained in the scientific method by his great analytic teacher Karl Abraham and by earlier teachers in biology and the basic sciences, from whom he received a sound fundamental scientific orientation ... The above influences are very evident in his writings, which are polished, couched in beautiful English prose and are models of scientific clarity. He did not believe that these factors, which were also characteristic of Freud's works, should ever become "old-fashioned". (p. 95)

And:

> Although he was a founding member of the British Psycho-Analytical Society and Institute, and had served as Director of Research, in 1944 Edward Glover resigned from the Society, retaining his membership of the International Psycho-Analytical Association through honorary membership in the Swiss and American Psychoanalytic Associations. In a dignified statement he explained that he could no longer subscribe to the training of candidates which did not clearly distinguish between fundamental Freudian concepts and what he regarded as unscientific and mythical concepts ... He felt that the training system had developed into a

system of power-politics which he could not condone, and which came into being under the prolonged and dominating influence of Ernest Jones. (pp. 98–99)

Fairbairn had been aware of Glover since at least the 1929 international IPA conference in Oxford, as in his notes on the conference under "Impressions of Psychoanalysts, The British Group", he remarks that "Edward Glover was intellectually the most impressive" (Birtles & Scharff, 1994, p. 455). In 1943 Glover delivered Fairbairn's only contribution to the Controversial Discussions, Fairbairn's important comments on unconscious phantasy and inner reality (Birtles & Scharff, 1994, pp. 293–294) where he proposes an object-relations based understanding of unconscious phantasy.

> In conclusion, I cannot refrain from voicing the opinion that the explanatory concept of "phantasy" has now been rendered obsolete by the concepts of "psychical reality" and "internal objects", which the work of Mrs Klein and her followers has done so much to develop; and in my opinion the time is now ripe for us to replace the concept of "phantasy" by a concept of an "inner reality" peopled by the ego and its internal objects. These internal objects should be regarded as having an organized structure, an identity of their own, an endopsychic existence, and an activity as real within the inner world as those of any objects in the outer world. To attribute such features to internal objects may at first seem startling to some; but, after all, they are only features which Freud has already attributed to the superego. What has now emerged is simply that the superego is not the only internal object … Inner reality thus becomes the scene of situations involving relationships between the ego and its internal objects. The concept of "phantasy" is purely functional and can only be applied to activity on the part of the ego. It is quite inadequate to describe inner situations involving the relationships of the ego to internal objects possessing an endopsychic structure and dynamic qualities. It would still seem legitimate, however, to speak of "phantasies" in the plural (or of "a phantasy") to describe specific inner situations (or a specific inner situation), so long as this limitation of meaning is appreciated. (King & Steiner, 1991, p. 360)

Fairbairn knew and corresponded with Glover and there are several letters between Glover and Fairbairn in Fairbairn's archive at the

National Library of Scotland (www.fairbairn.ac.uk), including letters dated during the period that Fairbairn was developing his own psychology of dynamic structure. Fairbairn's son, Cosmo, also confirmed that Glover often visited Fairbairn in Edinburgh (personal communication).

More significant than the letters, or the personal visits perhaps, Fairbairn's 1941 paper on a revised psychopathology of the psychoses and the psychoneuroses on its original publication in the *International Journal of Psycho-Analysis* (IJPA) includes comments on Glover's 1932 paper on the classification of mental disorders in its introductory passages. I argue that Fairbairn's revised psychopathology is closely parallel to Glover's 1932 suggestions for a developmental approach to the classification of mental disorders. The significant differences are that Fairbairn rejected Abraham's classification of the erotogenic zones and their developmental progression apart from the oral and the genital stages. In the oral stage Fairbairn retains Abraham's distinction between the early (sucking) and the late (biting) stage. Between the oral and the genital stages Fairbairn introduces a transitional stage, while Glover, following Abraham, has an anal and a phallic stage. For Fairbairn these transitional stages are about the way that internal objects are dealt with and give rise to the neuroses—obsession, hysteria, phobia, and paranoia—each of which is an "alternative technique, all belonging to the same stage in the development of object-relationships ... [which] cannot be classified in any order corresponding to presumptive levels of libidinal development" (Fairbairn, 1952, p. 46) (see more detailed discussion below).

I will quote Fairbairn's remarks, from his original 1941 paper, on Glover and ego-nuclei, in full, because these are the only examples I have been able to find of either man talking about the other's work and in particular the classification of mental disorders and ego-nuclei.

> The significance of splitting the ego can only be fully appreciated when it is considered from a developmental standpoint. As has been well described by Edward Glover (1932, J. Ment. Sci., 78, 819–842), the ego is gradually built up in the course of development from a number of primitive ego-nuclei: and we must believe that these *ego-nuclei* are themselves the product of a process of integration. The formation of the component nuclei may be conceived as a process of localized psychical crystallization occurring not only within zonal, but also within various other functional distributions.

Thus there will arise within the psyche, not only e.g. oral, anal and genital nuclei, but also male and female, active and passive, loving and hating, giving and taking nuclei, as well as the nuclei of internal persecutors and judges (super-ego nuclei). We may further conceive that it is the overlapping and interlacing of these various nuclei and classes of nuclei that form the basis of that particular process of integration which results in the formation of the ego. Schizoid states must, accordingly, be regarded as occurring characteristically in individuals in whom this process of integration has never been satisfactorily realized, and in whom a regressive disintegration of the ego has occurred ... The account given of the formation of the *ego-nuclei* falls naturally into line with Freud's conception that the libido is originally distributed over a number of bodily zones, some of which are specially significant and are highly libidinized. There is a common element also between the conception that successful development of the ego depends upon an adequate integration of the *ego-nuclei* and Freud's conception that the success of libidinal development depends upon the integration of the various libidinal distributions under the mastery of the genital impulse ... The inherent weakness of the libido theory is best appreciated, however, when we consider it in the form in which it emerged from Abraham's revision ... There can be no question of the correctness of relating schizoid conditions to a fixation in the early oral (incorporative and pre-ambivalent) phase characterized by the dominance of sucking. Nor, for that matter, can there be any doubt about the correctness of attributing manic-depressive conditions to a fixation in the later oral (ambivalent) phase characterized by the emergence of biting. For the dominant *ego-nuclei* in the schizoid and the manic-depressive are found to conform in character to these respective attributions ... There can be no doubt that, as Abraham pointed out so clearly, the paranoiac employs a primitive anal technique for the rejection of his object, the obsessional employs a more developed anal technique for gaining control of his object and the hysteric attempts to improve his relationship with his object by a technique involving a renunciation of the genital organs. Nevertheless, my own findings leave me in equally little doubt that the paranoid, obsessional and hysterical states—to which may be added the phobic state—essentially represent, not the products of fixations at specific libidinal phases, but simply a variety of techniques employed to defend the ego against the effects of conflicts of an oral origin. The conviction that this is so is supported by two facts: (a) that the analysis of paranoid, obsessional, hysterical and phobic symptoms invariably reveals the presence of an underlying oral conflict, and (b) that paranoid, obsessional, hysterical and phobic symptoms are such common accompaniments and precursors of schizoid and depressive states. By contrast, it is quite impossible to regard as a defence either the schizoid or the depressive state in itself—each a state for which an orally based ætiology has been found. On the contrary, these states have all the character of conditions against which the ego requires to be defended. (Fairbairn, 1941, pp. 251–252, emphasis added.)

When in 1952 Fairbairn reprinted his 1941 paper on a revised psychopathology as chapter two of his only book *Psychoanalytic Studies of the Personality* (1952) his original comments on Glover and ego-nuclei were excluded. This might have been akin to Fairbairn's failure to cite the influence of Suttie on any of the ideas he was developing, as I have already explored elsewhere (Chapter One), or it may well have been because Glover left the British Psychoanalytic Society in 1944 after long and bitter disagreement with Klein as to what constituted psychoanalysis. Roazen in his *Oedipus in Britain* (2000) argues that Glover got "... singularly stigmatised as a malevolent influence" (p. 147), the chief architect of which in Roazen's account being Jones (op. cit., pp. 147–149). "Jones use of the word 'sordid' was designed to help in what became, I think, the demonisation of Glover" (op. cit., p. 148). Jones did, of course, provide the preface to Fairbairn's only book.

One question that might arise is the degree to which Glover was still committed to a theory that he had initially outlined in 1932. He was certainly still committed to the ideas when he collected and published some of his papers in his books *On the Early Development of Mind* in 1956 and *The Birth of the Ego* in 1968. Both of these books contain the work on, and the diagrams related to, the classification of mental disorders used in this chapter. That this work was important to Glover can be judged from a letter that he wrote to Freud in November 1938, quoted by Roazen in his *Oedipus in Britain* (2000). In it Glover includes a copy of his paper on "The Concept of Dissociation" (1938) and points Freud to "The part on 'ego-nucleation', 'synthesis', 'splitting', and 'dissociation' ..." (Roazen, p. 113) and comments on another enclosure as follows: "I enclose also an earlier paper on classification written many years ago. It was at this time that I was first impressed by the concept of ego-nucleation and synthesis" (op. cit.).

In her highly influential and widely read paper "Notes on Some Schizoid Mechanisms" (1946) Melanie Klein acknowledges the primacy of the schizoid suggested by Fairbairn (and consistent with Glover's classification) and changes her label for the earliest "position" to the paranoid-schizoid. She does however reject both Glover's and Fairbairn's models of early ego development explicitly. Klein's first remarks on recent papers by Fairbairn (1941, 1944, 1946) are:

> ... Fairbairn has given much attention to the subject-matter with which I am dealing to-night ... It will be seen that some of the conclusions which I shall present in this paper are in line with Fairbairn's conclusions, while others differ fundamentally. Fairbairn's approach is largely from the angle of ego development in relation to objects, while mine was predominantly from the angle of anxieties and their vicissitudes. He calls the earliest phase the "schizoid position" and states that it forms part of normal development and is the basis for adult schizoid and schizophrenic illness. I agree with this contention and consider his description of developmental schizoid phenomena as significant and revealing, and of great value for our understanding of schizoid behaviour and of schizophrenia. I also consider Fairbairn's view that the group of schizoid or schizophrenic disorders is much wider than has been acknowledged, as correct and important; and the particular emphasis he lays on the inherent relation between hysteria and schizophrenia deserves full attention. His term "schizoid position" seems adequate if it is meant to cover both persecutory fear and schizoid mechanisms. (Klein, 1946, p. 100)

Having agreed with some aspects of Fairbairn's approach and changed her own categorisation accordingly (i.e., the introduction of the paranoid-schizoid position), Klein goes on to address areas where she is not in agreement with him.

> I disagree ... with his revision of the theory of mental structure and instincts. I also disagree with his view that to begin with only the bad object is internalized ... I also dissent from Fairbairn's view that "the great problem of the schizoid individual is how to love without

destroying by love, whereas the great problem of the depressive individual is how to love without destroying by hate" (cf. Fairbairn, 1941, p. 271). This conclusion is in line not only with his rejecting the concept of primary instincts but also with his under-rating of the rôle which aggression and hatred play from the beginning of life. As a result of this approach, he does not give enough weight to the importance of early anxiety and conflict and their dynamic effects on development. (Klein, 1946, p. 100)

And:

We know so far little about the structure of the early ego. Some of the recent suggestions on this point have not convinced me: I have particularly in mind Glover's concept of ego nuclei and Fairbairn's theory of a central ego and two subsidiary egos. (op. cit.)

What I am suggesting in this chapter is that a careful reading of Glover's developmental theory of the ego-nuclei and its relationship to the psychoneuroses and the psychoses is isomorphic with Fairbairn's own revision of the psychopathology of the psychoneuroses and psychoses (1941). Glover's theory can be seen as offering an understanding of the detailed internal working of Fairbairn's central and subsidiary egos, and Fairbairn's theory offers a higher level ordering of Glover's model, an absence noted by Rayner (1990, p. 147). It is also worth noting, as Padel suggests, that:

Winnicott's paper entitled "Primitive Emotional Development" (1945) was an attempt to get Klein to accept his formulation of the earliest stages of an infant's development. Padel believes that Klein's "Notes on Some Schizoid Mechanisms" (1946) was a response to Winnicott's paper, but he also notes that, according to Grosskurth (1986), Klein had also been spurred to write the paper by Fairbairn's publication in 1944 of his paper on endopsychic structure. (Clarke, 2014, p. 303)

Fairbairn and Glover

I think there is a direct parallel between Glover's 1932 classification of mental disorders and the developmental framework into which he cast them and Fairbairn's own revised psychopathology in 1941, although there is nothing that I know of to suggest that either man publicly acknowledged this, apart from Fairbairn's reference to Glover and ego-nuclei in the initial publication of his paper on the revised psychopathology discussed above.

At the highest level Glover suggests a developmentally based schema for his attempt at the classification of mental disorders that is based in Abraham's series (see Table 2.1 below, A). On page 260 of his revised psychopathology paper (1941) Fairbairn outlines his view on the development of object relationships, which is then reproduced in a slightly modified form on pages 38–39 of Fairbairn (1952) (see Table 2.1 below, B). On page 263 of his revised psychopathology paper (1941) Fairbairn goes on to consider the natural object appropriate to the various developmental stages, which he reproduces in a modified form on page 41 of Fairbairn (1952) (see Table 2.1 below, C).

It is instructive to compare these schema to the Figure 2.2 below, which Glover first used in his 1932 paper and which was reproduced in both of his collections of papers *On the Early Development of Mind* (1956) (as his Figure 3) and *The Birth of the Ego* (1968) (as his Figure 1). Even a cursory glance will show how similar Fairbairn's developmental schema is to Glover's. The biggest difference is that what Glover describes as the Anal Sadistic (B) and the Genital Sadistic (C) stages have been treated as different aspects of the transitional stage in Fairbairn's theory. Glover himself refers to these as "transitional states" (Glover, 1956, p. 81 and p. 183), so there is justification for seeing Fairbairn's transitional techniques as replacing stages B and C in Glover's schema.

N.B. I have *redrawn* Glover's diagrams and I have *inverted* these diagrams to draw attention to the similarities between them and Fairbairn's model, which I have interpreted as follows (Clarke, 2005; Chapter Three) and reproduced here to help the reader interpret Glover's diagrams as possible precursors to Fairbairn's diagrams (Figure 2.1 below).

Fairbairn's table on page 37 indicating how the accepted and rejected objects are disposed in the psychoneuroses—obsession, paranoia, hysteria, and phobia—as described on page 267 of his revised psychopathology paper (Fairbairn, 1941) and page 46 of Fairbairn (1952), can be profitably related to Glover's diagram. Fairbairn derives this table from considering the way that internalised objects are treated using terms like those Glover uses in his diagram; for example, expulsion, retention and restitution, the latter being a key term in his theory of art (1938b).

Table 2.1. Comparison of Fairbairn and Glover's developmental schemas.

A

[Abraham's series]
A. ORAL
   (1) PREAMBIVALENT [SUCKING]
   (2) SADISTIC   [BITING]
B. ANAL-SADISTIC
   (1) EXPULSION-DESTRUCTION
   (2) RETENTION-MASTERY
C. GENITAL
   (1) PHALLIC
   (2) FINAL-POSTAMBIVALENT

B

In accordance with what precedes, it is now submitted that the norm for the development of object relationships conforms to the following scheme:
  I. Stage of Infantile Dependence, characterised predominantly by an Attitude of Taking.
    (1) Early Oral—Incorporating—Sucking or Rejecting (Preambivalent)
    (2) Late Oral—Incorporating—Sucking or Biting (Ambivalent)
  II. Stage of Transition between Infantile Dependence and Mature Dependence, or
    Stage of Quasi-Independence—Dichotomy and Exteriorisation of the Incorporated Object.
  III. Stage of Mature Dependence, characterised predominantly by an Attitude of Giving—Accepted and Rejected Objects Exteriorised.

C

In the light of what has just been said, the natural objects appropriate to the various stages of development may be indicated as follows.
  I. Infantile Dependence
    (1) Early Oral—Breast of the Mother—Part-Object
    (2) Late Oral—Mother with the Breast—Whole Object treated characteristically as a Part-Object
  II. Quasi-Independence (Transitional)
    Whole Object treated characteristically as Contents.
  III. Mature Dependence.
    Whole Object with Genital Organs.

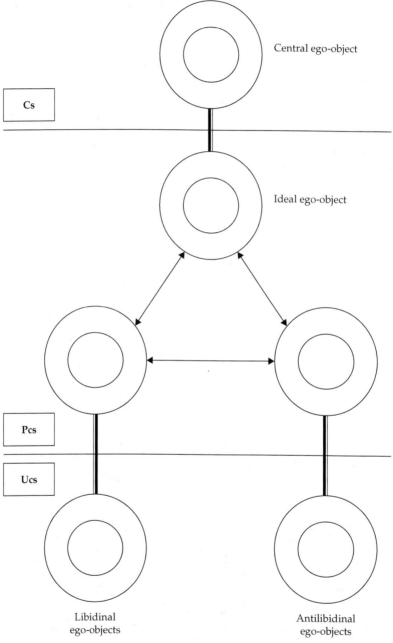

Figure 2.1. Fairbairn's model incorporating the topological categories.

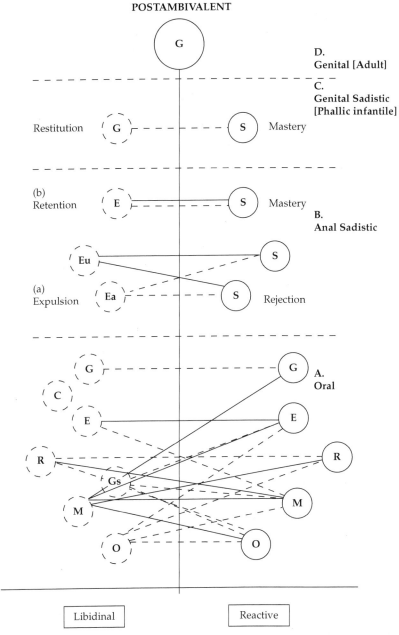

Figure 2.2. Glover's diagram of libidinal primacies and ego-nuclei (redrawn).

Table 2.2. Key to Figure 2.2.

> **Libidinal primacies and ego-nuclei**: Based on Figure 3 from Glover's 1932 paper on the classification of mental disorders from *On the Early Development of Mind* (p. 172).
>
> Explanatory notes and key taken from *The Birth of the Ego* by E. Glover (p. 25).
>
> **Illustrating the relation of libidinal primacies to ego formations**:
> A view of ego development in longitudinal section: *ego-nuclei bisected and reflected* to show libidinal and reactive constituents; note the relative lack of organisation of the oral phase, emphasising the importance of the other zonal components during that stage. Interrelations of different libidinal and reactive zones are indicated by plain and dotted lines (emphasis added).
>
> In stages B, C and D the attitude to the instinctual object (or part-object) is indicated.
>
> *Key*: O Oral; M Muscular; Gs Gastric; E Excretory; Ea Anal (Excretory); Eu Urinary (Excretory); R Respiratory; C Cutaneous; G Genital; Oth Other zonal organisations; S Sadism.

Having interpreted both the hysterical and paranoid techniques in terms of the acceptance and rejection of objects, we can now obtain interesting results by applying a similar interpretation to the phobic and obsessional techniques. The conflict underlying the phobic state may be concisely formulated as one between flight to the object and flight from the object. In the former case, of course, the object is accepted, whereas in the latter case the object is rejected. In both cases, however, the object is treated as external. In the obsessional state, on the other hand, the conflict presents itself as one between the expulsion and the retention of contents. In this case, accordingly, both the accepted and the rejected objects are treated as internal. If in the case of the phobic state both the accepted and the rejected objects are treated as external and in the obsessional state both are treated as internal, the situation as regards the hysterical and paranoid states is that one of these objects is treated as an externalized object and the other as an internalized object. In the hysterical state, it is the accepted object that is externalized, whereas, in the paranoid state, the object which is externalized is the rejected object. The nature of the object relationships characteristic of the four techniques may be summarized in the following table:

Technique	Accepted object	Rejected object(s)
Obsessional	Internalized	Internalized
Paranoid	Internalized	Externalized
Hysterical	Externalized	Internalized
Phobic	Externalized	Externalized

The chief features of the stage of transition between infantile and mature dependence may now be briefly summarized. The transition period is characterized by a process of development whereby object-relationships based upon identification gradually give place to relationships with a differentiated object. Satisfactory development during this period, therefore, depends upon the success which attends the process of differentiation of the object; and this in turn depends upon the issue of a conflict over separation from the object—a situation which is both desired and feared. The conflict in question may call into operation any or all of four characteristic techniques—the obsessional, the paranoid, the hysterical and the phobic; and, if object-relationships are unsatisfactory, these techniques are liable to form the basis of characteristic psychopathological developments in later life. The various techniques cannot be classified in any order corresponding to presumptive levels of libidinal development. On the contrary, they must be regarded as alternative techniques, all belonging to the same stage in the development of object-relationships. Which of the techniques is employed, or rather to what extent each is employed would appear to depend in large measure upon the nature of the object-relationships established during the preceding stage of infantile dependence. In particular it would seem to depend upon the degree to which objects have been incorporated, and upon the form assumed by relationships which have been established between the developing ego and its internalized objects. (Fairbairn, 1952, pp. 45–46)

In the diagram of libidinal primacies and ego-nuclei Glover uses the terms "libidinal" and "reactive" to describe the different aspects of the instincts as he sees them. Fairbairn (Birtles & Scharff, 1994, pp. 133–141) gives an extensive discussion of Drever's account of the "appetitive" and the "reactive" instinctive tendencies in his 1930 paper on the libido theory published as chapter 3 of *From Instinct to Self Vol II*. The distinction between libidinal and reactive in Glover becomes the distinction between libidinal and antilibidinal in Fairbairn.

Glover provides what he calls a "workable definition" of ego-nuclei in the following words taken from his paper on the classification of mental disorders:

> Any psychic system which (a) represents a positive libidinal relation to objects or part objects; (b) can discharge reactive tension (i.e. aggression and hate against objects) and (c) in one or other of these ways reduces anxiety, is entitled to be called an ego system or ego-nucleus. Thus an oral system gratifies instinct on a part-object (mother's nipple), it can exert aggression towards the nipple (sucking, pulling, biting) and it is able to prevent some degree of anxiety. This is the model or prototype of an independent, autonomic, primitive ego-nucleus. (Glover, 1968, p. 28)

This describes an ego, which is related to an object by affective links (initially instinctual to some degree) or, in other words, an object relationship. Since Glover was a follower of and defender of Freud the idea of component instincts giving rise to ego-nuclei, which subsequently cluster and integrate to produce more and more complex egos, came quite naturally to him. But Fairbairn had already criticised Freud's libido theory and had come to the conclusion that it is object relationships that are foremost, that the ego is object seeking, and that it is *egos that have instincts not instincts that have egos*. As a consequence he sees internalised object relationships as generating the ego-nuclei (object relations-based internal working models of reality) of which Glover's developed model is comprised. In this regard Fairbairn's 1944 comments on the question of instincts versus object relationships is pertinent.

> In actual fact, the "object-relationship" standpoint which I have now come to adopt has resulted from an attempt, imposed upon me by circumstances, to gain a better understanding of the problems presented by patients displaying certain schizoid tendencies, i.e. a class of individuals for whom object-relationships present an

especial difficulty; and here, in parenthesis, I venture to express the opinion that psychoanalytical research in its later phases has suffered from too great a preoccupation with the problems of melancholic depression. Previous to my reaching the above-mentioned standpoint, however, I had already become very much impressed by the limitations of "impulse psychology" in general, and somewhat sceptical of the explanatory value of all theories of instinct in which the instincts are treated as existing per se. The limitations of impulse psychology make themselves felt in a very practical sense within the therapeutic field; for, whilst to reveal the nature of his "impulses" to a patient by painstaking analysis is one proposition, to enable him to know what to do with these "impulses" is quite another. What an individual shall do with his "impulses" is clearly a problem of object-relationships. It is equally a problem of his own personality; but (constitutional factors apart) problems of the personality are themselves bound up with the relationships of the ego to its internalized objects—or ... the relationships of various parts of the ego to internalized objects and to one another as objects. In a word "impulses" cannot be considered apart from the endopsychic structures which they energize and the object-relationships which they enable these structures to establish; and, equally, "instincts" cannot profitably be considered as anything more than forms of energy which constitute the dynamic of such endopsychic structures. (Fairbairn, 1952, pp. 84–85)

In his books *On the Early Development of Mind* and *The Birth of the Ego* Glover reproduces the following diagram (Figure 2.3 below) from his 1932 classification of mental disorders paper. As you can see from the labels that Glover has added to the diagram, the sequence he assigns to the different stages of development are as follows: Dementia Praecox, Melancholia, Paranoia, Obsession, Phobia, and Hysteria. This is the same order that Fairbairn argues for on the basis of his developmental theory except that he thinks that the psychoneuroses all represent transitional techniques for avoiding the psychoses and are therefore not ranked.

Perhaps the best way to think about this diagram is as an outline of the way that, as we develop, we go through more and more complex forms of internal organisation or synthesis, which are represented here by the major categories of mental disorder—the psychoses and the psychoneuroses ending with mature dependence in Fairbairn's schema or genital primacy in Glover's outline. If we have not thoroughly worked through each stage as we develop then there is a possibility that under stresses, internal and external, we can revert to an earlier form of organisation. Of interest to Glover was the way that drug addiction, alcoholism and perversion, which could seem to involve a number of different stages of development, might be seen as "transitional".

> ... it was much more important to examine conditions which, however infrequent in incidence, lay between the great disorder groups. These "transitional" states ... tell us more of the gradual process of mental development than the major groups of mental disorder ... it is a significant fact that although alcoholism constitutes on the whole a transitional group, it is nevertheless itself capable of subdivision in terms of varying depth of defence, e.g. hysterical, obsessional, depressive and paranoid types. (Glover 1956, p. 81)

And further on:

> ... I believe that in transitional states such as alcoholism and drug-addiction, we can observe, in some cases, a curious interplay between repression and introjection and in others between repression and projection. *If this be the case we ought to be able to establish the original transitional phases of mental development during which these combinations first operated.* (Glover, 1956, p. 342, emphasis in original)

I conjecture that it was these and other similar comments that Glover made about transitional states that prompted Fairbairn's own reframing of the developmental process on object relations lines and his formulation of the characteristic treatment of objects for the neuroses.

Figure 2.3 is a precursor to Fairbairn's own diagram of a central self and its (ideal) object, and two subsidiary selves—libidinal and antilibidinal—and their objects, based in early object relationships internalised but never properly integrated into the central self. The clusters of ego-nuclei in the infant stage can be seen to form the two unconscious ego-object dyads—the libidinal and the antilibidinal. The primitive ego of the first anal stage would represent the earliest form of the central self, which, as in Glover's diagram, becomes progressively more complex and mature as development of the child proceeds. In particular, as the organisation of the ego becomes more complex, and the association

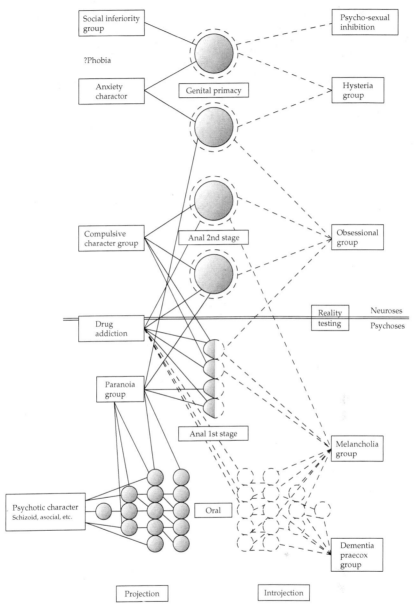

Figure 2.3. Glover's classification of mental disorders (redrawn).

42   THINKING THROUGH FAIRBAIRN

Table 2.3. Key to Figure 2.3.

[Figure 6 from Glover's 1932 paper on classification]

Illustrating the application of three primary factors in classification, (a) descriptive, (b) degree of ego development, (c) qualitative reality testing; ego seen in longitudinal section; *earlier nuclei bisected and reflected* to emphasise (a) lack of organisation of oral stages and (b) relative independent action of processes of introjection and projection. Approximate fixation points indicated by plain and dotted lines. [Emphasis added].

The oral "cluster" is represented in five separate layers to suggest a preliminary expansion of ego interest followed by a gradual contraction prior to the establishment of anal-sadistic primacy (see Table 2.3 below for detail).

The Key is the same as for Figure 2.2 above.

between word and thing presentations takes place in the preconscious, this will become the seat of the ego-ideal in Fairbairn's theory.

I will attempt to illustrate these parallels by describing an approach that my colleague Paul Finnegan and I have used recently to try to understand multiple personality disorder (MPD) from a Fairbairnian perspective (Chapters Three and Four). The diagrams below show first the initial development of the self, based upon Fairbairn's account of the internalisation of object relations (ego-nuclei) as a defensive measure against an unsatisfactory early relationship with a pre-ambivalent mother. N.B. Object relationships are represented as follows:

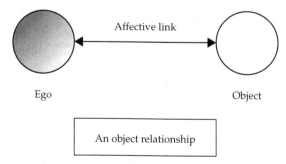

Figure 2.4. Representation of an object relationship for Fairbairn.

Table 2.4. Expansion of Figure 2.3.

The cluster of ego-nuclei that Glover places in the Oral stage (see diagram and notes above) is difficult to include in the diagram itself, so I am going to represent these using a table. I have used italics to represent the group of ego-nuclei involved in projection and those in bold font as involved with introjection. As noted above each row in the table represents a developmental stage of the early ego with the bottom row being the earliest.

		Genital	*Anal (Excretory)*	**Anal (Excretory)**	**Genital**	
	Genital	*Anal (Excretory)*	*Oral*	**Oral**	**Anal (Excretory)**	**Genital**
Other	*Genital*	*Excretory*	*Oral*	**Oral**	**Excretory**	**Genital**
	Muscular, etc.	*Excretory, Genital*	*Oral*	**Oral**	**Excretory, Genital**	**Respiratory, Cutaneous, etc.**
		Muscular, etc.	*Oral*	**Oral**	**Respiratory, Muscular etc.**	

44   THINKING THROUGH FAIRBAIRN

This is followed by the splitting of the ambivalent object and the consequent splitting of the ego to form the basic endopsychic structure.

This leads on to a recasting of Fairbairn's diagram to incorporate the topographic categories (Clarke, 2005). This was then extended to take into consideration our attempts to understand MPD using Fairbairn's model (Chapter Four). We concluded that an alter was a dynamic structure based upon previous object relations that had never been totally integrated into a higher level dynamic structure and because of environmental stress had become independently active. We gave a number of examples based upon clinical work of how this might happen. I think that the relation between Fairbairn and Glover explored

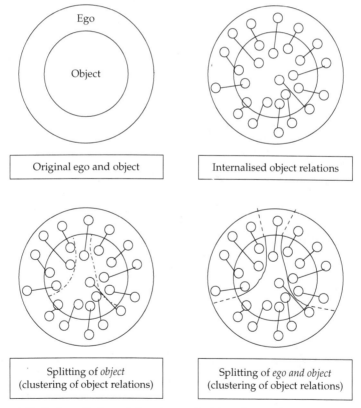

Figure 2.5. Early splitting of the ego and object for Fairbairn.

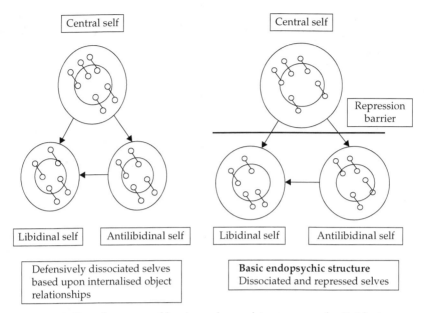

Figure 2.6. Development of basic endopsychic structure for Fairbairn.

above does help us to understand the detailed lower level workings of Fairbairn's endopsychic structures and how they could dis-integrate or come apart under pressure leading alters to dissociate.

Figure 2.7 below is a generalised version of the diagram Paul Finnegan and I used in our 2012 paper offering a Fairbairnian understanding of alters. By combining the underlying ego-nuclei approach of Glover with Fairbairn's endopsychic structure model we can see that alters are based upon ego-nuclei/object-relations based dynamic structures, which are affectively based and incompletely integrated into higher level endopsychic structures.

Conclusion

I think this illustrates quite clearly the parallels between Glover's Freudian, component-instinct based classification of mental disorders and Fairbairn's object-relations based approach to the same problem. The significant differences being that Fairbairn starts with a pristine ego that becomes attuned to the world by incorporating object-relations

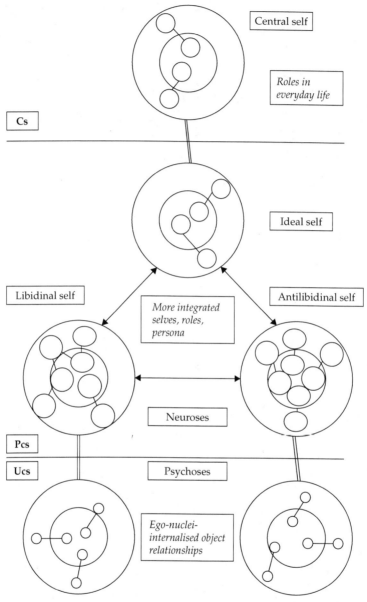

Figure 2.7. The developed model of inner reality based on Fairbairn.

based experience of the world as dynamic structures upon which the later complexities depend.

By relating Fairbairn's object relations approach to Glover's Freudian component-instinct based approach, it becomes possible to indicate how Fairbairn produced a synthesis of Freud's structural- and instinct-based theories in a relational form that does not have to dispense with instinct, since that is now seen to be intrinsic to affect within object relationships, albeit subordinate to object relationships. As such I would maintain that Fairbairn's theory is a true candidate for a synthesis of the classical and the relational.

I could have written this chapter from a different perspective, using, for instance, Glover's book *The Birth of the Ego* and his discussions of ego-nuclei, the process of ego nucleation, his ideas on ego-differentiation, the concept of dissociation, ego-synthesis, and a "primary functional phase". This would show in detail the striking parallels there are between the two men's thinking, which is captured in their diagrams despite Glover's acknowledgement that the diagrams can never capture all of the detail of the relationships between the different structural components of the mind. Glover makes an important plea for the combination of Freud's structural and topographical approaches, which he says are not contradictory but complementary, in particular in the attention they can give to the development of the preconscious in the overall development of the mind. This has interesting echoes in Fairbairn's combination of the structural and the topographical in his own diagram and his placing of the ego-ideal in the preconscious. I think there is a great deal more to be discovered in relating Fairbairn's and Glover's work and that this could be the basis for a true synthesis of the classical and the relational.

I have argued that there is a very close relationship between Fairbairn's and Glover's developmentally based models using the tables and diagrams that both men used to represent their respective approaches. I have suggested that the major difference between the two views is that the lowest level building blocks of each are different but also closely related, Fairbairn's object relationship and Glover's ego-nuclei being different only in the focus of attention—Glover's on component instincts and affect and Fairbairn's on object relationships, which are affect based. I believe that the resulting model contradicts the "relational turn" to some degree and makes Mitchell's characterisation of Fairbairn as being between paradigms (classical and relational) much more open to question.

If this combination of Fairbairn and Glover is agreed to be useful then it would also shed light on the origin of alters in MPD/DID, since these can be seen as ego-nuclei or object relationships that have not been reliably integrated into higher level structures, like the libidinal, antilibidinal and ideal—egos and objects of Fairbairn's endopsychic model—and are capable of independent activity under appropriate circumstances.

It should be noted that Winnicott was thinking along similar lines concerning the early development of mind and used the idea of ego-nuclei to explore similar problems. See the section on "Primitive Stages of Emotional Development" in chapter XVII of his *Through Paediatrics to Psychoanalysis* (1975, pp. 221–228) for explicit reference to ego-nuclei and diagrammatic representation of early developmental processes directly comparable to those developed by Glover.

It seems to me that a full understanding of the combination of ego-nuclei and object relationships must include the recognition that each is not simply an affectively coloured self-object relationship but involves a complex manifold of sensory strands going even further than the more recently developed ideas of "haptonomy—the science of affective contact" (see www.haptonomie.org/en/).

PART II

MULTIPLE PERSONALITY DISORDER

CHAPTER THREE

Fairbairn's thinking on dissociative identity disorder and the development of his mature theory

Co-author Paul Finnegan

Introduction

While investigating a new interpretation of Fairbairn's theory by Clarke (2005) paying closer attention to the (Freudian) topographic categories that Fairbairn included in his original diagram we became convinced that this revised version of Fairbairn's diagram of endopsychic structure was ideally suited to the understanding and treatment of multiple personality disorder (MPD), which has been renamed dissociative identity disorder (DID) in DSM-IV. We became convinced that looking at the way that Fairbairn addressed multiple personality throughout his work would provide fresh insight into the development of his model of endopsychic structure.

> The theory which I now envisage is, of course, obviously adapted to explain such extreme manifestations as are found in cases of multiple personality … (Fairbairn, 1952, p. 159).

MPD represents one extreme end of a spectrum of dissociations that Fairbairn saw as the foundation of inner reality and its dynamics—his "psychology of dynamic structure" (Fairbairn, 1952, p. 128). In this chapter we show that the development of Fairbairn's thinking about the structure of inner reality—from his MD thesis in 1929 (Fairbairn, 1929) through to his 1954 paper on hysterical states (Fairbairn, 1954)—is explicitly related to his thinking about MPD. We also show that Fairbairn's thinking about dissociation and its relationship to repression, his investigation into the nature of the Freudian super-ego, and his analysis of a patient with a "physical genital abnormality"—all of which took place before 1931—were intrinsic to the development of the mature model that he put forward in a series of papers that started in 1940, which comprise Part One of his only book, *Psychoanalytic Studies of the Personality* (Fairbairn, 1952).

After an historical review of the development of Fairbairn's mature theory, and the importance of multiple personality to that process, we outline a Fairbairnian framework for the understanding and treatment of MPD.

Fairbairn's thinking about multiple personality

Fairbairn provided very little clinical material related to MPD, so we cannot be certain that he ever treated a fully fledged case of MPD. However, his repeated references to multiple personality and his account of a female patient with a genital abnormality (Fairbairn, 1931), who was the subject of a paper in the clinical section of his book (Fairbairn, 1952), make it seem likely that he was familiar with one of the most common clinical experiences of the condition—the taking over of a person by an alternative personality. This is the main criteria for the identification of MPD or DID in DSM-IV. As we illustrate below, Fairbairn's experience with this patient was very significant in the way he came to understand endopsychic structure, and she seems to have given him the idea that dreams are about the relationship in inner reality between dynamic structures (ego-structures and internal objects) rather than about wish fulfilment (Fairbairn, 1944, pp. 98–99).

Fairbairn was deeply interested in dissociation—the concept Breuer and Freud had taken from Janet and used in their early work on hysteria (Freud & Breuer, 1895d). While Freud later introduced the term "repression", giving it a key place in psychoanalytic theory, Fairbairn argued that dissociation and repression were closely related and he developed his own psychology of dynamic structure based upon the dissociation and repression of mental structures.

Fairbairn came to see MPD as one part of a continuum into which the various object-relations-based "partitions of mind" (Davidson, 1982) might fall, or be cast. Our historical review of the importance of Fairbairn's thinking on MPD to the development of his model of endopsychic structure begins with Fairbairn's (1929) earliest mention of MPD, in his 1929 MD thesis, where he took for his subject two key concepts in psychoanalytic theory: dissociation and repression.

"Dissociation and repression" (1929)

During the course of investigating what Janet had meant by dissociation, Fairbairn (1929) considered whether or not the dissociated elements of a person would still have some consciousness of their own. He cited Bernard Hart (1926) to support the view that this was what Janet had meant, even though Fairbairn could find no explicit statement to this effect (Fairbairn, p. 30). He went on to look at the work of people who had been influenced by Janet and discussed the work of Morton Prince, who he argued was "perhaps the most notable of those who have applied the idea of dissociation to the explanation of abnormal mental states" (Fairbairn, p. 30). Most of Prince's work involved cases of multiple personality. In one of them, "Miss B" had a totally different personality ("Sally"), with a different set of memories. Prince argued that each personality had a different consciousness, and concluded that both were what he called "co-conscious". That is, each was aware of what was going on but only one was in charge at any particular time. However, "Where the dissociation involved elements too few to constitute a separate personality, he [Prince] believed that there resulted such phenomena as the anaesthesiae, paralyses, amnesiae, etc., to which Janet had called attention ..." (Fairbairn, 1929b, pp. 30–31). Nevertheless, Prince also regarded each of these sub-personal, dissociated elements as still having a consciousness of their own as well as being co-conscious.

Fairbairn (1929) looked at the views of his contemporaries, Rivers (1924, as cited in Fairbairn) and McDougall (1926, as cited in Fairbairn), and agreed with McDougall that the term "dissociation of consciousness" should be replaced by "dissociation of the personality". He argued that "what is distinctive about the dissociated elements is not independent consciousness but independent activity" (Fairbairn, 1929b, p. 31), and cited multiple personality as a disorder in which independent consciousness and independent activity were both present.

Fairbairn seemed closer to Prince in that he thought each of these dissociated elements had a consciousness of his or her own, but, like McDougall, he saw this as a dissociation of personality; for him, each of these dissociated structures was a personal structure. Fairbairn's conclusions regarding dissociation—and repression, as he conceived it—are important for understanding his mature model of mind, which he only made fully explicit fifteen years later in his paper on endopsychic structure (Fairbairn, 1944), but which he seems to have been using implicitly from 1929 onwards. For example, in his MD thesis, after a long discussion he concluded that dissociation could be defined as:

> ... a *mental process whereby unacceptable mental content or an unacceptable mental function becomes cut off from personal consciousness*: such mental content or function being regarded as unacceptable if it is either irrelevant to an active interest, incompatible with an active interest, or unpleasant in relation to an active interest. (Fairbairn, 1929b, p. 51, Fairbairn's emphasis)

Fairbairn defined repression as "*an active mental process whereby certain mental elements, the appearance of which in consciousness would cause unpleasure, are excluded from personal consciousness without thereby ceasing to be mental*" (Fairbairn, 1929b, p. 69, Fairbairn's emphasis). He argued that dissociation was a defence "directed against mental content determined ultimately by *events that happen* to the individual", whereas repression was a defence "directed against *tendencies which form part of the mental structure* of the individual himself" (Fairbairn, 1929b, p. 77, Fairbairn's emphasis). Thus the repression of mental structure (by mental structure), discussed further in his paper on the super-ego (Fairbairn, 1929b, p. 101 ff), is a second line of defence; it operates on previously dissociated mental structures, enabling a stable, basic endopsychic structure to form and be sustained.

Despite his argument that repression was a special form of the dissociation of the unpleasant, the basic distinction between dissociation and repression concerned the phenomena that were being defended against. In the case of dissociation these were external, thus accounting for Fairbairn's insistence on the importance of what had really happened to the child. Repression, on the other hand, was seen as defending against unpleasant phenomena generated internally. That is, content generated by the activity of dissociated mental structures would need to be defended against, thus accounting for the dynamics of the multiplicity of (dissociated) egos.

"The Superego" (1929)

The same year that he wrote his MD thesis, Fairbairn (1929) wrote two papers on the super-ego, its nature and function. Having already established that it "does not originate through being repressed and nor is it by nature repressed", he sought to explore the process whereby the super-ego is cut off from consciousness (Fairbairn, p. 112). In investigating this question he referred to a passage in *The Ego and the Id* (Freud, 1923b) where Freud makes reference to multiple personality. Fairbairn noted that "references to this remarkable phenomenon are conspicuous by their absence in Freud's writings" (Fairbairn, p. 112). He regarded this as odd, since, as far as he was concerned, cases of multiple personality "provide the most striking examples known to psychopathology of the wholesale cutting off of mental elements from the rest of the mind" (Fairbairn, p. 112).

Fairbairn's explanation of why the problem of multiple personality had been relatively neglected may still be relevant today. The first reason for this neglect, he said, was partly because such cases had not been brought into analysis. The second reason—which may well help to explain this relative avoidance of multiple personality by analysts—goes deeper and returns us to the discussion of dissociation and repression. After reviewing Freud's thesis that "the doctrine of repression is the foundation-stone upon which the whole structure of Psycho-Analysis rests" (1914b, p. 297, as cited in Fairbairn, 1929a, p. 113), Fairbairn argued that the reason why the phenomenon of multiple personality received "so little attention at the hands of Freud" was because multiple personality did not involve repression, but dissociation (Fairbairn, 1929a, p. 113). In a search for some evidence in support of this view he suggested the following passage from *The Ego and the Id*:

> Although it is a digression from our theme, we cannot avoid giving our attention for a moment longer to the ego's object identifications. If they obtain the upper hand and become too numerous, unduly intense and incompatible with one another, a pathological outcome will not be far off. It may come to a disruption of the ego in consequence of the individual identifications becoming cut off

> from one another by resistances; perhaps the secret of the cases of so-called multiple personality is that the various identifications seize possession of consciousness in turn. Even when things do not go so far as this, there remains the question of conflicts between the various identifications into which the ego comes apart, conflicts which cannot after all be described as purely pathological. (Freud, 1923b, 38–39, as quoted in Fairbairn, 1929a, p. 113)

Fairbairn noted that this passage came from a section of Freud's account of the development of the nucleus of the super-ego from the child's first identifications with his/her parents. Fairbairn argued that the process that gave rise to the super-ego was of a similar nature to the process that gave rise to multiple personality. He reiterated his conclusions from his MD thesis, noting the similarities and differences between dissociation and repression, and argued that the way the super-ego was cut off from the ego was through *"dissociation of the incompatible"* (Fairbairn, 1929a, pp. 113–114, emphasis added).

"Clinical Case" (1931)

In a 1931 paper on the analysis of a female patient with a genital abnormality, Fairbairn (1931) introduced the idea of "functioning structural constellations" (Fairbairn, 1931, pp. 221–222), which the authors believe is a direct precursor to the idea of endopsychic structure in his mature theory. Fairbairn said that through the analysis of the patient's dreams he could identify dynamic structures corresponding to the ego, the id, and the super-ego. He argued that Freud's tripartite division of mind could be taken to represent "a characteristic functional grouping of structural elements in the psyche" (Fairbairn, 1931, p. 218), and commented that although the dynamic structures of Freud's structural model were indicated in the case he was analysing, the possibility of other dynamic structures was also indicated.

Referring back to the passage from Freud's (1923b) *The Ego and the Id* quoted above, and using the idea of personification as the consequence of close identification, he argued that the personifications encountered in the patient's dreams might throw some light on multiple personality: "The characteristic personifications which have been described all presented the appearance of separate personalities; and this fact suggests the possibility that multiple personality may be merely an advanced product of the same process that created such personification in the present case" (Fairbairn, 1931, p. 218).

He then looked in detail at each of the personifications that appeared in the patient's dreams and concluded that while some of them might be understood as being based upon identifications, others seemed to be dynamic structures ("structural units") that had gained a degree of independence within the total personality for economic reasons. Fairbairn commented: "… it seems reasonable to suppose that the mental processes which give rise to multiple personality only represent a more extreme form of those which produced 'the mischievous boy', 'the critic', 'the little girl' and 'the martyr' in this patient's dreams" (Fairbairn, 1931, p. 219). He noted that these personifications were confined in large measure to the unconscious as revealed in dreams but could see no reason why similar personifications should not invade the conscious field in waking life. Towards the end of the case study Fairbairn noted that:

> it seems important to draw attention to another remarkable feature of the case—viz. The tendency of the patient to personify various aspects of her psyche. This tendency first manifested itself in dreams; but it came to be quite consciously adopted by the patient during analysis. The most striking and the most persistent of these personifications were two figures whom she described respectively as "the mischievous boy" and "the critic". (Fairbairn, 1931, p. 216)

He later commented that in the case of this patient there was a prolonged period in the analysis when "the mischievous boy" had taken "almost complete possession" of the patient's conscious life: "she later volunteered the statement that for the time being she was a totally different person" (Fairbairn, 1931, p. 219). Here are concrete examples of personifications that had appeared in the patient's dreams and then had taken over as the dominant personality of the person, at least during their relations with the therapist. While Fairbairn did not describe this patient as being multiple personality, the basis for such a diagnosis is present in the clinical material presented.

Fairbairn argued that the personifications in the patient's dreams had something in common with both the mental structures of Freud's structural theory and with the phenomena of multiple personality. For Fairbairn, the same process of differentiation led to both: to the structural elements of Freud's theory and to multiple personality. He went on to suggest that some aspects of multiple personality might be the consequence of a "temporary invasion of the conscious field on the part of 'the super-ego' or 'the id' ..." (Fairbairn, 1931, p. 219) but that multiple personalities were not necessarily consistent with the tripartite division of mind that Freud described. He suggested that manic states might be due to "the invasion of the conscious field by a formation of the nature of the id" (Fairbairn, 1931, p. 220) but resisted the conclusion that melancholia might be an equivalent invasion of the conscious field by the super-ego.

These thoughts and the model they imply are clear precursors to the mature model Fairbairn put forward in his 1944 paper on endopsychic structure, despite the absence of the exact terminology of that later model. The mature model presented a clearer distinction between ego-structures and internal objects, and used such descriptive labels as "libidinal", "antilibidinal", and "ideal", which might have allowed a more precise understanding of the different (preconscious and unconscious) personae represented by the personifications in his patient's dreams. From the mature model's perspective, "the mischievous boy" is clearly a libidinal ego figure; similarly "the critic" is clearly an antilibidinal ego; "the little girl" is probably a libidinal ego; and "the martyr" is probably an ideal-ego based figure. If his mature model had been available to Fairbairn in 1931, he might well have been able to bring a greater understanding to these unconscious personae and in the process encourage better understanding of the way the patient was splitting up the world and her role(s) in it, thus enabling splitting to be reduced and some greater degree of integration to be achieved.

"Schizoid Factors" (1940)

Fairbairn argued that a wide range of phenomena are based upon splitting, or on what he called the schizoid position, which is what became the basic endopsychic situation in the later papers. In the following quotation, he lists a wide range of phenomena that might be understood on the basis of the schizoid position, including multiple personality at one end of the continuum through depersonalisation, derealisation and other disturbances of the reality sense to déjà vu at the other.

> A similar view must be taken of such dissociative phenomena as somnambulism, the fugue, dual personality, and multiple

personality. So far as the manifestations of dual and multiple personality are concerned, their essentially schizoid nature may be inferred from a discreet study of the numerous cases described by Janet, William James, and Morton Prince. And here it is apposite to remark that many of the cases described by Janet as manifesting the dissociative phenomena on the basis of which he formulated his classic concept of "Hysteria" behaved suspiciously like schizophrenics—a fact which I interpret in support of the conclusion, which I have already reached on the basis of my own observations, that the personality of the hysteric invariably contains a schizoid factor in greater or lesser degree, however deeply this may be buried. (Fairbairn, 1940, pp. 5–6)

We take this to mean that the processes that lead to the establishment of the basic endopsychic structure and its subsequent development can go wrong in a wide variety of ways, including full-blown MPD and a variety of neurotic symptoms. We understand this range of different symptoms to be produced by different (internal) economic necessities and different relational contexts.

"Controversial Discussions" (1943)

During the protracted discussions between Anna Freud, Melanie Klein, their followers and members of the indigenous group of British analysts, which took place after Freud died, known as the Controversial Discussions (King & Steiner, 1991), Fairbairn made one contribution, in 1943, read in his absence by Edward Glover. In this, Fairbairn argued that the explanatory concept of "phantasy" had been rendered obsolete by the work of Klein and her followers and that the time was ripe for the replacement of:

> the concept of "phantasy" by a concept of an "inner reality" peopled by the Ego and its internal objects. These internal objects should be regarded as having an organised structure, an identity of their own, an endopsychic existence and an activity as real within the inner world as those of objects in the outer world. (Fairbairn, 1943b, p. 294)

Susan Isaacs rejected Fairbairn's suggestion on behalf of the Kleinian group and there was no further discussion recorded. In her rejection of

Fairbairn's interpretation of Klein, Isaacs argues that Fairbairn "oversubstantifies internal objects and makes them far too independent" (King & Steiner, 1991, p. 458). This is of great significance, since we argue that Fairbairn remained true to his idea of the real independence of dynamic structures and that the ontological status of internal objects and ego-structures remains a significant difference between Fairbairnian and Kleinian thinking, as in the latter they are understood to be the product of phantasy.

"Endopsychic Structure" (1944)

Continuing the refinement of his critique of Freud's account of repression, Fairbairn (1944) developed his view that mental structures are what repress mental structures. He saw a fundamental error in Freud's structural model: it failed to recognise that it is mental structures that produce what Freud called "impulses". In this passage, Fairbairn uses multiple personality to illustrate the view that mental structures are what is repressed and that mental structures produce "impulses":

> ... the phenomena of multiple personality, in which the linkage of repressed "impulses" with a submerged ego structure is beyond question; but such a linkage may also be detected in the less extensive forms of dissociation, which are so characteristic of the hysterical individual. In order to account for repression, we thus appear to be driven to the necessity of assuming a certain multiplicity of egos. This should not really prove a particularly difficult conception for anyone familiar with the problems presented by schizoid patients. (Fairbairn, 1944, p. 90)

He developed this theme throughout his book (Fairbairn, 1952); it will be seen again in the section entitled "Synopsis", below.

Fairbairn's theory of dreams, also developed in this paper, argues that dreams are the dramatisation of situations in inner reality, where ego-structures and internal objects are personified and dreams represent the relationships between these endopsychic structures. Interestingly, this has resonances with the view that Brenner develops (2001) in his chapter on "Trauma and the Dream Ego", where he suggests that "self-state" dreams are common. Brenner argues that it is of benefit to view the dreams of patients with severe dissociative pathology from this perspective.

> In a number of cases I have ... observed striking similarities between the manifest content of traumatic dreams and the first hand accounts of the personifications themselves ... The massively traumatised child who has recurrent dreams at night of his defensive altered states during the day may thus become further confused by the mutual influences of one or the other. (Brenner, 2001, p. 77)

"Object Relations" (1949)

In a paper reviewing the development of his mature theory of a psychology of dynamic structure, Fairbairn (1949) made perhaps the clearest statement of the relationship between his mature theory and multiple personality:

> *The theory which I now envisage is, of course, obviously adapted to explain such extreme manifestations as are found in cases of multiple personality;* but as Janet has pointed out, these extreme manifestations are only exaggerated examples of the dissociation phenomena characteristic of hysteria. Thus, if we implement the slogan "Back to hysteria", we find ourselves confronted with the very phenomenon of splitting upon which my theory of repression is based. (Fairbairn, 1949, p.159, emphasis added)

This is consistent with the way that Fairbairn understood and discussed MPD over a twenty-year period.

"Synopsis" (1951)

In the synopsis of the development of his views at the end of his metapsychology section in Fairbairn (1952) revisits the whole of the process we have followed from his 1929 work forward. First he argued that impulses necessarily involve object relationships and cannot be considered apart from ego-structures; they are thus the dynamic aspects of ego-structures. This led to his replacement of an impulse psychology with that of a "psychology of dynamic structure". He criticised Freud's structural theory for not being consistent with the modern scientific understanding of the relationship between energy and structure. He also argued that the original ego is oriented towards the external world and is thus, initially, reality-seeking as opposed to pleasure-seeking.

This reality principle is immature but under favourable circumstances can mature as experience grows. However, he argued that under inimical situations the reality orientation can deteriorate to a pleasure orientation.

This idea of dynamic structure led to a revision of the idea of repression, which was that repression is exercised primarily against bad internal objects, which are themselves allied to internalised ego-structures. Splitting of the ego is the mechanism that can account for the process of repression. Freud had postulated the existence of a structure capable of instigating repression (i.e., the super-ego) and Fairbairn's psychology of dynamic structures is based upon internalised object-relationship-based entities, like the super-ego, where one dynamic structure can repress another dynamic structure.

> *Such a conception would throw light not only upon the phenomena of multiple personality and hysterical dissociation, but also upon the practical difficulties experienced over the process described as "sublimation" in impulse-psychology* (the "impulses" to be "sublimated" being no longer regarded as separate from ego-structure). (Fairbairn, 1951, p. 168, emphasis added)

Fairbairn repeats his criticism of Freud and Klein for developing their theories too exclusively in relation to melancholia and the depressive position when in his view they should have paid more attention to hysteria and schizoid phenomenon. Fairbairn's suggestion that repression involves the splitting of the ego will come as no surprise to anyone familiar with schizoid patients. This summary by Fairbairn of the development of his theory has multiple personality at its heart.

"Hysterical States" (1954)

In his paper on hysterical states reprinted in volume 1 of *From Instinct to Self*, Fairbairn (1954) discussed Janet and dissociation before reiterating:

> Further consideration reveals that the process of dissociation, as conceived by Janet, carries with it the implication of *a split in the personality*, variable in its extent and often multiple; and the view that such an underlying splitting of the personality is implied in

hysterical phenomena is a view which I sought to substantiate in a paper written in 1944. (Fairbairn, 1954, p. 14, Fairbairn's emphasis)

Fairbairn commented in the next line that this is a view Freud himself "entertained" in his 1893a paper "On the psychical mechanism of hysterical phenomena":

> Indeed, the more we occupied ourselves with these phenomena the more certain did our conviction become that splitting of consciousness, which is so striking in the well-known classical cases of *double conscience*, exists in a rudimentary fashion in every hysteria and that the tendency to dissociation … is a fundamental manifestation of this neurosis. (Freud, 1893a, as quoted in Fairbairn, 1954, p. 14, Freud's emphasis)

Throughout his clinical and theoretical work, Fairbairn looked critically at Freud's model-building. Based in particular upon his detailed thinking about repression and dissociation, with the example of multiple personality as a real and logical limit at one end of a continuum, he cited Freud's own formulations to help produce a rational reconstruction of Freud that became his own psychology of dynamic structure. The importance of personifications based upon identifications was another key aspect of this recasting of Freud's theory. One aspect of this process, which did not come out clearly in these papers, but which was argued in Padel (1985), was Fairbairn's understanding that object relationships are internalised as a whole, so that people can use either side of the internalised object relationship in understanding, making or entering other object relationships. This approach can be traced back to Freud's (1914c) paper on narcissism, where alternate forms of identification (narcissistic or anaclitic) are possible to the child who has internalised the nursing couple. Multiple personalities can arise from narcissistic and anaclitic identifications (in Freud's terminology), or from ego identifications and object identifications (in Fairbairn's terminology).

Fairbairn's consideration of multiple personality throughout his working life leads to his proposing the following mechanisms, chronologically over a thirteen year period: (a) dissociation of mental structure (splitting), (b) the personification of dissociated mental structure and the development of functional structural constellations of dissociated mental structures, leading to (c) the proposal that inner reality is peopled by a constellation of real dynamic structures and that phantasy reflects the affective relationships between such dynamic structures. His overall proposal for the understanding of inner reality as an endopsychic structure is represented in his diagram (Figure 3.1).

Fairbairn's revision of Freud

Fairbairn was a Freudian, but he thought that Freud's structural model needed to be modified to make it more self-consistent and in line with twentieth-century science. This was the focus of all his theoretical work.

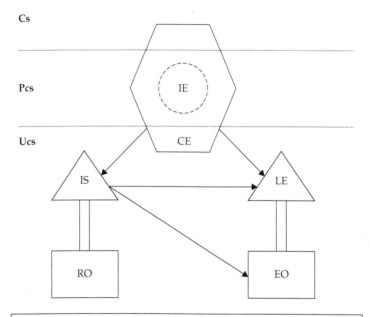

Figure 3.1. Fairbairn's original diagram (1944) (redrawn).

While Fairbairn concentrated most on bringing some rigour to the structural theory he was himself less consistent about his use of the topographical aspects of Freud's earlier model. A modification to Fairbairn's model of inner reality based upon the development of the role of the preconscious has been made recently (Clarke, 2005) and the resulting model can be seen as the incorporation of Freud's topographical categories into Fairbairn's model of endopsychic structure to produce a new model of inner reality.

Understanding this model as a representation of highly dynamic sets of object relationship structures and their interrelations is of the utmost importance and one needs to see each of its components as constantly in process as a person goes about their daily business. It is important to remember that "the map is not the territory". But the map does provide places for these dynamic structures to be situated in relation to each other, even if the dynamic nature of the processes involved cannot be adequately represented within the diagram. When it comes to psychic change there are two different ways in which Fairbairn's theory has been understood, one developed by Padel and the other by Rubens.

Padel (1991) suggested that in Fairbairn's theory psychic change and psychic growth in particular come about by the transformation of split off, repressed, libidinal and anti-libidinal dynamic structures whose *object relationships* are worked over and become (re)incorporated into the central ego/object and ideal ego/object. Similarly, he suggested that unacceptable aspects of day-to-day object relations are split off and appropriately directed during sleep to split off, repressed libidinal and antilibidinal subsidiary selves. There is thus a two-way process in Padel's model: in a repressive move, conscious experience is turned into unconscious (split off, dissociated) experience associated with either the libidinal or antilibidinal subsidiary selves; in an integrative move, (object-relations) aspects of these repressed, split off subsidiary selves are brought to consciousness, transformed, and reincorporated into the central self.

In Freud's topographical theory these transitions would usually be via the (system) preconscious (*Pcs*). Padel did not employ the preconscious consistently, but Fairbairn acknowledged the existence of the preconscious by placing the ideal self there. When Padel (1991) talked about the repressed selves not being absolutely split off from the central ego, or not being equally repressed, he was implying that some aspects of these selves could become conscious or potentially conscious; that is, they become preconscious. A full description of the processes Padel described, without using the concept of the preconscious, would show conscious (Cs) experience being transformed into unconscious (Ucs) material without mediation. It seems much more reasonable, given that the preconscious is a part of Fairbairn's model, to see the preconscious playing a mediating role between the central self and the unconscious libidinal and antilibidinal selves. Given that there are two levels of censorship (Freud, 1915e, p. 153) and that the ideal ego/object is most closely associated with the second level, between the Pcs and the Cs, it seems reasonable to suggest that there are Pcs representatives of the libidinal and the antilibidinal selves.

Rubens (1984) suggested that in Fairbairn's theory, structure is pathology and that psychic growth, in a developmental sense, takes place by means of non-structuring internalisations. To accept that structure is pathology *and* have no way to ameliorate this process other than the development of non-structuring internalisations and the internalisation of the good object as a defence against bad internal objects (cf. Mitchell, 1994) seems to us to be a counsel of despair. While we accept that Rubens' account captures an important aspect of the process of maturation we suggest that Padel's notion of psychic growth—that the unconscious libidinal and antilibidinal structural elements "like the Zuider Zee" can be drained and reclaimed as productive aspects of the central and ideal selves—is an attractive and convincing hypothesis, producing a more realistic ideal self (ideal ego plus ideal object) and a central self with more (realistic) powers. Our suggestion, which might perhaps provide a common basis for these different approaches to agree upon, is to modify Fairbairn's original model so that the *topographical* distinctions between the Ucs, Pcs and Cs are incorporated into the model consistently. Each of the selves represented should be regarded as comprising object relations. Thus, we would have a Cs central self with a Pcs ideal self as per Fairbairn's original diagram, but now we would also have Pcs and Ucs libidinal selves, and Pcs and Ucs antilibidinal selves.

When Fairbairn came to discuss the Oedipus situation, which he believes is an internal situation that is constituted by the child himself (Fairbairn, 1944, p. 119ff), he argued that the child has to make sense of the internalisations of the two most significant figures in his/her life, mother and father. In order to do this the child has to resolve the problem of having contradictory and disturbing bad objects at the centre of the libidinal and antilibidinal selves.

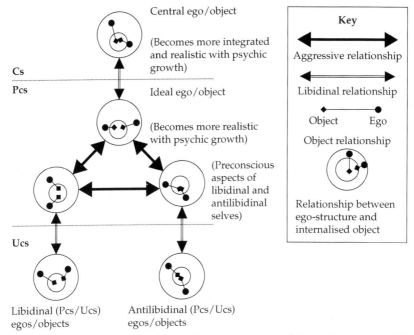

Figure 3.2. Fairbairn's endopsychic structure and Freud's topographic categories.

> Before the child is very old, these internal objects have already assumed the form of complex composite structures ... built up partly on the basis of the superimposition of one object upon another and partly on a basis of the fusion of objects. The extent to which the internal objects are built up respectively on the basis of *layering* and on a basis of *fusion* differs ... from individual to individual ... (Fairbairn, 1944, pp. 122–123, Fairbairn's emphasis)

Thus the child:

> ... for all practical purposes, comes to equate one parental object with the exciting [libidinal] object, and the other with the rejecting [antilibidinal] object; and by so doing *the child constitutes the Oedipus situation for himself*. (Fairbairn, 1944, p. 124, Fairbairn's emphasis)

It is through these means and in relation to the family situation that the child constitutes their own gender identity. From this time onwards, the complex composite objects are still subject to non-structuring internalisations, and the degree to which the layering and fusion of the parental objects can accommodate these will help to determine the future stability of inner reality.

One question that arises within Fairbairn's work itself is whether or not the internal objects (as opposed to ego-structures) are also autonomous personal structures. This is answered affirmatively in the last section of his 1944 paper on endopsychic structure and in his response to some critics of his view of endopsychic structure (Scharff & Birtles, 1994, p. 152ff). In this latter context he addresses Sutherland's argument that, with some patients at least, the libidinal and antilibidinal egos are much less well organised as in the case of "advanced hysterics", where the antilibidinal ego appears to be "composed of (or at any rate contain) several active sub-structures" (op. cit., p. 153). Fairbairn goes on to say that he has no difficulty "in accepting the proposition that the internal objects are composite structures ... [which] may undergo both disintegrative change under pathogenic conditions and integrative changes under therapeutic conditions" (op. cit., p. 154).

A Fairbairnian perspective on MPD

The extension of Fairbairn's theory that we propose addresses the question of the origins of alter personalities from within the theoretical framework of the endopsychic structure developed above. What we are proposing are new *structure generating processes* uniquely associated with trauma and dissociation as an explanatory extension of Fairbairn's theory. In order to develop this extension to the theory we need first to revisit the structure-generating aspects of the theory according to Fairbairn.

For Fairbairn, the development of the basic endopsychic structure is a once and for all process, which he sees as being stable up to the point of psychosis, even if all of the components are themselves dynamic. Once the basic endopsychic structure is developed then, as Rubens (1984) and Padel (1985, 1991) argue respectively, psychic growth occurs through either non-structuring internalisations or the growth of the central and ideal selves at the expense of the libidinal and antilibidinal selves. There are, however, examples of multiple personality that seem to go beyond this process. For example, clinically there may be paired same age personalities, one libidinal and one antilibidinal, and there may be two alter personalities, derivative of the same endopsychic structure, each of a different age, the younger personality having no knowledge of the older personality, while the latter has some awareness of the former. The specific development of dissociated sub-selves that are paired and/or age-specific in their behaviours and experience seems to suggest a more radical form of dissociation in response to trauma than is included in the model as we have developed it so far.

If we imagine an antilibidinal ego that is already to some degree subdivided (layered and/or fused) relative to the various antilibidinal objects that the person has encountered, so that each of these partial divisions of the antilibidinal ego might act independently, then this would go some way in explaining the dissociated selves of MPD. In Fairbairn's formulation it is the splitting of the *object* that leads to the splitting of the ego; therefore, we hypothesize that in overwhelmingly traumatic circumstances at the hands of another person, the splitting off of a traumatizing object-structure from the originating antilibidinal object-structure would be accompanied by the splitting off of a traumatized antilibidinal ego-structure from the originating antilibidinal ego-structure, leading to the formation of *a split off/dissociated ego-object sub-structure*. (see Figure 3.3)

It has been recognised for a long time that multiple personalities occur in clusters. Ellenberger in a section entitled "Personality Clusters" argues that:

> For quite a long time the only cases to be published were those of "dual personality". But it was later realised that the human mind was rather like a matrix from which whole sets of subpersonalities could emerge and differentiate themselves. (Ellenberger, 1970, p. 139)

We argue, based upon the model we are developing, that there can be severe vertical splitting in multiple personality, which leads to a duplication of the endopsychic structure. This duplication of endopsychic structure is another extension of Fairbairn's theory advanced for the express purposes of understanding clusters or "whole sets of subpersonalities". Furthermore, clinically it appears that alters based upon the ideal ego or ideal object are often the initial conduits or "gatekeepers" through which the analyst first comes into contact with these hidden clusters of other alters.

In a review article MacGregor (1996) describes characteristic alter personalities as follows: (a) child personalities, which are often paired, one

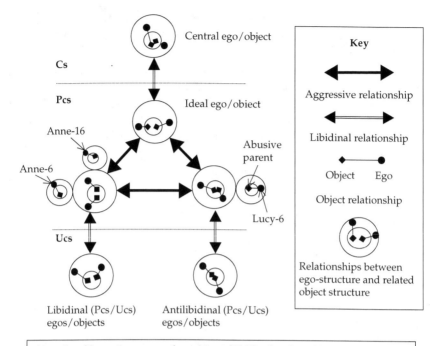

Figure 3.3. Trauma-induced vertical splitting of dynamic structures (1).

good, one bad; (b) protector personalities; (c) persecutor personalities, which "sabotage the patient's life"; and (d) opposite-sex personalities.

On the basis of Fairbairn's model as we have developed it above, different personalities may be located within the structural model of inner reality. Within this model each of the personalities is libidinal, antilibidinal or ideal, and based upon either an ego or an object identification. These include: a) child personalities derived from the libidinal or antilibidinal ego, which, when paired, are often engaged in a persecutory relationship; (b) protector personalities derived from the ideal ego and ideal object; (c) persecutory personalities derived from the antilibidinal ego and antilibidinal object; and (d) opposite-sex personalities derived from object-based identifications.

Importantly, in keeping with Fairbairn and Padel's emphasis on the importance of the libidinal aspects of endopsychic dynamics,

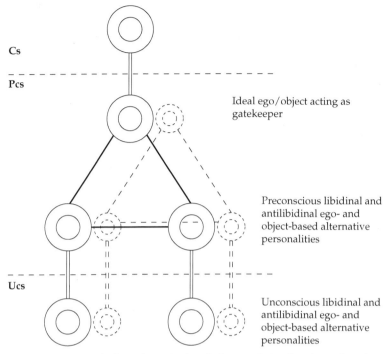

Figure 3.4. Trauma-induced vertical splitting and duplication of endopsychic structure (1).

this model also suggests that there are personalities derivative of the libidinal ego and the libidinal object as is also borne out in our clinical experience. Consequently, the model we are proposing is well suited to the "mapping" of alter personalities (MacGregor, 1996), as it locates alters in terms of their endopsychic structure of origin and facilitates the understanding of the relationships that exist between them. The model may also guide analytic inquiry with respect to alter personalities that have remained repressed and/or split off. This model also provides a framework for the understanding of the transference/countertransference dynamics that emerge as internal object relationships become externalised.

Conclusion

We have reviewed the role that Fairbairn's thinking about MPD had on the development of his own thoroughgoing theory of object relations.

We have suggested developments to his model to include Freud's topographic categories and Padel's understanding of psychic growth. We have agreed with Fairbairn's statement that his psychology of dynamic structure can be used to understand the structural origins of the various personalities that are characteristic of MPD and the relationships that exist between them. Further, the model may guide analytic inquiry with respect to alter personalities that have remained repressed and/or split off. This model also provides a framework for the understanding of the transference/countertransference dynamics that emerge as internal object relationships become externalised. The next chapter outlines the application of this theoretical approach to some cases of MPD treated by Paul Finnegan.

CHAPTER FOUR

Evelyn's PhD in Wellness—a Fairbairnian understanding of the therapeutic relationship with a woman with dissociative identity disorder

Co-authored with Paul Finnegan

Fairbairn's thinking about dissociative identity disorder (DID) played an important role in the development of his own distinctive formulation of object relations theory (Chapter Three). In this chapter we present clinical material from Dr Paul Finnegan's work with Evelyn, a patient with DID, to illustrate how an extended version of Fairbairn's model of endopsychic structure might be used. First, to map particular commonly occurring alter personalities; second, to formulate an understanding of the relationships between alter personalities; third, to understand the transference-countertransference dynamics that emerge as internal object relations are externalised, and finally, to conceptualise the process of psychic growth as it takes place during the process of working with someone who has DID. The presentation of the clinical material will be followed by a brief introduction to the extended Fairbairnian model and a discussion of the clinical work from this perspective. The approach that we are presenting will then be discussed in relation to some other psychoanalytic approaches. Dr Paul Finnegan was Evelyn's analyst and the clinical material is reported from his perspective.

Evelyn

Evelyn was referred by a retiring colleague with the suggestion that I continue the twice-weekly supportive psychotherapy that he had provided for several years. He described Evelyn as a woman who was inhibited about her sexuality, had great difficulty expressing her anger, and experienced intense separation anxiety.

Evelyn's perspective on therapy was that she continued to need someone to help her deal with the difficulties she faced in her life—particularly marital difficulties. Evelyn was married to a rather overbearing and controlling man, who tended to treat her "like a child in his protective custody".

Evelyn was the eldest of two children and had a brother two years younger. When Evelyn was a year old her mother's father died, which led to her mother becoming "depressed and unresponsive" and Evelyn's care being given over to her grandmother. Evelyn saw her mother as always having been "self-absorbed" and there being "no emotional connection" with her. Evelyn said: "This is how it was in our family—no one could stand this sad, pained and lonely child … [my mother's] … response to this would be just to space out."

Evelyn had always had trouble being close to her father, as he was often absent, and when he was at home with his family he was ill-tempered, threatening, and sometimes violent. "He would fly into terrible and unpredictable rages and destroy everything in sight … I would be so frightened …" Evelyn's mother remained passively submissive to this threatening and violent father—never addressing the impact of his behaviour on their children.

We began meeting twice weekly and although Evelyn initially presented as described by the referring therapist, over the next few months she began to reveal strikingly different aspects of her personality. While sometimes she was lively, warm, engaging, and explicitly seductive, at other times she was demanding, furiously angry, and vengeful. I initially thought Evelyn to be a woman with overwhelming attachment needs and I felt quite challenged, and sometimes overburdened, by the demands that she made on me. I later came to understand that what she was demanding of me was an expression of attention, interest and caring that had been missing in her relationship with her mother. The rage with which she responded to my empathic failures also had its origins in her identifications with her demanding and violent father.

Meeting twice weekly left her feeling "lost" between sessions, and feeling that she had "lost" me, and she dealt with this by leaving notes and letters outside my office door and many phone messages at my office and at my home, all expressing her feelings about what had happened during the previous session. From time to time she left letters at my door that thoughtfully and intelligently explained what had happened in the more chaotic sessions and these letters were signed Martha. One of these letters read:

> The well part of me has to write, when I am able, as there are only a few times when I'm in control to write. She was angry at you again today. That is the child part of her that was never allowed.

Sessions were soon increased to five times weekly, as the sessions would sometimes be characterised by such chaos that neither of us felt we could manage without meeting daily. Evelyn's impact on me was so cognitively and emotionally disorganising that I could not work well with patients seen after her, so I booked her appointments as the last of my day. On her own initiative, Evelyn began to use the couch. The transferences continued to oscillate between libidinisation and idealisation when I pleased her and vengeful fury when I failed her. Within the context of these transferences, and while they were in occasional abeyance, we were gradually able to develop a space in which we could work creatively and effectively together.

When Evelyn learned that I was about to begin working with a new patient she exhibited rage of an intensity far greater than anything I had met with before. She felt betrayed, abandoned, despairing, vengeful and murderously destructive. She screamed at me: "How could you? You make me think you care about me and you do this! You can go straight to hell and so can your new baby!" And then she pleaded for my exclusive attention: "I'm just a little baby. I need you for me. Please don't do this to me." And she seethed: "I could kill you both. I hope she chokes on your milk." And she begged: "Don't give the baby your breast! Save your breast for me." When she later realised that I had taken this "second" patient into my care she exploded with:

> Fuck the mother and fuck the child ... where is my father? ... gone away as usual ... who is going to tend to me? ... I'll have to tend to myself ... you're too busy with your new baby. ... I wish you and your damn baby were dead ... I can't take any more of this shit.

During the first three years of our work we engaged in a re-enactment of Evelyn's first two years of life, the early dynamics of her relationship with her mother, to the time of the birth of her brother and the first year of her adjustment to his presence in the family. During this phase there was a sustained symbiotic merger over a long period, with urgent demands for my undivided attention, empathic responsiveness, and participation in the regulation of her affective states. There was also intense despair and violent rage when I failed her, as I often did, leading her to feel utterly abandoned by me. There was then a gradual movement from this symbiotic merger through play and on to a slow and painful engagement of the process of separation. A process of profound and painful disillusionment accompanied the gradual transformation of our relationship from one of alternating engulfments and abandonments to one of communication between us as separate and different selves.

On the communication and recognition of the multiplicity

During the first years of our work Evelyn dismissively denied any knowledge of the many letters signed "Martha" clearly explaining the chaotic and confusing events of a previous session that were left at my office door. A letter received at a time of crisis, and signed Martha, read as follows:

> I don't know how well you understand the part of her named Martha who is me. I write on her behalf. I am a well part of her but I am not quite strong enough yet to be in control of these fits of hers.

Later, at another time of chaotic confusion, another letter signed Martha was received and read as follows:

> You don't know me very well ... right now she feels a sick part of her is taking over ... You must intervene. If you can't reach her please try to reach me. Yes, right in front of her. That might make her wake up to reality.

In the next session Evelyn was in a screaming rage and I was in a state of overwhelming confusion. In desperation, and without conscious thought or reflection, I asked: "Is Martha here?" The patient immediately stopped screaming, paused for a moment and answered: "Yes." After a brief period during which she shut her eyes and took a deep breath she said very quietly:

> Hello, Dr Finnegan. Now you have finally got it. I have been here before. You just haven't recognised me. There are many others and you will meet them all in time.

When Evelyn emerged from the dissociated state in which she had been Martha she had no memory of what had happened but she was aware that she had lost some time. Later that day a letter signed Martha was left at my office, which read as follows:

> Today you saved the day by appealing to me, Martha. That really shocked her because she never felt you believed I existed. She doesn't want you to know about me ... she is jealous and frightened of me. She wants to be well but doesn't want to get lost either.

In the months that followed, Martha presented spontaneously during many sessions and after each such occurrence Evelyn would be amnesic about what had happened during the time that Martha had been present. Martha was always intelligent, thoughtful, emotionally stable and fully collaborative in her conversations with me. She regularly helped me to understand Evelyn's thoughts, feelings and behaviour in ways that were far beyond Evelyn's capacity to grasp. Many months passed before Evelyn could acknowledge the existence of Martha and she was initially hostile in her attitude toward Martha, thinking that the "calm, thoughtful and intelligent one" would be preferred over herself, whom she thought of as "always angry, demanding, and dependent". Evelyn would eventually say of Martha: "She shares my body with me but she's *not me!*"

The emergence and dynamics of three clusters of alternative personalities

Several months after the first appearance of Martha Evelyn squatted in the middle of the office and then gradually stood erect and trembling with her neck extended and from her mouth she suddenly blew a glob of sputum and then she collapsed to the floor in a heap. Following my interpretation of her primary identification with the penis of her father she said: "I know that was him. I hate that part of myself. Robert is the sick, evil, angry destructive, penis part of me." And Robert hated Evelyn as well. She often heard his voice screaming at her with contempt calling her a "stupid bitch". At times Robert evoked in Evelyn a sadness, pain and loneliness that were too much for her to handle and she would feel like a helpless child pleading with him to stop being so cruel to her. One time after Robert had left a phone message for me full of screaming profanity and invective, Evelyn called a little later to say; "That is not me. That is my father. That is his kind of rage. I am just like him."

Later I began to get phone messages in the voice of a young child pleading: "Daddy, please hold me and tell me that you will come back." And: "Daddy, it is night time. Please come over and touch me and tell me not to hurt." Other messages were left in the voice of an angry child; "You son of a bitch! You son of a bitch! You are never going to touch me again!" When I played these messages for Evelyn to hear she would be stunned by them and have no memory of having made the calls.

I began to think that there could have been a history of sexual abuse by her father but when I raised this possibility with Evelyn she was defiant and oppositional. That night phone messages were left saying; "Daddy, I love you so much. Please care about me. Love me Daddy, please. I love you Daddy. Please be there for me". A few days later there was a call in which Evelyn said she felt she was "in a trance" and that she was Sara. When the adolescent Sara presented in sessions during the following months she was explicitly sexually seductive. There were times when she would call out to me to join her on the couch saying: "Fuck me! Do it! Move, damn it!" Sara left messages saying how devastated Evelyn had been by her sexualised behaviour and that: "If we can get rid of Evelyn you and I have got it made". As Evelyn heard the phone messages left by Sara, with their invitations to, and demands for, sexual intercourse, Evelyn said: "I'd rather die, I'd rather be crazy, than face my shame and guilt". After several months of seductive behaviour Sara finally grasped that her sexual offers would not be accepted and that her sexual demands would not be met.

Sometime later six-year-old Georgina presented spontaneously as the patient sat on the side of the couch with her legs spread wide, and in the manner of an innocent and charming child invited me to touch her "down there". Georgina idealised and loved her father and, in the transference, eagerly sought the love of "Dr Daddy". She said: "It's fun and nice before it goes in the bum ... but it's *not my bum* it goes into!" Georgina had developed in the context of repetitive paternal seduction, which had taken place during the patient's early childhood. In her dissociative response to this invasive and overstimulating experience of seduction Evelyn had experienced a loss of personal identity and later adopted the identity of *Georgina*, the name of the patient's rag doll, both to relieve the anxiety attendant upon her recognition of the loss of her identity and to express the idea that the secretive and conflict-ridden seductive molestation was happening not to her but to her doll. Georgina offered that she had once "been" the doll but later "became" herself. It had been Georgina who had left the telephone messages months before asking for her father/analyst to be with her and to hold her.

One day Georgina spoke of feeling "all warm and wet inside" when her father was touching her and then she suddenly turned onto her stomach and abreacted a terrifying and painful anal rape, as Geraldine. Geraldine hated the man who "stuck it in my bum," saying, "He's *not my* father". In the transference Geraldine experienced me as "Dr Fuckfinnegan!" Geraldine brought to the transference her pain, helplessness and despair as well her rage, hatred and fears of the repetition of traumatic experiences. The choice of the name Geraldine expressed an aggressive and retaliatory wish against a little boy who had been the patient's childhood playmate. Gerald sometimes hit his little girlfriend and made her cry—but she never hit back. The experience of her father's violent abuse precipitated a dissociative response accompanied by a regressive loss of personal identity. The patient wished that the overwhelmingly painful and terrifying anal rape was happening, not to her, but to Gerald. "When it hurt I became him so he'd hurt." It had been Geraldine who months earlier had left the telephone messages calling me, in a paternal transference, a son of a bitch and telling me that I would never touch her again.

While Georgina knew very little about Geraldine, Geraldine knew about Georgina and resented her for "hoarding" all the good experiences with the exciting father. Further, Geraldine hated Georgina for dumping onto her all of the painful experiences with the man who she saw as "*not my* father".

Evelyn also had an alter based on an identification with her mother, Mrs R. This alter treated me with contempt, saying "It is none of your business what is going on in this house". Mrs R. expressed Evelyn's mother's long-standing attitude towards the sexual abuse of her daughter by her father: it was never to be acknowledged. However, there was ample evidence that the mother had known that incest had been occurring throughout Evelyn's childhood and later in the course of treatment Evelyn was furiously enraged with her mother for "not throwing her body between mine and his."

In the context of analytic work with Georgina and Geraldine, Robert suddenly appeared at the end of a session, grabbed me by the throat and pushed me against the office wall, saying "Keep your hands off my kid!" Martha later reported that Robert felt threatened; he felt that the control he had over Geraldine was being eroded by my developing relationship with her. Evelyn was later to write:

> My inner Robert got a hold of me again and told me you didn't want to hear from me and that you didn't care and that you were disgusted with me ... he said you never wanted to hear from me again.

Robert clearly wanted to maintain his relationship with, and control over, Geraldine. It took a great deal of time and effort to establish a relationship with him that allowed more frequent direct engagement with the child personalities and steps to be taken towards more integrative functioning.

Later in the analysis a second cluster of alters presented themselves, an adolescent group. These alters had developed during a period of time when Evelyn had lived away from home in a boarding school where she was regularly visited by her father and taken to a nearby hotel to have sexual relations with him.

Helen presented in the context of our work on this period in Evelyn's life and she functioned in a manner similar to Martha. Sara—who had presented earlier on in our work—and Sarah participated in the progressive phases of sexual relations with the father during this time. Of these sexual encounters Helen wrote:

> After it was over the others gave her [*Sarah*] a really hard time blaming her for the mess and telling her how bad she was and it was her fault and all the screaming and yelling caused extreme headaches. Linda holds the extreme

sadness and pain that cannot be tolerated for long periods of time by the others as the pain and sadness is too deep.

Sara and Sarah each presented themselves seductively, demanded my undivided attention, and pressed for some explicit statement of my sexual interest in them. When I failed to respond to these insistent demands for sexual attention and affirmation a sudden switch would take place leaving Linda in a state of anguished humiliation and sometimes suicidal despair. Linda knew that she was hated by the others and only Helen was able to offer some understanding and comfort to her. Following upon the affectively charged transference circumstances in which Sara, Sarah and Linda would appear, it often happened that Helen would then declare that the emotional upset of the other alters had been "their own fault" and that she was deeply sorry for their behaviour in my office and for any upset they might have caused me. The analysis of this cluster of adolescent alters—of which I have mentioned only a few—required that attention be paid to the needs and feelings of each one individually and that the relationships that existed between them be understood, interpreted and slowly moved towards understanding, reconciliation, and more integrative functioning.

Later on in the analysis there emerged a third cluster of alters that had developed in Evelyn's early twenties during the first years after her marriage. During this time Evelyn had an ongoing sexual relationship with her father and Sandra became pregnant by him. Christine [Christ-teen] "sacrificed" herself and carried the child, and Mary, "a virgin mother", gave birth to the child and in breastfeeding reached "perfection as a mother with a perfect child." Helen guided Sandra, Christine and Mary through the course of the pregnancy, childbirth, and subsequent care of the child, a daughter who was later diagnosed with cystic fibrosis. Initially Evelyn had reluctantly reported that this child had been given up for adoption at the age of somewhere between six months and a year because of its ill health and Evelyn's inability to provide adequate care. Much later in the analysis Helen revealed that Mary had cared for the child until it was given up for adoption at the age of three. Evelyn was astonished to hear this and proud to have Helen's revelation confirmed by her mother.

I will return to the account of my continuing work with Evelyn at the end of this article. In this next section we are going to examine the work from a Fairbairnian perspective.

An alternative version of Fairbairn's model incorporating Freud's topographic categories

Graham Clarke (2005) has suggested that Fairbairn's use of Freud's topographic categories should be more consistent and that the object relations basis of each of the ego-structures and internal objects needs to be made both clearer and more consistent. The diagram illustrating this model (Figure 4.1) is used (a) to describe the whole of the endopsychic structure, (b) to indicate the location within the endopsychic structure of the various alters and (c) to thus reveal their relationships with each other.

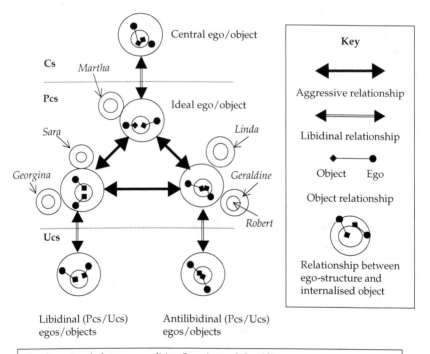

The dissociated alter personalities *Georgina* and *Geraldine* represent paired alternative personalities of the same age, one libidinal and the other antilibidinal. *Sara* (libidinal) and *Linda* (antilibidinal) represent the development of later alter personalities. It may be the case, as we have described, that all of these alternative personalities are known by an ideal alter personality such as *Martha* but not really known to each other or the central ego until much later in the analysis.

Figure 4.1. Trauma-induced vertical splitting of dynamic structures (2).

The subsidiary, ideal, libidinal and antilibidinal egos and internal objects form a repository of object relations possibilities that are respectively acceptable, idealised, overexciting or over-rejecting and frustrating. For Padel (1991), one important component of psychic growth within Fairbairn's theory is achieved by allowing or enabling the unconscious overexciting or over-frustrating object relations to be considered consciously and (re-)incorporated within the range of object relations possibilities available to the conscious part of the person, the central ego. If these prove to be unacceptable to the ideal self then they become submerged again into the preconscious (*Pcs*) or the unconscious (*Ucs*) libidinal and antilibidinal selves.

Under this view of psychic growth the movement of object relations possibilities from the *Ucs* via the *Pcs* to the conscious (*Cs*), negotiating as it goes the two censorship barriers at the *Ucs/Pcs* and the *Pcs/Cs* levels, is essential. There is also, as Rubens (1984) and others have argued, another form of psychic growth—non-structuring internalisations—where the person internalises good object relations directly into the ego-ideal, after the basic endopsychic structure has developed.

It is important to recognise that the identification of alters and their histories is a crucial aspect of the psychic growth of the person suffering from DID. Through therapy, alters can become familiar with each other; intercommunication between alters becomes feasible and psychic growth becomes possible. The expanded representation of the elements of Fairbairn's model we are using here can be used (a) to map the alters as they are discovered during therapy, (b) to identify the relationships between and among the alter personalities, (c) to further an understanding of the varied and complex transference and countertransference dynamics encountered in the treatment of DID and d) to track the process of psychic growth during the course of the analytic relationship.

A Fairbairnian approach to understanding Evelyn and her alters

Our initial hypothesis, based on Fairbairn's model of endopsychic structure, was that various alter personalities were derivative of, and traumatically split off—or dissociated—from the individual dynamic ego and object structures that comprise the overall endopsychic structure. From this perspective Martha, the first alter personality to present during the course of the work, is understood to be an ideal ego alter based on the internalisation of experiences with good objects. Martha originally appeared during Evelyn's latency period and was modelled on positive aspects of her experience of her mother, her grandmother, and a much-admired woman who was a neighbour. Martha's appearance followed upon the development of a "good enough" therapeutic relationship and she functioned to assist in the management of the analyst's relationship with Evelyn. Martha typified ideal ego alters in that while she was aware of the travails of the "others inside" and could offer some guidance and support, she operated at a considerable emotional remove. Such ideal ego alters are commonly found in people who identify as having multiple personality and can act as gatekeepers to the internal realm of other alter personalities and clusters of alter personalities.

Robert was the second alter to present and we understand him to be an antilibidinal object alter based on Evelyn's identification with her phallic, aggressive, abusive and controlling father. His aim was to demonstrate his power, to frighten and control the analyst, and to maintain his relationship with his "kid" (Geraldine). We understand the resistance manifested in Robert's attitude and behaviour as deriving from the wish to perpetuate "the relationships prevailing between the various ego-structures and their respective internal objects, as well as between one another" (Fairbairn, 1958, p. 380) and that this necessitates "... the maintenance of the patient's internal world as a closed system ..." (op. cit.). A second antilibidinal object alter, Mrs R, based on an aspect of Evelyn's identification with her incest-denying mother, presented later in our work and clearly also wanted Evelyn's inner world preserved as a closed system, for as she said to the analyst: "It is none of your business what is going on in this house." Antilibidinal object alters such as Robert and Mrs R. present formidable resistances to analysis—particularly in the control they have over child alters due to the attachment of the child alters to such internalised bad objects.

Sara's presentation as the third alter personality followed upon the question of incest having been raised and the subsequent phone calls that were much later recognised to have been made by Georgina and Geraldine. We understand Sara to be a libidinal ego alter, as in her explicitly seductive manner she sought the sexual love of the analyst as a libidinal object. Given the timing of her presentation she may have been functioning to protect the child alters from the threat of sexual abuse by the analyst.

The child personalities Georgina and Geraldine can be understood to be libidinal ego and antilibidinal ego alters respectively. Georgina expressed her transference love for the analyst as the libidinal object "Dr Daddy" and Geraldine expressed her transference hatred towards the analyst as "Dr Fuckfinnegan!" Consistent with Fairbairn's (1963) idea that "the antilibidinal ego, in virtue of its attachment to the rejecting (antilibidinal) object, adopts an uncompromisingly hostile attitude to the libidinal ego …" (Fairbairn, 1963, p. 224), on the basis of additional experience with DID we offer that antilibidinal ego alters are typically aware of, resent, and hate their libidinal ego counterparts. As indicated above, Geraldine bore a hateful resentment towards Georgina, seeing her as being the cause of the terrifying and painful anal rapes perpetrated upon her by the antilibidinal object Robert, who she saw as *"not my father"*. Some antilibidinal ego alters may cling with near-psychotic conviction to the idea that the other alter personalities are *"not me"*; and out of their envious, homicidal rage they may inflict grievous bodily harm on the body of an "other" such as Georgina.

Further, it often happens that libidinal ego alters, such as Georgina, know little or nothing of the lives of the "others inside"—of Geraldine, for example—with the exception of their awareness of their related libidinal object alter to whom they are bonded with a loving hope that knows no end. A "need and expectation" of a libidinal ego alter that has not been met by the related libidinal object alter brings upon the antilibidinal ego alter an unending agony of humiliation, anguish, and despair experienced at the hands of the related antilibidinal object alter. Fairbairn's (1944) outline of this dire situation captures the essence of its horror:

> In virtue of these experiences of humiliation and shame he feels reduced to a state of worthlessness, destitution or beggardom … The child's experience is one of, so to speak, exploding ineffectively and being completely emptied of libido. *It is thus an experience of disintegration and of imminent psychical death.* (Fairbairn, 1944, p. 113, emphasis added)

In terror of such catastrophic, objectless psychic death, an antilibidinal ego alter such as Geraldine clings in desperation to her related antilibidinal object, Robert—and in the transference, to her analyst. This bond of need for, and of loyalty to, a bad object yields a powerful form of resistance to therapy and to psychic growth.

86   THINKING THROUGH FAIRBAIRN

Our initial hypothesis that alter personalities were traumatically split off or dissociated from the individual dynamic ego and object structures that comprise the overall endopsychic structure was helpful in understanding basic characteristics of various alters, the relational dynamics that were found to exist between them, and aspects of the transferences and countertransferences. The dynamics of the relationship that we have illustrated to exist between an antilibidinal object alter, Robert, and an antilibidinal ego alter, Geraldine, led us to our second hypothesis: that under particular circumstances there could be the splitting off of related ego-object substructures.

The fact that there were three clusters of alter personalities—child, adolescent, and early adult—led to our third hypothesis: that under particular circumstances there may emerge complete alternative endopsychic structures vertically dissociated from the original or main endopsychic structure. This would be the case for the cluster of adolescent

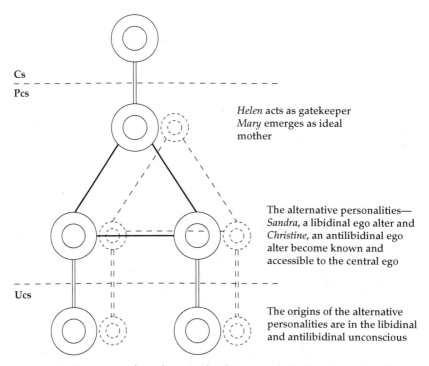

Figure 4.2. Trauma-induced vertical splitting and duplication of endopsychic structure (2).

alters that emerged in the context of Evelyn's father visiting her while she was away at boarding school and the continuance of their sexual relationship. Helen, an ideal ego alter, emerged in this context and functioned in a manner similar to Martha. While Helen knew a great deal about Martha and the child alters, Martha and other alters having their origins in the original endopsychic structure knew nothing of Helen or of any of the adolescent alters. The alter personalities Sara and Sarah, who participated in sexual relations with the father during Evelyn's adolescence, can be understood to be libidinal ego alters, and Linda, who held "the extreme sadness and pain" can be understood to be an antilibidinal ego alter.

The third cluster of alters, the young adults guided by Helen, included: 1) Sandra as a libidinal ego alter in her sexual relationship with and impregnation by the father; 2) Christine as an antilibidinal ego alter who sacrificed herself and carried the child; and 3) Mary, as an ideal ego alter personality and the infant's principal caretaker.

The symptoms that Evelyn's original therapist had described on her referral—inhibited sexuality, difficulty in expressing anger, and intense separation anxiety—may be understood in terms of the dynamics found to exist between Evelyn and the alter personalities derivative of the ideal, libidinal and antilibidinal substructures. Her inhibited sexuality can be seen to be in consequence of her guilt and shame related to her sexual relationship with her father and by the dread of repetition of sexual assault. The sexuality of the libidinal ego alters Georgina, Sara, Sarah and Sandra had been repressed by the central and ideal egos in what Fairbairn referred to as "direct repression". Further, the central and ideal egos' direct repression of the antilibidinal egos and objects—Geraldine, Robert, Mrs R., Linda and Christine—can be seen to have been manifested in Evelyn's difficulty in expressing anger. In addition, the libidinal substructures are subjected to "indirect repression" through the aggression directed at them by the antilibidinal substructures. Through the dynamics of both direct and indirect repression Evelyn's internal world had long been maintained as a "closed system"—with the relations between the alter personalities derivative of the various egos and objects being preserved intact.

Evelyn's intense separation anxiety can be seen to derive from the intense longings of the libidinal ego alters such as Georgina and the desperate clinging attachment to antilibidinal objects such as Robert on the part of antilibidinal egos alters such as Geraldine. It may well have been that many of these dynamics came into play in Evelyn's relationship with her husband, where he treated her "like a child in his protective custody".

It is clear that during the course of the analysis all of these previously repressed relational dynamics were encountered in the transferences and countertransferences prior to the presentation of the related specific alter personalities. For example, in the early period of the analysis Evelyn's presenting as sometimes lively, warm, engaging and explicitly seductive and at other times as demanding, furiously angry and vengeful preceded the presentation of any of the libidinal and antilibidinal alter personalities.

While all of the alters are dissociated aspects of the unconscious, during the course of the therapy they rise to the preconscious and have a profound influence on conscious mental functioning and can then move into full consciousness and demonstrate a specificity of identity and of agency. In the case of Evelyn the processes of the progressive coming into consciousness of all of the alter personalities seems to have been guided in each instance by an ideal ego alter functioning as a gatekeeper and minder to an oedipally organised set of alters—Martha with the cluster of child personalities and Helen with the cluster of adolescent personalities and then again with the cluster of young adult personalities. The processes through which the alter personalities come into consciousness—develop therapeutic relationships with the analyst, come to know more of one another with the reduction of dissociative splitting, progressively develop increased capacity for integrative affect regulation, and engage in the resolution of inter-alter conflicts—are processes of psychic growth as discussed above.

Discussion

We have retrospectively illustrated the most common features of alter personalities based upon the different dynamic structures of Fairbairn's theory as they appeared in this one clinical example. Based upon additional clinical experience of working with DID patients we argue that ideal, libidinal and antilibidinal ego and object alters typically share certain characteristics and perform similar functions that are related to the dynamic structures from which they have been dissociated. Ideal ego alters are typically thoughtful, helpful and emotionally detached and may act as "gatekeepers" to the clusters of alternative personalities with whom they are associated; whereas ideal object alters are typically ineffectual. Libidinal ego alters present relational dynamics of need, idealisation, hopefulness and excitement as well as, sometimes, explicit expressions of sexual excitement and the expectation of sexual responsiveness from the analyst as a related libidinal object; whereas libidinal object alters present as seductive and alluring and typically have no regard at all for the well-being of any other alter. Antilibidinal ego alters present relational dynamics including murderous rage, vengefulness, fury, malignant envy, and profound distrust—as well as vulnerability, helplessness, hopelessness, and despair at being abandoned in an objectless world; whereas antilibidinal object alters are aggressive, contemptuous and controlling and present profound resistances to the process of psychic growth and integration.

We have also illustrated that alter personalities may take full control of consciousness and we have offered examples of some of the typical relational dynamics occurring between alters derivative of the ideal, libidinal and antilibidinal dynamic structures. We have also given examples of some of the typical transferences that emerge during the course of analysis and highlighted some of the resistances, which derive from the maintenance of ties to bad objects and the wish to preserve the inner world as a closed system. Finally, we have given some indication of the process of analysis and of the need to address alter personalities directly, respectfully and analytically prior to interpretation more specifically intended to facilitate integrative functioning.

As well as being able to allocate the various alter personalities to particular ideal, libidinal and antilibidinal dynamic structures in Graham Clarke's expansion of Fairbairn's model, we have shown that clusters of such alter personalities could be readily identified. We are suggesting that these clusters of alternative personalities operate as the equivalent of alternative endopsychic structures for the person involved. As we have illustrated in our clinical material, these alternative endopsychic structures characteristically involve an ideal, a libidinal and an antilibidinal component.

In summary, we are suggesting a spectrum of dissociated alters:

(a) Individual examples related to specific dynamic structures;
(b) Multiple dissociated alters related to the same dynamic structure;
(c) Paired ego and object alters related to the same substructure; and

(d) The partial or complete replication of an endopsychic structure comprising a constellation of different dynamic structures yielding a cluster of personalities—such clusters being a common finding.

Keeping in mind that Fairbairn thought of dissociation as a defence "... directed against mental content determined ultimately by *events that happen* to the individual" (Fairbairn, 1929b, p. 77), we have noted the radical traumatic dissociation of alter personalities—engendered by the splitting of dynamic structures—and the resultant resistances to their becoming known. Repression for Fairbairn involves the action of dynamic structures on other dynamic structures: namely the *direct* repression by the central and ideal egos of the libidinal and antilibidinal ego-objects and the *indirect* repression of the libidinal ego-object by the antilibidinal ego-object.

Davies and Frawley (1992b) explicitly distance themselves from Fairbairn's view of the processes involved in generating the original endopsychic structure, where dynamic structures are split off and then repressed: "Unlike Fairbairn, we do not believe the dissociated ego state(s) is repressed; rather, *we stipulate that repression never occurs* and that the ego states coexist, each with its own consciousness" (Davis & Frawley, 1992b, p. 80, emphasis added). They argue that in circumstances of childhood sexual abuse there is a defensive vertical splitting of the ego, which serves both to manage overwhelming affects and to protect against knowing. One of the coexisting ego states knows about and affectively reacts to the trauma while the other ego state, although somewhat depleted, is ignorant of the trauma. Our interpretation of Fairbairn's view of dynamic structures is consistent with Ogden's recent comments when he says that, "for Fairbairn, internal objects are thinkers with impulses" (Ogden, 2010b, p. 1003)—this being at odds with the concept of ego states. Differently from Fairbairn, dissociation is seen by Davies and Frawley as:

> ... a vertical split of the ego that results in two or more ego states that are more or less organized and independently functioning ... [and that] ... These ego states alternate in consciousness, and, under different internal and external circumstances, emerge to think, behave, remember and feel. (Davis & Frawley, 1992b, p. 80)

In consequence of this vertical splitting, the abused child self—which exists in "the context of perpetually abusive object relations"—and the related aspect of the object are "… literally ejected from the patient's more integrated personality functioning and allowed to set up an independent existence for the sake of pursuing its separate needs" (Davies & Frawley, 1992a, p. 21). Under these circumstances the dissociated self is not repressed but coexists with its own consciousness. Dissociation, then, is "… a process that preserves and protects, in dissociated form, *the entire internal world* of the abused child" (Davies & Frawley, 1992a, p. 8, emphasis added).

In light of the clinical material we have presented above, this restatement of the function of dissociation under trauma for survivors of childhood sexual abuse is convincing. Some aspects of the clinical material we have offered can certainly be understood within the perspective of the "vertical split"; for example, the sudden switches between Georgina and Geraldine as well as those that took place between Evelyn and Martha. However, we also think there is a more far-reaching dissociative vertical split between endopsychic structures in many of the patients that are diagnosed with multiple personality. And, we also think that there is clear clinical evidence of repression—a point to which we will return below.

Grotstein has described Fairbairn's theory of endopsychic structure as "the unsurpassed metapsychology of child abuse and of multiple personality" (Grotstein, 1991, p. 140), and, "the most apposite paradigm yet proffered for child abuse, child molestation, post-traumatic stress disorder and multiple personality disorder" (Grotstein, 1994b, p. 123). Within this Fairbairnian perspective he has stressed the autonomy of the endopsychic structures—"… each structure has its own autonomy, provenance, innocence, will (intentionality), rationale (*raison d'etre*), birthright, blessing, or curse … [and] … 'I'-ness" (Grotstein, 1994a, p. 183)—and discussed "the dialectics of endopsychic relationships". Grotstein (1992) has noted, in a discussion of psychoanalytic work with survivors of childhood sexual abuse, that:

> … these patients experience themselves to be discontinuous; each of these apparently disconnected selves lives autonomously and independently of each other and may not even know of one another's existence, yet they seem at the same time to have some unconscious relationship with one another. (Grotstein, 1992, p. 71)

Although he does not present clinical material from work with a person with multiple personality, Grotstein does explicitly acknowledge that "in cases of extreme dissociation such as those occurring in multiple personality, that subpersonalities can be independent of each other" (Grotstein, 1994a, p. 182).

We greatly appreciate Grotstein's Fairbairnian approach and, at the same time, think it is insufficient to fully explain the radical traumatic dissociation of alter personalities that we have illustrated above. Working within this Fairbairnian approach we posit the traumatic dissociation of endopsychic structures and we suggest that such dissociated/split-off endopsychic structures may be repressed for long periods of time prior to the repression being lifted and the endopsychic structure, and its related personalities, again becoming conscious and functioning in a manner indicated by the concept of a vertical split. In the case of Evelyn there emerged three, previously long-repressed, distinct constellations of ideal, libidinal and antilibidinal selves—one of children in the latency period when the abuse began; one of adolescents when Evelyn was away at school and the abuse resumed; and one of adults when Evelyn bore and independently cared for her father's child for three years. Upon their return to consciousness during the course of analysis these constellations of alternate personalities presented clinically in states characterised by vertical splits.

Conclusion

We have provided an account of Fairbairn's model of endopsychic structure and used it to retrospectively analyse the work with a person with DID. We hope that our preliminary illustration of the clinical application of Fairbairnian thought to DID has suggested the usefulness of this approach in developing a structural dynamic understanding of the disorder and that it offers a productive approach to developing effective ways of working with those who have survived appalling abuse through the processes of dissociation.

We now return to concluding the story of Evelyn.

Evelyn's analysis continued for several years and she made substantial progress in her self-understanding and in her mastery of the impact of her cumulative traumatic experiences. Her relationships with family, friends and colleagues improved and she developed a "peace of mind" that she experienced as both soothing and satisfying. In the middle phase of the analysis (which lasted in total for ten years) she developed metastatic breast cancer. Although there was initially some understandable denial of the implications of this illness, given what she had already been through, she went on to have surgery, radiation and chemotherapy and to offer considerable emotional support and understanding to other women with this illness. During this period she was able to locate the daughter she had initially cared for and had then given up for adoption. She calmly absorbed her daughter's expressions of hatred and rage toward her, achieved a sense of reconciliation with her and was with her during the final days of her life as she was dying from cystic fibrosis. As therapy was concluding, and her life was drawing to an end, Evelyn reflected that in the process of therapy she had achieved her "PhD in Wellness" and took great pride in having done so. Prior to her death she left a document stating that she hoped that the telling of her story would be helpful to others who had experienced physical and sexual abuse and who had gone on to develop multiple personality as well as to those who are involved in their treatment. We are deeply appreciative of Evelyn's generosity.

PART III

FILM

CHAPTER FIVE

Failures of the "moral defence" in the films *Shutter Island* (Scorsese, 2010), *Inception* (Nolan, 2010), and *Memento* (Nolan, 2000): narcissism or schizoid personality disorder?

Introduction

I am going to look at the three films in the title from the perspective of Fairbairn's object relations theory and in particular his concept of the moral defence. I will argue that the three films mentioned are centrally concerned with a dynamic of this sort and it is in exploring this dynamic and its difficulties, as they are portrayed in the films, that some understanding of the often complex action of the films may be reached. The idea of using Fairbairn's concept of the moral defence as a prism through which to view these three films was prompted by the question that Teddy Daniels (Leonardo Di Caprio), the main protagonist of *Shutter Island* (Scorsese, 2010), asks his "sidekick" (and psychiatrist) at the end of the film: "Which is best, to live as a monster or die as a good man?"

The moral defence

In Fairbairn's account of the moral defence against bad objects (1952, p. 65 ff) the "delinquent child" is reluctant to admit that his parents are bad but is prepared to admit that he is bad. Fairbairn argues that the child seeks to purge his objects of their badness by taking this badness upon himself and is rewarded by a sense of security that an environment of good objects confers. However, this outer security is purchased at the price of inner security, as his ego is henceforth left at the mercy of a band of internal persecutors. These internalised bad objects are repressed but when repression fails the four classic psychopathological defences are called into operation—phobic, obsessional, hysterical, and paranoid.

Fairbairn suggests that there is another form of defence, which he variously calls the moral defence, the defence of the super-ego or the defence of guilt. In order to develop this further Fairbairn distinguishes between two kinds of badness—unconditional and conditional. Unconditional badness is badness from a libidinal point of view. The bad objects the child internalises are unconditionally bad and since the child has internalised them, and thus identifies himself with them, then he is unconditionally bad. In order to be able to redress this unconditional badness, Fairbairn argues that the child internalises his good objects, which assume a super-ego role. In Fairbairn's model of endopsychic structure there are unconscious libidinal and antilibidinal selves into which the bad objects are internalised and a preconscious ideal self, which is the equivalent of Freud's positive super-ego, into which the good objects are internalised. The punitive super-ego is part of the antilibidinal self. The central self is equivalent to Freud's ego. All selves are object-relationship based. So the child becomes conditionally bad or good, according to the degree to which he leans towards his internalised bad objects. Fairbairn explains that it is preferable to be conditionally rather than unconditionally bad by reference to religion; "better to be a sinner in a world ruled by God than to live in a world ruled by the Devil" (pp. 66–67).

Fairbairn argues that it is the child's need for its parents, however badly they treat him, that compels him to internalise bad objects, and it is because this need remains attached to them in the unconscious that he cannot bring himself to part with them. Fairbairn discusses guilt as a defence against the release of bad objects and argues that the process of moving from object relationships where your external objects are bad into a situation in which you internalise your bad objects and transform your external objects into good objects and then internalize those good objects results in a moral situation at a higher level of mental development than the original level at which the super-ego operates. It is, he suggests, at this higher level that analytic interpretations in terms of guilt and the Oedipus situation are alone applicable; and the level at which psychotherapy is often rather exclusively conducted. Fairbairn thinks this is undesirable because, in his view, under these circumstances guilt operates as a resistance in psychotherapy. He discusses the difficulties for psychotherapy of dealing with the release of bad objects from the unconscious, which he believes is one of the chief aims the psychotherapist should set out to achieve, but he suggests this can only happen if the analyst has become a sufficiently good object for the patient. Fairbairn cautions against over-interpretation at the guilt or super-ego level, since he says the defence of the super-ego and repression are separate defences and the relief of guilt might actually intensify the repression of internalised bad objects. That is, strengthening the super-ego can lead to a reinforcement of the repression of the bad objects in the unconscious. For Fairbairn it is the coming to consciousness of the internalised bad objects and their subsequent successful release that is crucial to achieving inner harmony.

I will suggest that in the films *Shutter Island* (Scorsese, 2010), *Inception* (Nolan, 2010) and *Memento* (Nolan, 2000) the defence of guilt against internalised bad objects is widely illustrated and that the release of the internalised bad objects, in each case associated with the death of the wife of the film's main protagonist, is resisted.

Shutter Island

At the end of *Shutter Island*, Teddy Daniels, who has just regressed again to a fully fledged delusional state, and is about to be lobotomised, asks his "shrink" (who is at this moment seen by him to be his sidekick—another federal marshal) a rhetorical question: "Which is best, to live as a monster or die as a good man?" Linking this to Fairbairn's notion of the moral defence I will rewrite the question as, "Which is best, to live as someone who is unconditionally bad or die as someone who believes that he is conditionally good?"

Teddy Daniels, an upholder of the law in his role as Federal Marshal, is searching the asylum on *Shutter Island* for a woman who has killed her three children and a man who is grotesque-looking and responsible for terrible crimes. While he seeks to solve the case of the missing woman he is beset by images and flashbacks of a concentration camp in Dachau in WWII and, separately, of his wife. These represent aspects of the internalised bad objects that his being a man of the law is unable to repress.

The main backstory is that he underwent traumatic experiences during the liberation of Dachau in WWII and has flashbacks of the piles of corpses in the death camp and of the death of a German commandant that he deliberately allowed to die in a long and lingering death when he could have put him out of his misery. Apparently provoked by the shock at the sights they have seen and panic at some suspected retaliation by the German guards, Daniels was also involved with other American soldiers in shooting down some unarmed German concentration camp guards.

Later, as a federal marshal, Daniels is a hard-working lawman with a drinking problem. He ignores his wife and family and she becomes mentally ill and burns down their flat. He moves the family to the country, which makes his wife even more isolated and, while mentally disturbed, she drowns their three children in a lake while he is away at work in the city. When he discovers his dead children in the lake he shoots and kills his wife.

Subsequently, he has been unable to accept that this is what has happened and lives in a delusional state where he is a good cop trying to find a patient who is missing from *Shutter Island*—a woman who killed her three children. He has a split personality and an alter ego who carries his real name and is terribly scarred and horrible to look at who is also at large in the asylum. His denial of this alter ego is compromised by the fact that the name he has adopted as his own is an anagram of his real name and, further, that the name of the woman who killed her children is an anagram of his wife's real name. For this lawman, killing his wife after discovering that she has killed their children is both unacceptable and inexcusable. He can neither accept that he did it, nor find any way of making restitution except by investigating the case of this missing woman as the federal marshal, a man of the law. This federal marshal is the good man he refers to at the end, the man making serious endeavours to find these missing persons—his wife and himself—and bring them both to justice, unaware that they are both aspects of himself.

Another dimension of the story is that his enlightened psychiatrists are instituting a more psychotherapeutic approach by letting him act out his delusional role while being maintained on a new (in the 1950s) tranquillising drug that prevents his worst excesses of unmanageable behaviour. This is being done in order for him to discover for himself who he really is and that the woman he murdered, and who murdered her children, was his wife. From a Fairbairnian perspective his wife is a projection of an internalised libidinal bad object and the scarred and horrible man is a projection of himself as an internalised antilibidinal bad object. The psychiatrist's aim, described in Fairbairnian terms, is to effect a cure by releasing the internalised bad objects, which are cathected by libidinal and antilibidinal parts of himself.

His ability, at the end of the film, to develop the question about living as a monster—that is, either accepting that he did what he did and being unable to make some restitution or dying believing himself to be a good man in his delusion that he is a blameless federal marshal trying to solve a mysterious disappearance—suggests that there is still some element of choice involved here. In choosing to "die as a good man" (i.e., be lobotomised), he is turning a "blind eye" to the reality that he has acknowledged at least twice previously, according to the film, when he was able to remember and recognised what he had done but was eventually unable to accept or find a way to live with this knowledge and so relapsed. He would rather die having a view of himself as a good man, however illusory this is, and which he knows at some level to be false, than admit his badness and try to make some restitution. In terms of Fairbairn's understanding of the balance between shoring up inner reality by reinforcing the super-ego (ego-ideal in Fairbairn's schema) versus releasing and learning to cope with the repressed bad objects, it seems as if the "defence of guilt" has gone too far and the internalised bad objects can *never* be released, faced, and understood.

It seems that making restitution is difficult, indeed impossible, so that there is no option but to be unconditionally bad, evil and unredeemable and therefore it is better to die deluded but conditionally "good". For Fairbairn the bad objects can only be released if "the analyst has become established as a sufficiently good object for the patient" (Fairbairn, 1952, p. 70). We might conclude that this has not happened in the therapy so far or that the good object in the protagonist was itself already compromised. What this might suggest, given the importance of the early choice of object (anaclitic or narcissistic) as developed by Freud in his paper "On narcissism" (Freud, 1914c) is that he had taken himself to be his own ideal, and to give that up would lead to actual madness and psychic death anyway, as a monster of unconditional badness. So the question he poses for himself at the end implies that his inner reality is based upon his having made himself his own ideal at an early stage and, having no alternative powerful internal good objects, or insufficiently strong internal good objects, he is unable to realistically recognise his own shortcomings without its fragmenting his inner reality totally.

What he did to the German guards pales into insignificance in relation to what the German guards did to their Jewish and other prisoners, and while this might trouble him it does not appear to undermine his ability to take himself as his own ideal. On the other hand, his love for his wife and children, and particularly his little girl, and the degree to which his wife's mental state, when she killed their children, is his responsibility, makes it impossible to accept what he did to her and for him to keep himself as his own ideal. Without himself as his own ideal the internal dynamic of his world is returned to what Klein calls the paranoid-schizoid position, a time before inner reality is stabilised by the realisation that the libidinal and antilibidinal objects are both based upon object relationships with mother and restitution to mother, as a unitary ideal (good) object can be established as what Fairbairn calls the accepted object.

His wife is, in part, like his mother during the paranoid-schizoid position in that he is ambivalent towards her and she has not become an ideal towards whom he might make restitution. On the contrary, in taking himself as the ideal it is to that self for his own self-serving ends that he must make restitution. This is why he preserves the illusion that he is a good man, which, for the psychiatrists, means a totally deluded man, unable to be honest or realistic about himself, a man in denial. Whether or not lobotomy is an appropriate therapeutic response to this condition is a different and problematic issue.

Fairbairn in characterising the moral defence suggests that children who have been abused are likely to internalise their abuser as a good object (which for Fairbairn goes into the ideal object) and make themselves conditionally bad, especially if the abuser is a parental figure. That is, they are better off choosing to be conditionally bad in a good world than being unconditionally bad in an evil world. This is an (internal) object relations approach to dealing with bad (external) objects. Daniels, in *Shutter Island*, cannot stand the thought of being unconditionally bad in an evil world or of having his name live on as someone who was unconditionally bad and this seems to be because he is unable to adopt the moral defence. He is unable to successfully use the moral defence because he has already taken his ego-ideal as his ideal and this is why he chooses the self-deluded option of acting out what could be seen as a phantasy of himself as a good man.

This slippage between Fairbairn's view of the moral defence and the defence being adopted by Daniels in *Shutter Island* is, I think, the same, or a similar, defence to that implied by Shelby and Cobb in the films *Memento* and *Inception* respectively and it is to the way this defence manifests itself in these films that I now turn.

Inception

> Dom Cobb (Leonardo Di Caprio) is a skilled thief, the absolute best in the dangerous art of extraction, stealing valuable secrets from deep within the subconscious during the dream state, when the mind is at its most vulnerable. Cobb's rare ability has made him a coveted player in this treacherous new world of corporate espionage, but it has also made him an international fugitive and cost him everything he has ever loved ... Now Cobb is being offered a chance at redemption. One last job could give him his life back but only if he can accomplish the impossible—inception. Instead of the perfect heist, Cobb and his team of specialists have to pull off the reverse: their task is not to steal an idea but to plant one. (Publicity blurb www.lovefilm.co.uk)

The basic premise of the film is that there are different levels of consciousness through which to work on someone's mind. Conventionally there are two or three levels before falling through into some form of madness in a deeply unconscious world that can appear to last forever and in which the person can become trapped. There is also an assumption that people can share these subconscious dream spaces through technical means and that the content of these shared dreams can be derived from different dreamers. There are dangers to using real memories, so the navigators of these different levels of consciousness invent architectures for these alternative realities as well as content. When someone who is involved in the collective dream space against their will becomes aware of the process they can direct projections of themselves in the form of people and objects against the interlopers.

The central difficulty is that Cobb, who is an expert at both travelling through these different layers of consciousness and who, in his time, has been the architect of some of these alternative realities, has a problem. He was married to a woman who killed herself in such a way that he is suspected of her murder and he is unable to return to the U.S. to be reunited with his children. His projected version of this woman, his wife, is active and disruptive in his below conscious lives and is capable of sabotaging things. She can thus be interpreted as a bad internalised object. She seems to dwell most persistently at the very deepest levels of consciousness, where she and Cobb once spent what seemed like ages together playing, building and growing old together before he convinced her that this level of reality was not real and they needed to commit suicide together in order to be restored to their real lives. Another important premise of these alternative universes is that time behaves progressively more slowly in the dreamtime at whatever level of consciousness you move to. In the film there is a mathematical relationship between these different layers that means that a short time at the level of conscious reality becomes aeons at the deepest level. This allows for different and complex actions, processes, and sequences to be nested as each level downwards is traversed. Interestingly, however, at each level although the architecture may be invented everything appears real and the activity between characters is like that in everyday reality. One difference is that death (or some other trigger) at a lower level of consciousness usually kicks you back up to the next higher level of consciousness. Parallels between this infrastructure and Freud's topographic understanding of the mind are clear enough.

As the film progresses, these different levels are engaged in order, ostensibly, to carry out the main object of the film—to plant an idea in a business man's mind in order to prevent his becoming a global dictator of energy policy, or perhaps more sanguinely to protect the interests of one of his competitors in the energy market. This is the "inception" of the title, which, if achieved, will allow Cobb to return home and be with his children again. However, as we follow Cobb into different states of consciousness it becomes clear that his "wife" is a continuing problem. As the film develops it is revealed that she killed herself believing that the current reality they lived in together (everyday reality) was a dream reality and that if they killed themselves they would reach reality proper. She does implore him to kill himself with her, as they had done before, so they can be together in this imagined higher reality but he refuses and she kills herself.

The shared dreams that occupy different levels of consciousness are based upon the minds of the people involved, and since, once they become aware of the shared nature of this dream space, individuals can generate or "project" figures to interrupt the dream and get rid of the "interlopers", these "projections" are usually agonistic and disruptive. Cobb's wife appears at various times in Cobb's memories of the past but also as a disruptive projection based upon Cobb's subconscious mind (I am using this term to apply to both preconscious and unconscious aspects of the mind in Freudian terms) at different levels during the running of his projects. In Fairbairn's terms, Mal (Marion Cotillard), his wife, is an internalised bad object with both an aggressive antilibidinal aspect and a libidinal aspect. She exists at all of the levels that they enter in the journey below consciousness but has her strongest hold on Cobb at the unconscious level where Cobb and Mal have lived in a world of their own making for what appears to have been aeons and which she wants him to return to and stay with her. At this level there is also a suggestion that she is an ideal figure for him. However she is a memory, or a projection based upon a memory, since the real Mal is already dead before the film starts.

Cobb has been unable to get rid of this internalised bad object in all its manifestations, indeed seems to be secretly encouraging it by using the technique he uses for stealing secrets to revisit his own memories and by so doing in some way reinforcing them or at the very least keeping them alive. This is the libidinal cathexis that Fairbairn talks about between the ego components (libidinal, antilibidinal, and ideal) and the bad internal objects to which they are attached, which works in therapy as a powerful resistance to cure.

We might ask why Cobb is committed to keeping Mal's memories alive like this even though they disrupt his work and cause him problems and prevent him from being able to be reunited with his children. And the answer within this view of the process is because he feels guilty about having planted the idea in her mind that their current reality was nothing but a dream and that they needed to kill themselves in order to escape back to reality. In his account he did this because the world they shared at the deep unconscious level *was* a phantasy and had palled and he wanted to get back to (everyday) reality. It is because of this experience that he knows that inception can work.

You can interpret this deepest layer as the real unconscious where space and time dissolve, or as Lacan's imaginary world of the dyad, Vonnegut's "granfalloon", or however you like to phrase it, but it seems to me to relate to the earliest experience of the (environment) mother and the "paradise" that has to be overcome, or lost, in order for real development to begin to take place. So here we have a wife who in some ways operates within Cobb's internal world like a libidinal object based upon the early relationship with the mother and who wants to keep Cobb at this level of infantile dependence. Cobb, on the other hand, wants to be able to overcome his guilt and remove the internalised bad object that is his wife (probably originally based upon his mother) from his inner reality, in order to be able to move on and be a father (and mother) to his children. He wants to be able to move on from her suicide, which he feels responsible for, having implanted in her mind the idea that current reality is a dream and one can make it back to the true reality by killing oneself. This may not be too far away from the sort of thinking that sees Jihad as an express route to heaven.

So the whole film is about Cobb taking Mal's [sic] badness into himself in order to make her good in the external world and then suffering the consequences of having internalised this bad object into himself, which is precisely the mechanism that Fairbairn describes as the moral defence.

Memento

Memento (Nolan, 2000) is an earlier film by the director of *Inception* and one which has been written about extensively and garnered many prizes. Ostensibly, it is the story of Leonard Shelby (Guy Pearce), whose wife was raped and killed in an attack that left Leonard with a head injury causing anterograde amnesia—the inability to lay down new memories subsequent to the injury. This diagnosis is not undisputed and a number of commentators have argued that there are significant variations from normal anterograde amnesia in Leonard's "condition" as he refers to it throughout the film (e.g., Noir Network, 2011). The film is notable for the way that it is constructed, involving as it does two different narrative threads, one going forward and the other going backwards in time, both of which are set after Leonard and his wife are attacked. The chronologically forward story is in black and white and shows Leonard in a hotel room talking to a cop on the phone about what happened to him and includes flashbacks to some of his memories of his life before the trauma up to and including aspects of the attack.

Leonard's project throughout the film is to track down and identify his wife's killer and to take revenge by killing him. As he accumulates evidence of who the killer might be he preserves this using Polaroid photos and tattoos. The chronologically reversed story shows Leonard's activities in short segments from the present until back to a point where he has avenged himself on someone he believes to be the killer of his wife. The film starts with Leonard shooting a policeman, Teddy (Joe Pantoliano), who is probably the undercover cop that Leonard talks to on the telephone in the parallel narrative. The audience has to work hard to both remember what has gone before and to then make sense of the story as it unfolds backwards, because of the short film shots showing Leonard's activity and because they are chronologically reversed, in sequence but not internally. This has been argued by some to be a process not unlike that faced by people with anterograde amnesia as they struggle to make sense of their world.

However, by the end of the film Leonard, who is an archetypally unreliable narrator because of his inability to lay down new memories, is revealed by Teddy to have been perhaps far more unreliable than we ever imagined. This reveal from Teddy's perspective on Leonard then opens up an alternative way of seeing the film. This alternative account of Leonard's "condition" and the story itself is consistent across a number of commentators (Bainbridge, Klein, Hutchinson and Read, Starfield) but interpreted differently by each. Andy Klein's paper explores the whole range of interpretations that have been developed and provides an overview of the different approaches to the film and its detailed structure. Klein argues that Leonard has exploited his own inability to remember as a way of setting up Teddy as the killer so that sometime later he will be able to "finally 'solve' his wife's murder again, and wreak vengeance on Teddy" (Klein, 2001). The "again" refers to the fact that Teddy's reveal suggests that Teddy has been using Leonard to kill people for some time, Teddy having already set these people up as being the killer of Leonard's wife. The people involved are in fact drug dealers and Teddy, as a corrupt cop, uses Leonard to kill them and then takes their money and/or drugs. There is a suggestion within the film that Natasha (Carrie-Anne Moss) primes Leonard to identify Teddy as his wife's killer and thus kill him. Leonard, who wears the boyfriend's clothes and drives his car, has killed Natasha's drug-dealing boyfriend. Andy Klein suggests that, in the end, "'Memento' rights itself, and the wronged will somehow be avenged, in a corrupt way that is the only way to achieve justice in a corrupt world". Starfield (2000–2002) meanwhile sees the film as Leonard's attempt to create an identity for himself: "Lenny takes over Teddy's life and invents a new identity for himself. With no past his future is an open book ... Lenny finds freedom at the end of the film by creating his own future".

More interestingly, from a psychoanalytic viewpoint, two of the commentators cited earlier see Leonard's condition following Teddy's reveal to be that of an hysteric. "In Memento, Leonard can be seen as adopting a hysterical masquerade of trauma in order to deflect the overwhelming sense of emptiness implied by the fact of his condition" (Bainbridge, 2003). In a similar vein, Hutchinson and Read suggest that Leonard's difference from ourselves may be "less neuro-cognitive and more moral-psychological" and their tentative diagnosis is that Leonard is a victim of "a hysterical amnesia resulting from the need to suppress the memory of a trauma and resulting in a continually-maintained bad faith" (Hutchinson & Read, 2005).

Teddy's reveal, as described by Andy Klein, is that Leonard's wife did not die and that Leonard himself killed her by administering too much insulin. Leonard had attributed this event to Sammy Jankis, someone with anterograde amnesia that Leonard had dealt with as an insurance agent before the attack happened and who accidentally killed his wife in the same way. It seems that Sammy Jankis might be a projection, an alter ego of Leonard, which would make some sense of the subliminal image of Leonard and not Sammy sitting in a hospital ward. That Leonard might have killed his wife because of his "condition" would go some way to explaining why he could never complete his project, since if he was ever convinced that he had avenged his wife's murder he might have to face up to the reality of his own condition or the recognition that he had no project. Perhaps also, to signal that revenge had been completed might open the possibility for grief and reparation, which, if it was indeed Leonard who killed her by injecting her with insulin over and over again at her instigation, would probably be unbearable.

Fairbairn argued strongly that hysteria is the way into understanding psychopathology, as his own thoughts on dissociation and repression based on a study of Janet evince; so too his "slogan" of "Back to Hysteria" originally published in his 1944 paper (Fairbairn, 1952, pp. 92–94 and pp. 158–159). If Leonard's condition is related to hysteria, what might we assume its defensive function to be? Not being able to remember beyond the fact of his wife's death at the hand of another means, in the law of the talion, having to take revenge upon her murderer. For Melanie Klein this is characteristic of the paranoid-schizoid position, while in

Fairbairn's language it represents the dominance of the unconscious libidinal and antilibidinal sub-selves. Not being able to remember that you have already taken your revenge upon your wife's killer means that the process of mourning and reparation or restitution is forever postponed; you can never be reconciled to her death, and your good object, your ideal ego, is forever denied, unreachable, unachievable. In Fairbairn's understanding of hysteria and the characteristic way that objects are deployed projectively and introjectively, the hysteric has their bad objects inside and their good objects outside (Fairbairn, 1952, p. 46). This would seem to fit with Leonard's own situation. But hysteria is a defence against something worse, which given the dissociative aspects of hysteria would be some sort of schizoid breakdown, some sort of fragmentation and potential annihilation. The primitive morality of the talion replaces the more advanced moral defence as a form of defence and the price is an inability to remember anything longer than about ten minutes.

There is, however, an image towards the end of the film, which in many ways fulfils Freud's claims for the wish-fulfilling aspects of dreams and daydreams and at the same time reflects Fairbairn's own conception of dreams as depictions of self states or situations in the internal world (Fairbairn, 1952, p. 99). This is a short clip of Leonard and his wife, alive and well, sitting together on the bed, smiling at the camera. The area above Leonard's heart has now been tattooed with the phase "I did it", signalling the fact that the murder has been avenged. Thus, we have the paradox that Leonard has killed his wife's killer—"I did it"—and the fact that she is alive and well. Alternatively, we have a confession and a wish fulfilment simultaneously. In terms of its reflecting Leonard's internal world, we have a couple, one of whom is dead but appears to be alive, with another who might have killed her killer, or killed her, or both. This is a primal couple that you would not want at the heart of your inner reality.

It is the likelihood that Leonard killed his own wife, and has revenged himself on a string of, probably innocent, others after being manipulated by Teddy, that Leonard is unable to face and why he has taken refuge in his hysterical amnesia. He is his own hero and villain and spends his time projecting his bad objects onto others on the slightest pretext in order to be able to sustain the self-deception. If we go down this route, then it was Leonard's original injury that led to his hysterical amnesia and may have led to his killing his wife, and the guilt he feels would be compounded. He could not protect his wife from the attack and rape, and he killed his wife because of the condition that developed subsequently.

In the moral defence the good object is internalised to provide a defence against the already internalised bad objects. In Leonard's case, as an hysteric, his good objects are outside and unattainable and he is driven by his internal bad objects to repeat the process of killing his wife's "killer", over and over again. Leonard is unable to internalise the good object into his ego-ideal and his developing a containing "second-skin" (Bick, 1968) to record the facts of the "case" (which might also be a mark of Cain), combined with his own mirroring self-regard, are clues to a deep-seated narcissism, which means that he projects all the blame onto the unknown assailant and Sammy Jankis, and remains free of guilt himself. Teddy's reveal opens up the possibility that Leonard is the guilty one and that is the unarticulated reason that Teddy has to be killed and the post-traumatic past cannot be remembered.

Regarding the structure of the film and the implied structure of the process in which Leonard is engaged, we could say that it strongly shares features with what, in Freudian theory, would be called the repetition compulsion, but Fairbairn's explanation of both the repetition compulsion and the death instinct is based upon attachment to internalised bad objects.

> if the effect of a traumatic situation is to release bad objects from the unconscious, the difficulty will be to see how the patient can get away from these bad objects. The fact is that he is haunted by them; and since they are framed by the traumatic incident, he is haunted by this too. In the absence of a therapeutic dissolution of the cathexis of his bad objects, he can only achieve freedom from this haunting if his bad objects are once more banished to the unconscious. (Fairbairn, 1952, p. 78)

Discussion

Crucially, the differences between the moral defence and the defence employed here concern the nature of the good object that is internalised defensively. In the moral defence this is usually an other and more often than not a parent that has been made good—that is, not a "naturally" or clearly good object. In the defence that is shared by Daniels, Cobb and

Shelby the good object that is identified with seems to be the libidinised ideal self—that is, a defence that, in classical language, would be called narcissistic. The object that has been libidinised is the ideal object/ego-ideal and not the libidinal object of Fairbairn's theory.

The implication of this view in *Shutter Island* is that Terry Daniels is unable to admit his own badness or failure and lives in his phantasy of being a good man, an upholder of the law. He is split between being the idealised upholder of the law and the ugly, scarred, completely bad alter ego whose name is an anagram of his own. He chooses his "mad" view of the world because he is unable to accept the guilt of having himself been monstrous—unconditionally bad—and has been unable to internalise any alternative good object so that he might just be regarded as conditionally bad and thus able, with difficulty, to accept and make restitution for his badness. This raises a number of questions regarding Fairbairn's object relations view of this process and of the process that is called narcissism in classical language.

If we look at Fairbairn's conception of the moral defence and strip it of its religious metaphors, the only way that this can operate is if the good object that is internalised is based upon a significant other. In a world without God it is significant others that need to be internalised to establish, and later shore up, the good object internally. In a world in which the family is riven with problems and there are no overarching grand narratives that can command undivided loyalty and respect and that themselves might support and encourage belief, then the internalisation and strengthening of the good object in the ideal object becomes problematic, and it is this problematic that these three films are all circling around.

In Fairbairn's theory the normal development of the good object is based upon successful and acceptable object relationships with mother or primary caregiver initially and can be strengthened and developed through experiences with other good objects subsequently. It is a failure, or rather an inversion, of this process, where the (libidinised, ideal) ego is taken as the good object, that seems to lie at the heart of these alternative formulations of the process.

What is the nature of the unconditional badness that besets Daniels, Cobb and Shelby in these films? It is a failure of the relationship between the main protagonist and his wife in each case that is the root cause of the difficulty, her fate depending upon and being the responsibility of the main protagonist. He is guilty of the problems that befell her and he has internalised her as a bad internal object.

In *Shutter Island* the wife, who is said to be suffering from manic depression, kills their children while Daniels, scarred by war and his experience of Dachau, and unable to cope, becomes an alcoholic, ignores her manifest problems, and buries himself in his job as a federal marshal, which he follows assiduously. When he discovers that in a fit of depression his wife has drowned their children he kills her. This might be seen to be a similar reaction to his earlier experience of Dachau, where he let the German Commandant die painfully and killed the death camp guards in cold blood, in that some of the imagery of the death camp shows the cold-blooded murder of children.

In *Shutter Island* Daniels chooses madness, and to be lobotomised, to have the hurt and the memory excised, cut out. In *Memento* Shelby chooses to forget so that he can keep on killing to expiate the guilt he feels. In *Inception* Cobb is left in limbo in a literal sense, since the film is unresolved; he might still be in a dream and not have overcome the guilt he feels at his wife's death. These all echo unrealistic responses to disillusionment as described by Macmurray (1961) (see the section on disillusion below).

In *Inception* Cobb has inadvertently caused his wife to kill herself by implanting an idea in her head using the very technique of manipulating the preconscious and the unconscious that he is currently employing to guarantee and expand his everyday business.

The main dynamic, then, in each of the films is guilt relating to the death of the main protagonist's wife. In each case the wife can be seen to operate as a bad internalised object to which the protagonist is strongly libidinally attached. All three films seem to represent failure to find restitution for the guilt the protagonist feels vis-à-vis his wife's untimely death, which suggests that she was also an ideal object for them. The wife also acts antilibidinally towards the main protagonist, directly or indirectly, meaning that she occupies the three basic relationships derived originally from the initial splitting of relations with mother during the development of the basic endopsychic structure.

An object relations approach to narcissism

Fairbairn discusses narcissism at a number of places in his 1952 book *Psychoanalytic Studies of the Personality* distinguishing between primary and secondary narcissism in the following manner, "… *primary narcissism may be simply defined as … a state of identification with the object, secondary narcissism being a state of identification with an object which is internalised"* (Fairbairn, 1952, p. 48, emphasis in original). He argues that there is no "… necessary incompatibility between the view that libido is primarily object-seeking and the conception of libido cathecting the ego, since there is always the possibility of one part of the ego structure treating another part as an object …" (Fairbairn, 1952, Footnote, p. 83).

For Fairbairn, then, narcissism is a state of identification with an internalised object. We have known, since Freud's paper on narcissism, that the child internalises the nursing couple and can make object choices on the basis of one or other party to this object relationship, one being the mother (anaclitic); the other being the child itself (narcissistic). It would appear that the sort of preferred object choice that the protagonists of these films are making is what Freud calls narcissistic object choice. However, this is not a homosexual choice, at least not as explicitly represented in these films, but it does suggest that the relations between the couples are based upon identification rather than difference, which would make decathecting the libidinised object that much more difficult, which it seems to be for all three of them.

In each of these films the central figure seems to have taken themself as their (libidinised) ego-ideal and this makes their admitting that they could have made a mistake exceptionally difficult for them. Whilst the ego-ideal/ideal object is not usually regarded as a bad object in Fairbairn's terms, even if attachment to bad objects is seen to be the origin of the utmost resistance to opening the closed world of inner reality to allow for some change to occur, the alliance between the central ego and an ego-ideal based upon identification with the self can provide a sufficiently repressed inner world so as to prevent any change from occurring and thus act as a bad object, as has been argued elsewhere (see Chapter Four).

At this point, and given that both Freud and Lacan have used ego-ideal and ideal ego and super-ego in quite specific ways, it is necessary to revisit another aspect of Fairbairn's model. For Fairbairn the ego-ideal and the ideal object are the repository of positive moral and value-laden examples based upon identifications with good objects through object relations, starting with the mother or primary caregiver. Meanwhile Fairbairn's equivalent of the punitive super-ego is the anti-libidinal ego and its object again based upon the internalisation of object relations characterised by rejection and frustration. Fairbairn's division of the super-ego between two distinct dynamic structures is consonant with Ferenczi's own understanding of this process when he says:

> my objective was to destroy only that part of the super-ego, which had become unconscious and was therefore beyond the range of influence. I had no sort of objection to the retention of a number of positive and negative models in the preconscious of the ordinary individual. (Ferenczi, 1928, p. 98)

This parallel can be clearly seen in a paper by the author attempting to consistently employ Freud's topographical categories within an extended version of Fairbairn's model (Clarke, 2005).

Fred Alford, writing of Fairbairn and Guntrip as the purest expression of object relations theory, comments that although they rarely write about narcissism "they see a schizoid split in the self as characteristic of virtually all emotional disorder" (Alford, 1988, p. 67) and points to the significance of Greenberg and Mitchell's view that what American analysts call "narcissism" British analysts tend to call "Schizoid personality disorder". "This insight allows us to connect the symptomatology of narcissism—feelings of emptiness, unreality, alienation and emotional withdrawal—with a theory that sees such symptoms as an accurate reflection of the experience of being split off from a part of oneself" (op. cit.). This view of narcissism "as an excessive attachment of the ego to internal objects ... resulting in various splits in the ego necessary to maintain these attachments, allows us to penetrate this confusion" (op. cit.).

Disillusion

Before returning to the moral defence, I want to introduce another strand of thinking within the British Object Relations Group (Independents or Middle Group) that is important for the internal dynamic we are considering. Originally formulated by Suttie (1935) and subsequently developed by Macmurray (1961) and Winnicott (1953), the concept of disillusion has deep significance for the films being considered. Although each of the central characters might be considered narcissistic they are different in the way they cast and respond to their circumstances. I have argued elsewhere (Clarke, 2003a) that Macmurray's development of Suttie's original approach to the consequences of disillusion for the internal dynamics of the child are more far reaching than Winnicott's view of disillusion but consistent with Fairbairn's understanding of endopsychic structure. The important point that Macmurray brings out is that there are three distinct ways of responding to a mother's attempts to disillusion the child— that is, gradually introduce them to reality and a realistic view of their own powers. The three outcomes are (1) to return to a loving, trusting relationship with mother understanding that she let the infant struggle for their own good, and it is this option in which the good object might be most strongly developed and internalised. The other outcomes are (2) to treat the mother and others as essentially bad and out to frustrate or deny the infant and for the infant to therefore adopt an agonistic approach to others and the world and to try to take whatever it wants rather than cooperate and work communally with and within it, and (3) for the infant to withdraw from the outside world and live in the inner world of imagination rather than work communally with others to achieve its ends.

If we were to try and characterise the three central characters of the films under discussion in terms of these three categories they clearly do not belong to the first category of successful adjustment to relating to others and working together without resentment. However, I think you could argue that each of the three characters in the films under discussion has withdrawn into their own inner world in order to live within their own imagination of what things are like rather than accept an independently existing reality. Daniels has clearly chosen to live in his internal world rather than recognise what has happened in reality. Shelby has decided to deny reality in order to allow him to repeat ad infinitum an act of revenge. Meanwhile, Cobb seems to be about living in the imagination and the only question is how do you know what the limit of that might be, since it is seen to be many-layered, and we are left at the end of the film wondering what the level of this particular reality is, quite literally. Insofar as Cobb appears to have rid himself of his internalised bad object by her having been shot and left at the lowest level of consciousness it might be argued that he has overcome his internalised bad object, but the film remains ambivalent about that. A dead spouse (or mother) in the deep unconscious could be the last manifestation of an attachment to a bad internal object and as such a powerful resistance to change (cf. Memento).

The moral defence revisited

When we return to consider the moral defence again it is clear that the nature of the process will depend to some degree upon the extent to which the development of the good object has been successful and the process of disillusion mastered without residual resentment and the choice of alternative ways of understanding and approaching the world. For the moral defence to work adequately there must be a degree of trust and dependence upon the (m)other already established, the alternative being one or other of the narcissistic or schizoid solutions to the problem, where you are in the right and the other is in the wrong, because you have taken yourself as your own ideal and not an other (usually a parental other). In this case, each of these films, while seeming at some level to involve the moral defence, actually illustrates the failure of that defence, because of the undeveloped nature of the dynamic structures that constitute the endopsychic structure due to a failure in the process of disillusionment during infancy. In that sense, and using Kleinian language, these characters have never successfully reached the depressive position; they have never accepted that mother was both good and bad but have maintained that split internally to their cost.

Conclusion

I have argued that each of these films in many ways seems to rehearse the moral defence, as Fairbairn called it, where you internalise the bad other as an internal object in order to have a world of good external objects. You take on that badness internally yourself and defend yourself against it by internalising the good other into your internal good object (ideal object and ego-ideal for Fairbairn). But after investigating the unfolding of the stories further and considering the process of disillusion as a significant process in the development of feeling real I have argued that none of these characters was able to reach a position in which they might employ the moral defence effectively, because they were still riven by failures at an earlier stage of development where they were unable to overcome the resentment and disappointment of disillusion and recognise mother as a whole good and bad other upon whom they could depend and who was the origin of their internalised good object. Significantly, instead each took *themselves* as their libidinised ideal object and retreated inside to achieve their own ends in their imagination, denying the separate existence of external reality. They are thus exemplars of failures of early infancy before the depressive position is reached and thus prone, as Fairbairn argued, to schizoid problems (Fairbairn, 1952, p. 55).

CHAPTER SIX

Trauma, dissociation, and time distortion in some "puzzle" films

Introduction

In his introduction to *Puzzle Films: Complex Storytelling in Contemporary Cinema* Warren Buckland (2009) argues that the "puzzle" film is of a different order of complexity to the Aristotelean notion of the complex narrative, in that puzzle films "embrace non-linearity, time loops and fragmented spatio-temporal reality ... they are riddled with gaps, deception, labyrinthine structures, ambiguity and overt coincidences ... characters ... are schizophrenic, lose their memory, are unreliable narrators, or are dead (but without us—or them—realising) ... it emphasises the complex *telling* ... of a complex *story*" (Buckland, 2009, p. 6). Thus the term "puzzle film" "names a mode of filmmaking that cuts across traditional filmmaking practices, all of which are becoming increasingly difficult to define: so-called American 'independent' cinema, the European and international art film, and certain modes of avant-garde filmmaking" (ibid., p. 6). I am going to look at a number of these puzzle films from a psychoanalytic perspective that is post-classical and relational in its intent, centrally concerned with trauma and dissociation, and based on the work of Ronald Fairbairn. I first outline an approach to film based on Fairbairn's object relations theory. I next look at the overall structure of some puzzle films. The main body of the chapter looks at psychoanalysis, trauma, dissociation, and time distortion. I end the chapter by looking at one film *The Jacket* using Fairbairn's "psychology of dynamic structure".

A Fairbairn-based object relations approach to film

I am going to develop some remarks I made in 1994 when I first tried to use Fairbairn's theory to understand film.

> I have treated the whole film as if it were a representation of unconscious phantasy, and also treated individuals within the film as if they had such an unconscious phantasy or such an endopsychic structure as Fairbairn described. (Clarke, 1994, p. 380)

Fairbairn's theory was centrally concerned with understanding trauma, multiplicity and dissociation (Chapter Three) and provides a model for creativity and psychic growth as restitution through his writings on art and creativity (Clarke, 2006, Ch. 5). This approach is predicated upon Fairbairn's view of (unconscious) phantasy first formulated during the Controversial Discussions.

> ... the explanatory concept of "phantasy" has now been rendered obsolete by the concepts of "psychical reality" and "internal objects" which the work of Mrs Klein and her followers has done so much to develop; and in my opinion the time is now ripe for us to replace the concept of "phantasy" by a concept of an "inner reality" peopled by the Ego and its internal objects. These internal objects should be regarded as having an organised structure, an identity of their own, an endopsychic existence and an activity as real within the inner world as those of any objects in the outer world ... (King & Steiner, 1991, p. 361)

This view, which was rejected by Klein and Isaacs at the time, has been supported subsequently by Ogden's paper on reading Susan Isaacs, where he concludes that:

> The movement from Freud's structural model to a model of internal object relationships structured by phantasy seems to me to be

a necessary implication of Isaacs's and Klein's work, but it is an implication that Isaacs seems to actively resist, perhaps for reasons having to do with the psychoanalytic politics of her time. (Ogden, 2011, p. 940)

Since for Freud,

the psycho-analyst must endeavour in the course of the treatment to unearth the phantasies which lie behind such products of the unconscious as dreams, symptoms, acting out, repetitive behaviour, etc. … [and] even aspects of behaviour that are far removed from imaginative activity, and which appear at first glance to be governed solely by the demands of reality, emerge as emanations, as "derivatives" of unconscious phantasy. (Laplanche & Pontalis, 1973, p. 317)

And for Klein, unconscious phantasy is the underlying origin of all symbolisation:

it seems to me that the artist is one who can, as it were, have a dream—let us say an unconscious phantasy—and can give it symbolic expression. (Segal interview, 1999)

For Fairbairn the concept of unconscious phantasy is replaced by endopsychic structure and it is the dynamics of endopsychic structure that lie at the origin of all of the products of phantasy as understood by Freud and Klein.

The model of endopsychic structure that Fairbairn derives from one of his patient's dreams is based upon the internalisation of object relationships experienced by the infant. An object relationship is an affective relationship between two people or a person and a thing that, when internalised, translates to an ego-structure affectively linked to an internal object, each potentially an active person-like structure. It comprises a conscious central ego libidinally linked with a preconscious ideal object, both based upon acceptable object relationships. Together these use aggression to repress two unconscious object-relationship based sub-selves, each an ego-object dyad linked libidinally. One sub-self is libidinal, based upon the internalisation of over-exciting object relationships, and the other is antilibidinal based upon the internalisation of over-rejecting or over-frustrating object relationships. The antilibidinal sub-self uses aggression to subject the libidinal sub-self to a secondary, indirect, form of repression. The antilibidinal self is the equivalent of the punitive super-ego, while the ideal object is the equivalent of the ego-ideal or positive super-ego. It is this system and its dynamics that Fairbairn suggests as a replacement for unconscious phantasy (see below).

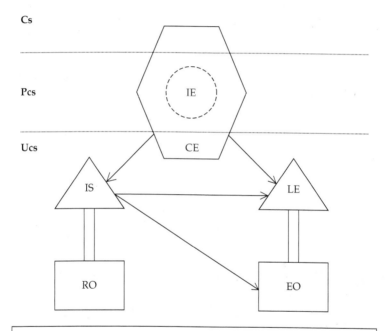

Key:
CE is Central Ego; IS is Internal Saboteur; LE is Libidinal Ego; RO is Rejecting Object; EO is Exciting Object.
Cs is Conscious; Pcs is Preconscious and Ucs is Unconscious.
→ Aggression; | | Libido.

In Fairbairn's original diagram, upon which this is based, although he described the ego-ideal (IE) as being in the preconscious he didn't represent it on the diagram.

Later on Fairbairn used libidinal ego and object for LE and EO respectively and antilibidinal ego and object for IS and RO respectively.

Figure 6.1. Fairbairn's original diagram (1944) (redrawn).

I should at this juncture make it clear that when I talk about object relationships I mean, and I think that Fairbairn means, the total breadth and depth of an affective relationship across a multi-modal manifold of cognitions, senses, and feelings; the touch, the taste, the smell, the sound, etc. between subject and object, between socially located persons or socially located persons and things.

Fairbairn's theory of art, developed in the 1930s, before WWII, is centrally concerned with symbolisation but contains within it a gradation of symbolisation that allows for the introduction of value (Read, 1951, pp. 79–80). Fairbairn's conception of "over-" and "under-symbolisation" and an "optimal synthesis" represented by the "restored object" allows for some relative responses in terms of the degree of fit between the artist and the "beholder" of the art work. I will discuss the application of Fairbairn's concepts of over- and under-symbolisation to cinema after describing the development of his psychology of dynamic structure, later in the chapter.

An approach that equates a film to a dream seems to me to be both the most productive and the most effective approach to take. Every film embodies, well or badly, someone's dream or phantasy of something. Thus a psychoanalytic approach to dreams can be a vital clue to how one might approach film psychoanalytically. Fairbairn's approach to dream is as follows.

> I tentatively formulated the view that all of the figures appearing in dreams represented either parts of the dreamer's own personality ... or else identifications on the part of the ego. A further development of this view was to the effect that dreams are essentially not wish-fulfilments, but dramatisations or "shorts" (in a cinematographic sense) of situations existing in inner reality ... therefore the situations depicted in dreams represent relationships existing between endopsychic structures; and the same applies to situations depicted in waking phantasies. (Fairbairn, 1952, p. 99)

When Laplanche and Pontalis conclude their entry on phantasy by discussing the relationship between phantasy and desire, their account seems to lend itself to representation and interpretation using an endopsychic structure like that described by Fairbairn.

> Even in their least elaborate forms, phantasies do not appear to be reducible to an intentional aim on the part of the desiring subject:
> a. Even where they can be summed up in a single sentence, phantasies are still *scripts (scénarios)* of organised *scenes* which are capable of *dramatization*—usually in a *visual form*.
> b. The subject is invariably present in these *scenes*; even in the case of the "primal scene", from which it might appear that he was excluded, he does in fact have a part to play not only as an observer but also as a participant, when he interrupts the parents' coitus.
> c. It is not an object that the subject imagines and aims at, so to speak, but rather a sequence in which the subject has his own *part to play* and in which *permutations of roles and attributions* are possible.
> d. In so far as desire is articulated in this way through phantasy, phantasy is also the locus of defensive operations: it facilitates the most primitive of defence processes, such as turning round upon the subject's own self, reversal into the opposite, negation and projection.
> e. Such defences are themselves inseparably bound up with the primary function of phantasy, namely the *mise-en-scène* of desire—a *mise-en-scène* in which what is prohibited is always present in the actual formation of the wish. (Laplanche & Pontalis, 1973, p. 318, emphasis added)

After introducing some of the common structural elements of the films I will look at the psychoanalytic background of the approach I have adopted and highlight some recent work on Pierre Janet's understanding of trauma, dissociation, multiplicity, and time distortions (Van der Hart & Steele, 1997). I will end by discussing the film *The Jacket* in some detail.

The assumption in this part of the analysis is that, following Fairbairn, dreams (daydreams, phantasies, etc.) are like (short) films of inner reality (Fairbairn, 1944), and Fairbairn's model of the basic endopsychic structure can be used to map the dynamics of the narrative. As I have also argued above, a dramatic narrative on film might be considered as a depiction of the dynamics of an endopsychic structure (Clarke, 1994). My main argument is that each of these films can be understood as an attempt to ward off psychic disintegration in response to a major trauma. These narratives are phantasies that are generated as part of a process whose function is to protect the main protagonist from madness and death, by dissociating and retranscribing the trauma in a restitutive move towards greater integration. Unpicking these phantasies involves a therapeutic journey, not unlike the journey described by T. S. Eliot in his poem "Little Gidding" (1942) where he writes:

> We shall not cease from exploration
> And the end of all our exploring
> Will be to arrive where we started
> And know the place for the first time.

Overview of the films under discussion

An exemplar of the "puzzle" films, both in structure and in terms of the time distortions involved, is *An Occurrence at Owl Creek Bridge*. This is based on an Ambrose Bierce short story and is just 23 minutes long but is the structural precursor of a number of the films being discussed. Indeed, with suitable adjustments it can be seen as the structural precursor of all the films discussed, since its narrative is more or less circular, involving as it does a time dilation that is the body of the film held between two contextual markers. "In my beginning is my end" (T. S Eliot, "East Coker", 1940). This structure, which involves time dilation around the trauma of death, means the story is the equivalent of an internal "state of affairs" dream (Fairbairn, 1944) generated by one mind and thus subject to analysis as if it is the dream or phantasy of one person. It might also be described as an "empty circle", since the story literally ends up back where it started.

Other films with a similar structure include *La Jettee* (Chris Marker, 1962), *Jacob's Ladder* (Adrian Lyne, 1990), *Twelve Monkeys* (Terry Gilliam, 1995), *Donny Darko* (Richard Kelly, 2001), *Mulholland Drive* (David Lynch, 2001), *The Machinist* (Brad Anderson, 2004), *The Butterfly Effect* (Eric Bress and J. Mackye Gruber, 2004), *The Jacket* (John Maybury, 2005), and *Dermaphoria* (aka *Desiree*) (Ross Clarke, 2014).

The constituents of the puzzle films that are being studied here are trauma and its resolution, dissociation, and restitutive phantasy. *Owl Creek Bridge* is the simplest of these films, since it contains these phases of the process in the order trauma, dissociation, restitutive phantasy, and resolution of trauma; the equivalent to a beginning, middle and end in conventional narrative. Other films have a structure that is like more complex forms of narrative where these elements are not necessarily in that order. In *Donnie Darko*, *Mulholland Drive* and *The Machinist* the trauma happened before the film starts or is only very briefly alluded to before the restitutive phantasy is developed. Here the original trauma and its resolution appear towards the end of the film. In *Jacob's Ladder* and *The Jacket* the context is a foreign war, which is the source of the trauma when the main protagonist is shot. The restitutive phantasy in all these films is of the making-good of the fragmented relationships that the main protagonist finds within himself.

The resolution for most of these films is the death of the main protagonist but at a higher level of integration. *La Jette* and *Twelve Monkeys* start and end with the trauma, and the restitutive phantasy that links the two traumas involves nothing less than restoring the world to a prelapsarian state before the catastrophe. *The Butterfly Effect* with its cyclic structure of traumas that seems to be going deeper and deeper into the past and the origins of the traumas, like a therapeutic regression, ends with an act of total negation. In *Dermaphoria* the trauma is followed by what might be called a restituitive phantasy—a choice between three fathers and a search for a lost love, the eventual fate of whom is not discovered until the end of the film.

In all but one of the films under consideration the main protagonist is masculine. In general all of the main characters are young. *La Jettee, Jacob's Ladder, Twelve Monkeys, Donnie Darko, The Machinist, The Butterfly Effect, The Jacket* and *Dermaphoria* all contain significant involvement with children as victims of abuse and aggression. The wider social significance of these films might be as exemplary forms of struggle against an inimical world in order to redress a wrong and make it right. In this they could be seen as offering encouragement to struggle to achieve some positive reconciliation of apparently warring factions within oneself and society despite the threats of loss and death.

The overall mechanism of the films starts on or around a trauma, leading to a dissociation that may spawn other traumas and dissociations, meaning that when you return to the beginning—that is also the end—with a greater knowledge and understanding than you had at the beginning, you can treat the intervening narrative as the phantasy of one mind, that mind being the mind of the main protagonist. This means that you can treat the narrative as a dream or a daydream, a narrative in any case produced by one mind in response to a trauma and motivated by a search for some form of restitution. The function of the dissociation in each case might be different but that will only become apparent when the dissociated reality and its transformations are analysed.

One argument about both the possibility, and the utility, of such time dilations—whatever their origin—is that the main protagonist can search for ways out of, or ways to understand, or make intelligible, and perhaps avoid, the worst outcome of the trauma that is upon him or her. Like the often reported cases of time slowing down when you are involved in a car accident and there being time to both consider and do things you would probably not have been able to do if still in your normal relation to time. These alternative narratives of an alternative life often involve alternative persona, and will have to be considered from this point of view too—that is, as the search for a solution or some restitution, depending upon how culpable the main protagonist feels themselves to be.

In *Owl Creek* a man is to be hanged off the Owl Creek Bridge during the American Civil War. As he is taken to the improvised gallows he remembers his wife and their home briefly. He has the noose put around his neck and the order is given for him to hang. He plummets towards the river below but the rope breaks and he lands in the river where he quickly struggles free of his bonds and swims for his life. The soldiers fire at him from the cliffs above but the river quickens over some rapids and he is swept a long way down stream where rifle fire can no longer reach him. The soldiers send cannon shots in his direction but miss. He climbs from the river and runs like mad but with intention. Throughout this section a song entitled "A Living Man"—a celebration of the beauty and complexity of the natural world—is playing. He runs through forest and woodland and eventually comes to the gates of a large house with a long drive. As he limps along the drive towards the house his wife comes out of the house and runs towards him. They are about to embrace when he is suddenly pulled up short and we cut to the bridge and the man jerked by the rope in the act of hanging. The whole of the story, from the point the rope breaks to his imagined reunion with his wife, is a defensive phantasy that protects him from the immediate knowledge of his own death and allows him to imagine a life restored by his reunion with his wife. He is not quite restored to his lost love but nearly so. This is an underlying pattern in many of the other films.

Closest to *Owl Creek* in my view is *The Jacket*, even though there are no explicit indications that the gap between the main protagonists being shot in Iraq in 1991 and his imagining himself slipping on ice and dying from a head injury on New Year's day 1993, are part of a similar alternative life running parallel to his dying from the original head wound in the Iraqi desert.

Whilst all of these films involve distortions of time in some form they do not all involve or require time travel as such. Time travel is a topic that is broached by *Donnie Darko* but apart from references to it in the film itself, it is not part of the story. On the other hand, *The Jacket* and *The Butterfly Effect* and *La Jettee* and *Twelve Monkeys* all involve some form of time travel and all under the same rubric, of trying to correct or compensate for, or otherwise make restitution for, something that has gone wrong in the past that is seen to be the root of a continuing problem in the present. As such these forms of time travel can be seen as being similar to the undoing of a trauma that has distorted or blighted a life and whose undoing might have a healing effect. This then has parallels with *The Machinist*, *Jacob's Ladder* and *Demaphoria*, which are about overcoming a dissociation caused by an earlier trauma and thus becoming able to see reality clearly again; *The Machinist* over an extended period of a year, *Jacob's Ladder* over a short period of hours, and *Dermaphoria* over days.

All of the films involve splitting (dissociation caused by trauma) where the protagonist appears in at least two distinct identities. In some, the alternative identity is contained within the time distorted narrative—*Owl Creek*, *Jacob's Ladder*, *The Jacket*—in others the multiplicity of the main character is more clearly expressed—*The Machinist* (Ivan), *Donnie Darko* (the rabbit), *Mulholland Drive* (Dianne becomes Betty and Camilla becomes Rita)—or, paradoxically, in the case of *La Jettee* and *Twelve Monkeys*, where the same person, as a child, witnesses their own death as an adult.

Overview of the general structure of the stories depicted

The dead narrator?

Part of the puzzling nature of these films is that at least two different perspectives are set in motion; one that is consistent with the apparent subjective experience of the lead character, which constitutes the body of the film, and one that is the view we take of that character when his or her subjective experience, as depicted, proves to be corrigible. That is when the altered state—the delusion or phantasy the lead characters are generating—is no longer able to sustain itself and the narrative collapses back to the choices we have to make about the lead character, on the basis of the information we receive or infer from the developed narrative. You might think of these as the subjective and objective poles of the narrative respectively. In all of the films we are returned to ourselves and the corrigible nature of the story we have been told by what turns out to be an unreliable and in some cases dead narrator. Since all of the stories are closer to a representation of what the lead character thinks and feels—that is, the subjective pole, these are also closer to psychosis understood in Fairbairn's terms as the process where inner reality determines the appearances of outer reality. At the objective pole these are also personal stories in which various forms of restitution are imagined and enacted in the dynamics of inner reality, this being understood as an attempted correction, in the internal world, to the various ills that the character is heir to, socially.

I think that each of these narratives can be seen as self-contained and as reflecting one person's imagination, and I see each of the films as depicting a dream or a daydream generated by one person—the main protagonist—and reflecting the dynamics of their internal world. The action of the films can be seen to echo a restitutive trajectory, so that the central characters make peace with themselves and their (imagined) others before dying or changing. That is, it follows the sort of trajectory that a therapeutic intervention might take but with a different overall outcome; death, in this case, representing something like the termination of the therapeutic process. As such, since each is regarded as a closed system associated with one individual, it can also be seen as an attempt at some form of self-healing or soul-saving given the presence of death. It might thus act as an encouragement to others to persist in trying to understand and endure what has happened to them, and there are a growing number of examples of people using film as a central part of therapy across a range of disciplines.

Over- and under-symbolisation in cinema

Herbert Read writes, quoting Fairbairn's paper on the ultimate basis of aesthetic experience (Read, 1951),

> He distinguishes between over-symbolization and under-symbolization—between the true work of art and those false works of art which do not function either because (1) "the censorship of the artist's super-ego is so rigorous, and necessitates such an elaborate disguise of the urges expressed, that the work of art is deprived of

almost all symbolic significance for the beholder"; or (2) the opposite case, "when the artist's super-ego is weak and his repressed urges are really 'urgent', these urgent urges express themselves in the work of art with a minimum of disguise". Then "the object is not sufficiently symbolic to pass the censorship of the super-ego. It is, so to speak, too like the real thing". (Read, 1954, p. 79)

Counter to these failed attempts, Read uses Fairbairn's principle of optimal synthesis where,

> The artistic activity "performs the double function of providing a means of expression for the repressed urges of the artist and of simultaneously enabling his ego to pay a tribute to the supremacy of his super-ego, the work of art ... essentially represents a means of restitution, whereby (the artist's) ego makes atonement to his super-ego for the destruction implied in the presence of repressed destructive impulses". "The under-symbolized work of art fails to produce the effect of restitution because the impression which it gives is one of more or less unmitigated destruction. ... On the other hand, restitution is meaningless apart from the presupposition of destruction; and, consequently, over-symbolization precludes the effect of restitution by excluding the impression of destruction too vigorously". So it is a case of not too much and not too little, and the work of art ... becomes "the highest unity ... reached through the full development and reconciliation of the deepest and widest antagonism". (Read, 1954, p. 80)

Fairbairn's papers on art were written before he developed his object relations theory in detail and they use classical language. I have attempted to rewrite his theory of art using his later nomenclature (Clarke, 2006, chapter 5). The id-structure that he refers to is later understood as the libidinal self, and the super-ego to which he must atone is a combination of a punitive unconscious super-ego in the form of the antilibidinal self and a positive, preconscious ego-ideal or ideal self. Terms like "primary" and "secondary process" and "sublimation", all of which are classical terms, are given a new object relations interpretation by Fairbairn. Artistic activity will come to be described "as an attempt to reconcile the primitive expression of a repressed id-structure with the requirements of a conscious ego-structure oriented towards external objects in a social milieu" (Fairbairn, 1953, p. 167). And, Fairbairn's revised understanding of sublimation involves

> [both] a change in the relationships existing between the artist and those objects who constitute society for him; and similarly ... a complex change (a) in the relationship of internally differentiated ego-structures not only with internal objects but also with one another, and (b) in the relationships of the conscious ego-structure with external objects. (Fairbairn, 1953, p. 167)

One could then classify films according to their place on the spectrum of over- to under-symbolised with a central ground of optimal synthesis for any specific culture. However it is also clear using these categories that innovation and novelty, changes in style, which might be characteristic of an era, do depend upon locating the films relative to this baseline, so that Italian neorealism and the nouvelle vague are under-symbolised but determine the direction of cinema for the next few decades—that is, they shift the centre ground—the optimal synthesis. It follows that the optimal synthesis is necessarily historical and subject to change. The puzzle film is probably over-symbolised, as it requires a great deal of work on the part of the viewer to make sense of it because of its relative distance from the optimal synthesis. In a review of Ernst Kris's *Psychoanalytic Explorations in Art* (1952), Fairbairn explains:

> The optimal itself does not ... represent any fixed standard. What is optimal for one artist may not be optimal for another. Similarly what is optimal for one audience may not be optimal for another audience; and what appears optimal in terms of the ethos of one age or culture may appear anything but optimal to those of a succeeding age or of a culture which is alien. Hence the notorious subjectivity of aesthetic judgements. The greatest works of art ... are those which have the most universal aesthetic appeal. (Birtles & Scharff, 1994, p. 430)

Fairbairn cites "the wilder productions of the Surrealists" as being under-symbolised and "Victorian art and other forms of art characterised by excessive formalism" as being over-symbolised. In a review, Fairbairn drew attention to the similarities between his work on aesthetics and Rickman's work on "ugliness".

> All things considered, there can be little doubt that both Rickman and the reviewer were simultaneously concerned with basic problems presented by the psychology of art, and that, whilst their approaches had much in common, they were essentially independent. (Fairbairn, 1959, p. 342)

Rickman concludes that:

> In the works of man, as in those which we separate and call the products of nature, we see creative and destructive forces in active interplay. When we discern the influence of creation predominating we are moved by something we call beauty, when we see destruction we recoil at the ugly. Our need for beauty springs from the gloom and pain which we experience from our destructive impulses to our good and loved objects; our wish is to find in art evidence of the triumph of life over death; we recognize the power of death when we say a thing is ugly. (Rickman, 1957, p. 88)

Psychoanalytic theory, trauma, and dissociation

The origins of psychoanalytic thinking according to Laplanche and Pontalis in their *The Language of Psychoanalysis* (1973) came from Freud's thinking about trauma.

> A classic description of the beginnings of psycho-analysis (from 1890 to 1897) runs as follows: theoretically, the aetiology of neurosis is related to past traumatic experiences whose occurrence is assigned to a constantly receding date according as the analytic investigation penetrates more deeply, proceeding step by step from adulthood back to infancy; technically, effective cure is sought by means of an abreaction and a psychical working out of the traumatic experiences. This traditional account adds that such an approach has gradually receded into the background. (Laplanche & Pontalis, 1973, p. 466)

Freud attributed the rehabilitation of hysteria as a topic for scientific study to the positive attention generated by Charcot's neuropathological investigations of hysteria during the last ten years of his life. Breuer, Freud's original collaborator, was more interested in trauma and dissociation than was Freud, and his approach is more closely related to Pierre Janet's work. It was, however, Freud's development of the idea of repression, which is intimately linked with his rejection of the "seduction theory", that came to dominate the classical metapsychology of psychoanalysis. This was not, however, the end of the story, and one of the most famous challenges to Freud's theory was Ferenczi's 1932 paper "Confusion of Tongues" (1949), proposing that the trauma of real child abuse led directly to the dissociation of person-like alternate selves, which was suppressed, in English, until 1949. Before this scandalous suppression of Ferenczi's paper Fairbairn had however written his MD thesis on the relationship between "Dissociation and Repression" (1927), which was only published in *From Instinct to Self Vol II* in 1994, suggesting that dissociation was a special form of repression. Fairbairn famously called for a "return to hysteria" when he put forward his model of endopsychic structure in 1944.

Work on the war neurosis—which had begun during the First World War (Ferenczi et al., 1920; Rivers, 1919) and was developed and expanded during the Second World War (Fairbairn, 1943a)—and work with survivors of the holocaust led to greater understanding of the disastrous consequences of real life events on the minds of their sufferers. In more recent years the development of attachment theory and the advancement of the understanding of inter-generational transmission of abuse have led to a great deal more interest being paid to both the real traumas being experienced and the dissociative consequences of these experiences. Subsequently the study of post-traumatic stress disorder, of dissociative problems in general and of multiple personality disorder or dissociative identity disorder have taken a place in parallel with more classical psychoanalytic approaches. This has not been without controversy and is still a site for discussion between these different strands of the psychoanalytic movement. A lot of post-Freudian psychoanalysis falls somewhere between these two approaches. An interesting and important relational perspective on these issues is developed by Jody Messler Davies in her 1996 paper linking the "pre-analytic" with the "post-classical". I think this approach opens the possibility for Fairbairn's theory to be read as providing a synthesis of the classical and the relational rather than being a stage in the development from the classical to the relational as she and Mitchell (2000) imagine.

The key to this understanding is the recognition that Glover's (1932) classically based paper on the classification of mental disorders is an exact precursor of Fairbairn's crucial revision of the understanding of psychopathology of the psychoses and the psychoneuroses (1941). I was only able to fully appreciate the parallels there are between these two views after I had looked at Fairbairn's use of Freud's topographical categories and seen that there was a need for a preconscious layer in Fairbairn's endopsychic structure (Clarke, 2005). I then went on in collaboration with my colleague Paul Finnegan (Chapter Four) to look at the use of this expanded version of Fairbairn's endopsychic structure in the understanding of multiple personality disorder, or DID, where each of the alters encountered clinically can be understood as an ego-nuclei acting independently of any of the other dynamic structures. Glover's concept of ego-nuclei can be seen as the atomic conception of object relationships, which contain affects, which are derivatives of instincts, and are the form that affect takes.

> "impulses" cannot be considered apart from the endopsychic structures which they energise and the object relationships which they enable these structures to establish; and, equally, "instincts" cannot profitably be considered as anything more than forms of energy which constitute the dynamics of such endopsychic structures. (Fairbairn, 1952, p. 85)

Distortions in time

In their "Time Distortions in DID: Janetian Concepts and Treatment", Van der Hart and Steele (1997) discuss Janet's concept of time and feelings of reality in relation to trauma and dissociation. They start by describing Janet's hierarchy of feelings of reality, and then go on to discuss the ways in which trauma can interfere with this hierarchy and the ways in which these distortions might be rectified. I think it is interesting to note that when Winnicott, at the end of his life, reflected on his criticisms of Fairbairn's book, that it was the importance of feeling real that he cited as one of Fairbairn's most important contributions (Clarke, 2006, p. 161). Fairbairn had of course written his MD thesis on the relationship between dissociation and repression to make good the fact that "when Freud introduced his theory of repression, he made no attempt to relate it to Janet's theory of dissociation" (Birtles & Scharff, 1994, p. 23). Fairbairn concluded that repression was a special form of "dissociation of the unpleasant", these dissociated elements consisting essentially "in tendencies belonging to the mental structure" (Birtles & Scharff, 1994, p. 79).

Some of the time distortions based upon dissociation that Van der Hart and Steele identify from Janet's writings are as follows: 1) automatic shifts in experiences of past and present events, 2) distortions in experiencing the future, 3) dominance of developmentally fixated time perspective, 4) identities that experience living in the past, 5) complete loss of sense of time, 6) reactivation and re-experience of traumatic memories, 7) amnesia for traumatic events, 8) amnesia for recent events. Many of these appear in the puzzle films under discussion.

> Van der Hart et al. (www.trauma-pages.com/a/vdhart-93.php) stated that "realization requires putting the event into words, relating it as a narrative, and reconciling the experience within the personality, thereby restoring continuity to the individual's personal history [i.e., the experience of time]. Non-realization of the trauma can exist to varying degrees" (p. 163). Janet (1935) stated that traumatized individuals have not "realized" the traumatic event, and referred to DID as a disorder of non-realization. Non-realization often results in a combination of amnesia and experiences that manifest major time disturbances. Realization is a necessary and crucial component of trauma work, and requires strong ego resources. Unfortunately, such resources are often disrupted by trauma, or in the case of long-term early trauma and neglect, may be non-existent or very poorly organized. (Van der Hart & Steele, 1997)

Realisation in this account means to put events in their proper place relative to the actual time that the person is living, so Van der Hart and Steele then consider treatment possibilities to encourage realisation.

> Treatment interventions are thus directed toward assisting the patient to relegate accounts to the proper place in time and resulting degree of reality, whether it means lowering the account or raising it on the hierarchy of feelings of reality. In any event, a primary goal of treatment would be to encourage full realization of traumatic events, which we have distinguished from abreaction or catharsis (Van der Hart & Steele).

The overall argument of the current chapter is that all of the films discussed can be regarded as presenting a trauma or a series of traumas that lead to dissociation or dissociations within the main character, and a consequent distortion of time. Furthermore, the film narratives rehearse the sort of process that would have to be undergone therapeutically if the person experiencing the dissociation were to try to come to an understanding of it and in so doing re-transcribe it, thus healing the dissociation and returning the (re)integrated person back to a conventional understanding of identity, time and reality as described by Janet. The films then, are a description of defensive strategies adopted by the person who suffers the trauma. They are centrally concerned with the realisation, or making real, of the traumatic events.

Some of the perplexity experienced by the viewer of these films is based upon the fact that the main protagonist is unaware of the real nature of what is happening, or has happened, to them. Something happens and the protagonist finds themselves struggling to make sense of it but the resolution of the puzzle only becomes clear at the end of the film when the person more or less returns to where they started, but this time with a fuller knowledge of what it all means. This might be compared to the Freudian notion of "nachträglichkeit" (which has also been called "deferred action") but is also consistent with the consequences of trauma and dissociation as originally described by Ferenczi.

> Deferred Action: Term frequently used by Freud in connection with his view of psychical temporality and causality: experiences, impressions and memory-traces may be revised at a later date to fit in with fresh experiences or with the attainment of a new stage of development. They may in that event be endowed not only with a new meaning but also with psychical effectiveness. Freud uses the term "nachträglich" repeatedly and constantly, often underlining it. The substantival form "Nachträglichkeit" also keeps cropping up, and this from very early on. Thus, although he never offered a definition, much less a general theory, of the notion of deferred action, it was indisputably looked upon by Freud as part of his conceptual equipment. (Laplanche & Pontalis, 1973, p. 111)

Faimberg (2007) made a plea for a broader conception of nachträglichkeit.

> ... the broader conceptualization of Nachträglichkeit ... can play an active part in the process of assigning new meaning retroactively (usually through interpretation)—and even giving a meaning, for the first time (usually through construction)—to what the analysand says and cannot say. It gives us a conceptual frame of unconscious psychic temporality with which to explore how psychoanalysis produces psychic change. Winnicott's "Fear of Breakdown" (1974) is paradigmatic of this broader conceptualization of Nachträglichkeit. (Faimberg, 2007, p. 1238)

In a wide-ranging and well-received book *Destructiveness, Intersubjectivity and Trauma* (2010) Werner Bohleber has written tellingly of the effects of trauma on the self and its ability to make and sustain relationships.

> For the ego, it is impossible to integrate the traumatic experience into the psyche. The assignment of meaning is interrupted because the coincidental and unexpected nature of the event cannot be absorbed by existing structures of meaning. One lasting effect, which is important for the definition of trauma, is that basic trust is destroyed, resulting in an enduring disruption of the understanding of oneself and the world ... Trauma is not just a relational term because it connects inside and outside, but because in trauma, a fundamental holding object relationship breaks down. (Bohleber, 2010, pp. 99–100)

And again in an echo of the problems attendant upon nachtraglichheit.

> The traumatic situation and its effect destroys the ability to symbolise it and grasp its meaning ... The trauma becomes the "black hole" in the psychic structure. Unintegrated trauma fragments later break into consciousness again and overwhelm the ego, which, however, cannot structure and integrate these fragments. They cannot be incorporated into the superordinate meaningful narrative without help. Since the traumatic experience disrupts the network of meaning for a human being, it is impossible to describe in a way that is bound to meaning. The support that meanings give no longer exists at this moment; the traumatic experience cannot be "contained". (Bohleber, 2010, p. 94)

Thus the pre-classical ideas of trauma and dissociation as they have been recuperated and redeemed by post-classical theorists and clinicians have reopened the possibility of approaching these puzzle films as the complex telling of complex stories of trauma and dissociation. To illustrate the application of this approach to cinema I am going to look at one of the films in some detail.

Analysis of The Jacket

I am using Ronald Fairbairn's object relations psychoanalytic theory or "psychology of dynamic structure" to look at these films from a dynamic perspective seeking to identify the libidinal, antilibidinal, ideal and acceptable relationships they depict and the ways these are developed and transformed as a way of understanding the underlying project of restitution that Fairbairn says characterises creative activity (Fairbairn, 1938b); attempts at the restoration of the original pristine self that has been sundered by early experience into multiple dissociated sub-selves.

I have chosen to look at *The Jacket* in greater detail to illustrate the approach outlined above, because it shares many of the characteristics attributed to puzzle films and also embodies some of the time distortions Janet says are characteristic of DID.

The way I have chosen to approach *The Jacket* means that for me the lead character (Jack Starks played by Adrian Brody) is dying on the battlefield throughout the film and is thus dead before any of the imagined action of the film actually takes place; it is all a (restituitive) phantasy.

Whilst the straitjacket that constrains the lead character is used for the title of the film, it is the mortuary drawer—the appropriate occupants of which are dead bodies—that facilitates his posthumous existence and his time travel and his active intervention in other people's lives. I regard this drawer as actually being a metaphor for his being dead or dying and coincidentally for his access to his unconscious, which is the true origin of the restituitive phantasies that constitute the body of the narrative.

Time travel here becomes the means whereby he can imagine putting things back together again, internally and externally, in a productive way, and can imagine them better, more integrated and more whole as his life ebbs away, having been shot in the head by a child soldier, an antilibidinal other, under the influence of an alien ideal in an unjustifiable military intervention in Iraq in 1991. A senseless killing in a massively destructive but unwinnable war leads on, back in the U.S., to another senseless killing in which he is again a victim and unjustly accused of murdering a policeman. (This is another life event in which Jack's sense of being rejected or frustrated could strengthen his antilibidinal self.) This is only possible because he is recognised as suffering from a brain injury that affects his memory. Just prior to his becoming involved in the murder of the policeman, he has helped a drunken mother (June Price) and her prepubescent girl (Jackie) to get their car started. (Despite his problems he remains positive and helpful, which suggests that both his libidinal and antilibidinal selves are under the control of his central self.) The mother, who has been either unconscious or throwing up most of the time that Jack and Jackie are becoming acquainted and he is fixing the car, assumes the worst of his friendliness towards the girl, and, when the car is started and she has recovered enough, she threatens him and sends him away without any thanks for his help. (This antilibidinal attack is based upon her own powerful antilibidinal self.) During his trial for murder it turns out that the mother and child might have been able to provide the court with some confirmation of his story but his memory is so damaged as to be unable to remember any detail that might allow the police to find them. Jack might feel that he has been rejected by a maternal antilibidinal object (June) but that he maintains a link with the libidinal object (Jackie), a token of which are the dog tags he gives her. The attack by June on Jack and Jackie can be seen as the antilibidinal self's attack on the libidinal ego and object.

Because of his brain injury, his possible "gulf war syndrome" (PTSD, which is characterised by dissociation), and his apparent involvement with the murder of a policeman, the authorities put him into a lunatic asylum. Here he encounters two very different approaches to therapy and the care of the inmates of the asylum. One exemplified by the behaviour of a female doctor (Dr Beth Lorenson played by Jennifer Jason Leigh, a maternal, an acceptable and potentially ideal object) is more sympathetic to various talking cures while the other, exemplified by a male doctor, (Dr Thomas Becker played by Kris Kristoffesen, a paternal, antilibidinal object) is committed to using physical therapies only—drugs, ECT, insulin coma, etc. Becker uses a combination of drugs, a straightjacket and a mortuary drawer to shock what he considers his less responsive, or more resistant, patients back to sanity. It is the experiences that Jack has while in the mortuary drawer that form the basis of the time travelling story.

The substance of the time travelling story is based upon a massive coincidence. While in the mortuary drawer, Jack travels forward in time by sixteen years to 2007 and meets and gets to know the little girl (Jackie), who is now a young woman. She is not happy or fulfilled but depressed and with very low self-esteem. Jackie works in a dead end job and has no hope for her future. Jackie tells him that her mother (June), while drunk, set herself on fire accidentally and died leaving Jackie with no one to care for her. Jackie is split, she is a libidinal object in relation to Jack but she is also in thrall to an active punitive antilibidinal ego based upon her relationship with her antilibidinal object—her mother—which prevents her from flourishing. Jackie has however kept the dog tags that Jack gave her when he fixed their car. He finds them in her flat and tells her that he is the man who helped her all those years ago. She does not want to believe this but is eventually convinced and then looks into his past and finds that he died Christmas 1992, soon after the time that he was put into the lunatic asylum. From her current perspective, he has been dead for years.

When Jack returns to the asylum he wants to find out how he died and starts to ask questions. There is a subplot about Lorenson (a potentially ideal object), who is in favour of the talking cure and is protective of him and opposed to the treatment he is getting from her male counterpart Becker (antilibidinal object). Lorenson is treating a child who is unable to communicate effectively with his mother or anyone else. She has tried all that she knows but is unable to make any progress in enabling the child to communicate. (The image of the isolated child unable to communicate with its mother suggests that Jack himself and as identified with Jackie may both have felt abandoned, unheld and unloved by their mothers.) The next time Jack travels to the future to see Jackie he asks her to find out about Lorenson and her child patient. Jackie finds this out and tells Jack what is wrong with the boy and how Lorenson manages to help him.

Meanwhile Jack and Jackie investigate what has happened to Becker and find him at a church where he appears to be a broken man, wracked with guilt, whose brutality (antilibidinal) was a consequence of his having been tricked by a child murderer who brutally killed another child after having been released by Becker. Jack sees his own grave and the date on it that is just a few days away from his asylum-based reality.

When Jack is back at the asylum he tells Lorenson what is wrong with the child and what she needs to do to help him. The solution is to administer a mild electric (ECT) shock, which, she does reluctantly, and successfully restores the child to normality. In this situation a small amount of maternal aggression is all that is required to help the child, like the process of benign disillusion, which enables the child to move on to higher stages of mastery and integration.

Jack subsequently asks Lorenson to help him contact Jackie's mother, June, who at this point is still alive. Lorenson agrees and Jack is able to visit June, and, after meeting Jackie as a little girl again, gives her mother a letter explaining what the consequences of her continuing to drink will be for her daughter. (He intervenes to interrupt June's antilibidinal behaviour and its profound long-term consequences for Jackie.) From his central self with the help and cooperation of his ideal self Lorenson, Jack engages his antilibidinal self (June) and provides guidance to lessen the neglectful aggression expressed toward the libidinal self (Jackie) in order to free her to develop and grow.

When Jack time travels next, just before the date he is due to die, while the place he arrives at in the future is the same, Jackie has changed. She is no longer harbouring a powerful antilibidinal self, based upon her relationship with her mother, as she was previously. She has changed and does not recognise him, but stops to give him a lift nevertheless, since she can see that he is injured; she has become empathic. In the course of their journey he discovers that her mother, June, has not died and that the girl and her mother have a very good and supportive relationship and that Jackie is flourishing and enjoying a productive and fulfilling life as a nurse now. June, as a stable and supportive mature self, a strengthed aspect of the central self in alliance with an ideal self, which has enabled her to incorporate the best from the subsidiary selves, has been able to allow Jackie to develop and to grow psychically.

Jack returns to the asylum, slips on some ice and bangs his head, which starts bleeding badly. He asks Lorenson to put him into the mortuary drawer, which she does and he travels forward in time to his journey in the car with the now flourishing Jackie. This becomes an ecstatic shot, lit in glowing colours with the song "We have all the time in the world" in the background as the film and Jack's life come to an end.

I suggest that the overall trajectory of the film is a depiction of a restitutive process and the various characters represent ego-structures and internal objects that he has worked to repair; the antilibidinal aspects of the mother, the daughter and the sick child having been transformed into positive libidinal objects, reintegrated into his central self. The antilibidinal paternal aggression of Becker is much reduced and has been replaced by guilt. The processes of retranscription, reintegration and restitution are depicted as painful processes that have to be gone through in the interest of cure, the transformation of ego-structures and internal objects in the process of psychic growth entailing as it does mental anguish. Jack has also come to love and be loved by Jackie, who is another powerful libidinal object that has become a real person to him so that he is able to die in a blissful state rather than in agony.

All this has happened by changing the nature of and the relationships between the characters in the internal world, the world of the unconscious that he has encountered and transformed during the process of dying. So the antilibidinal characters, the drunken mother and the punitive doctor, have also been transformed, turned from bad to good, or, at the very least, guilty—that is, moral characters.

One further question remains about the coincidence of the names Jack and Jackie. Is Jackie perhaps a female aspect of himself who he imagines will live on productively after he has gone? Is she someone who he has had to work hard to bring into existence as a well-balanced and flourishing character by intervening in her mother's life? So Jack and Jackie, as they drive off into the sunset with "all the time in the world", are perhaps an idealised and ideal couple, thus resolving the conflict within himself based upon his early experience with an "absent" mother. His ego-ideal and his ideal object are fused as the guide to a full life; the primal couple restored.

Conclusion

I have described a psychoanalytic approach to understanding some puzzle films grounded in Fairbairn's psychology of dynamic structure view of unconscious phantasy, dream, endopsychic structure, trauma, and dissociation. From this viewpoint, personifications of aspects of the self and their transforming relationships represent both characters in a drama and the economy of dynamic endopsychic structures. The sequence from trauma through dissociation and restitution-oriented phantasy and dreams allows for the reordering of the internal world in the direction of greater integration and synthesis. These are stories of creativity and psychic growth even as the possibility for growth appears to be foreclosed. Puzzle films as a genre seem to be about restitution even at the point at which all possibility of change has gone. Their social function might be to allow people to empathically struggle with the sorts of deprivation and trauma, experienced by some, and to witness the overcoming of these difficulties, even if the person dies after having achieved a more integrated self.

I have indicated how this approach might help us to comprehend the complex *telling* of complex *stories* as tales of our own mutability under trauma and the attempted recovery from trauma. This "state of affairs" approach to dream and phantasy takes our multiplicity for granted and shows the ways in which self-healing and self-transcendence are represented as the reintegration of previously dissociated powers into the central self. I have also suggested that Fairbairn's idea of over- and under-symbolised forms of art might provide a way of introducing value into the assessment of films within a psychoanalytic theory of art as the creation of objects for fun, and for the fun of others.

I have only very recently come across the concept of "embodied affect" in film theory (Rutherford, 2003), which is consequently absent from the analysis presented above but does suggest itself as a potential supplement to the further development of an object relations approach, in particular an object relations approach to the relationship between the viewer and an object or objects and their depiction on film.

PART IV

RELATIONAL PSYCHOANALYSIS

CHAPTER SEVEN

A modest proposal: Fairbairn's psychology of dynamic structure is not "between paradigms" but already a synthesis of classical and relational thinking

Introduction

No doubt like Swift's modest proposal (1729), my attempt here at a reinterpretation of Fairbairn's theory as already being a synthesis of classical and relational thinking before relational psychoanalysis was "invented" by Mitchell and Greenberg (1983) will provoke incredulity, but unlike Swift there is no satirical intention on my part. I am serious in believing that Fairbairn's theory can be interpreted in such a way as to demonstrate this synthesis. The incredulity at this project will come in equal measure from both classical and relational psychoanalytic thinkers despite the fact that the Kleinians and the Winnicottians (among others) have strayed far from classical Freudian understanding—an accusation that was originally levelled at Fairbairn by Winnicott and Khan (1953)—and that post-Freudian psychoanalytic thinking, as a whole, has already moved a long way from the original classical formulations of psychoanalysis, in so far as it ever accepted them. Contemporary Freudians in their attempts to future-proof Freud have incorporated aspects of Fairbairn's thinking on energy and structure into their own understanding of Freud's structural theory to its advantage. But I want to look again at the whole of Fairbairn's developed theory and its embeddedness in a distinctively Scottish approach to society and psychoanalysis as exemplified by Suttie and Macmurray in particular but emerging from Scottish Enlightenment thinking on society and approaches to the arts and creativity as reflected in the work of Herbert Read (1951). A major reason for this attempted reinterpretation was my recent realisation of the striking parallels between Fairbairn's model of endopsychic structure and the developmentally based, ego-nuclei model of the classification of mental disorders of his fellow Scot, colleague and friend, Edward Glover (Chapter Two).

Mitchell and Greenberg (1983) in their book *Object Relations in Psychoanalytic Theory* can be said to have initiated a purely relational (relational/structure) approach as an alternative to classical (drive/structure) psychoanalysis. Mitchell, whilst being the most consistent and sympathetic supporter of Fairbairn of all the relational thinkers (1983, 1994, 1995, 2000), rejects Fairbairn's account of the early formation of endopsychic structure and substantially rejects the further development of and reasoning about that structure (post 1943), with its close combination of structure and motivation, for precisely that reason in my view. Consequently the discussion will concern itself centrally with our origins as social creatures, the place of the good object in early development and beyond, and whether the dynamics of multiplicity are due to dissociation, repression, or a system that has a place for both.

I would like to look at Stephen Mitchell's view of Ronald Fairbairn's theory as represented by his chapter on Fairbairn in his book *Relationality: From Attachment to Intersubjectivity* (2000) where he describes Fairbairn's theory as being "between paradigms". Mitchell paints Fairbairn's theory as being between classical and relational or intersubjective approaches to psychoanalytic theory whereas I want to suggest that, when understood fully, it was already a synthesis of classical and relational insights and arguments well before the development of relational theory.

There are two substantive issues for Mitchell regarding Fairbairn's theory and these are: (a) Fairbairn's view of the good object, and the internalisation of the good object in his theory, and, (b) the usefulness of Fairbairn's model of endopsychic structure as it was described in Fairbairn's 1944 paper and used subsequently by him, though still never fully developed in my view.

There are at least two consequences of Mitchell not finding the 1944 paper and the fully developed endopsychic structure model useful.

One is that it is through this model that one can see the parallels between Fairbairn's revised psychopathology and Glover's classification, which opens the way to seeing Fairbairn's model as a synthesis between classical and relational approaches. The second is the often forgotten use by Fairbairn in the development of his endopsychic approach of three different levels of analysis of the patient's dream, which alerts him to the endopsychic structure interpretation he develops. The argument being that the endopsychic structure (object relational) interpretation is better but exists alongside other (classical or existential) ways of interpreting the dream.

Mitchell described Fairbairn's 1944 model of endopsychic structure as reflecting Fairbairn's "characteristic tendency to become absorbed in schematic, intricate theoretical constructs which drift away from their clinical and developmental referents" (Mitchell, 1994, p. 80). It is worth reminding ourselves of what Fairbairn thought about the relationship of Freud's instinct-based theory with the theory of object relationships that he was putting forward. In that 1944 paper Fairbairn spells out the relationship he sees between object relationships and impulses in the following terms.

> The theory of object-relationships thus inevitably leads us to the position that, if "impulses" cannot be considered apart from objects, whether external or internal, it is equally impossible to consider them apart from ego structures. Indeed it is even more impossible to consider "impulses" apart from ego structures, since it is only ego structures that can seek relationships with objects. We are thus brought back to the conclusion, already recorded, that *"impulses" are but the dynamic aspect of endopsychic structures* and cannot be said to exist in the absence of such structures, however immature these may turn out to be. Ultimately "impulses" must be simply regarded as constituting the forms of activity in which the life of ego structures consists. (Fairbairn, 1944, p. 88, emphasis added)

And, further on in the same 1944 paper Fairbairn makes it even clearer that the energy of impulses is absolutely necessary but that they are in the service of object relationships.

> In order to account for repression Freud found himself compelled to postulate the existence of a structure capable of instigating

> repression—viz. the super-ego. It is, therefore, only another step in the same direction to postulate the existence of structures which are repressed. Apart from any theoretical reasons such as those already advanced, there are very good clinical reasons for making such an assumption. Prominent among these is the difficulty experienced in effecting the "sublimation" of libidinal "impulses". This difficulty cannot be adequately explained as due to an inveterate and inherent obstinacy on the part of "impulses" themselves, especially once we have come to regard "impulses" *as just forms of energy at the disposal of the ego structure*. On the contrary, it can only be satisfactorily explained on the assumption that the repressed "impulses" are inseparable from an ego structure with a definite pattern. The correctness of this assumption is confirmed by the phenomena of multiple personality, in which the linkage of repressed "impulses" with a submerged ego structure is beyond question; but such a linkage may also be detected in the less extensive forms of dissociation, which are so characteristic of the hysterical individual. (op. cit. p. 90, emphasis added)

The rejection by Mitchell of the post-1943 basic endopsychic model is an effective way of removing all of the economic arguments concerning libido and aggression and the ways in which these are distributed and controlled using dissociation and repression, as well as effectively removing the notions of libidinal, antilibidinal and ideal egos and objects from any discussion as deeply significant motivating factors.

The critique of Fairbairn's understanding of the good object and the summary rejection of Fairbairn's endopsychic structure can then be seen as the attempt to remove the notion of the unconscious along with the remnants of some underlying set of affective processes from the theory. But, as Fairbairn comments in his addendum to the 1944 paper on acceptable object relationships (precursor to the instantiation of the ideal object), once the libidinal (over-exciting) and antilibidinal (over-rejecting) object relations aspects have become dissociated and repressed, these then (acceptable object relations) become idealised, as their sexual and aggressive aspects are occluded.

This is not to say that Fairbairn's theory does not need further research, merely that the basis for such an attempt was already provided by Fairbairn and it is the absence of an organised group of followers or "school" that has proved the most significant obstruction to its being worked on more fully.

Because Fairbairn published his theory in a piecemeal way and only ever restated it, albeit in a simplified form, towards the end of his life (Fairbairn, 1963), the work required to take it further was never done in his lifetime and the usefulness of his insights into the relational approach helped others more than his own supporters to extract the full relational ramifications of his theory.

Fairbairn's theory is both classical and relational; it has an unconscious and explicitly accepts that the two main motivating factors are libido and aggression. All object relations have an underpinning in affect that qualifies as a form of drive theory and is much broader than the any simplistic component instinct-based drive for the breast or to suckle. The underlying motivation is the multi-modal object relations' need for company.

A comparison of Fairbairn's revision of the psychopathology of the psychoses and the psychoneuroses (Fairbairn, 1941), with Glover's classical developmental model of the growth of ego and the classification of mental disorders (Glover, 1932), to which it is closely related in my mind, could also provide the different modes that Mitchell cites and uses in his interactional hierarchy (Mitchell, 2000).

Self and society

Fairbairn (1944) quotes Aristotle to the effect that we are social creatures first and foremost who come to be who we are in a society and can only flourish fully within a community, a viewpoint that is echoed by both Suttie and Macmurray. This underlying belief that we are social creatures is rehearsed in the Scottish Enlightenment by James Dunbar as I have described elsewhere (Clarke, 2008b). It is therefore interesting to say the least that Mitchell defends Fairbairn against a critique from Greenberg, his erstwhile colleague, concerning the instinctual basis, or not, of Fairbairn's understanding of ourselves as object-seeking and object-relating by referring to the theory that we are all essentially social creatures (Mitchell, 2000, p. 106).

In Suttie's view, what we seek is company, whilst Macmurray suggests it is our lack of instinctual adaptation that drives our need for relationality. Both, however, agree that it is not a matter of instincts but object relationships, starting with our relationship with mother or mother substitute. We need someone who will cherish and protect us, feed us and keep us warm and safe from harm as much as they are able.

This first social and personal relationship and its outcome provide us with an insight into the sorts of character and personality that we might develop. I have written elsewhere about what I believe to be Suttie's influence on Fairbairn (Chapter One) and about the parallels between Fairbairn's model of endopsychic structure and Macmurray's Suttie-influenced understanding of the tripartite split, internally, and its relationship to the process of disillusionment (Clarke, 2003b).

It is also crucial at this stage to point to another common aspect of these theories. We are dealing with an active self-regulating system that will be influenced by its experience of the world it encounters, and it will achieve this by internalising object-relations aspects of its experience, initially, and later by discriminating between these internalised object relationships, to produce separate person-like centres of activity and understanding.

Like Gregory Bateson (1979) I believe that mental processes require collateral energy so that psychoanalysis is an understanding of bio-psycho-social processes in which energy is crucial but not finally determining, a viewpoint that my earlier quotation from Fairbairn's 1944 paper supports.

In line with the development of affective neuroscience, one might argue that the underlying motivation is *seeking* (an object) and that once unified with the object (relational) *play* is the predominant motivation (Panskepp). In terms of a theory of potential powers, the child will be able to develop its powers and flourish in an environment that is sensitive to its needs and willing to support its activities. The world is, however, a more difficult place than this, so only some of the child's potential powers will be encouraged and allowed to flourish while others will be, consciously or unconsciously, blocked or frustrated or, as can be the case in disillusionment, encouraged inappropriately and/or prematurely. This will lead to a splitting, or dissociation, of powers that will be unique to each person's particular experiences and what they make of them. It is this process that gives rise to the basic endopsychic structure of Fairbairn's model. For Fairbairn, developmentally, we pass through a stage of what he calls the "transitional techniques", where, as we grow and develop, the particular way that we chose to deny or encourage our specific powers is open to change, but with these changes comes the possibility of neurotic response. As we become increasingly independent, the dangers attendant upon our increasing independence present themselves as the possibility of withdrawal back to an earlier level of integration. Negotiating these difficulties successfully and achieving a relative independence on the way to a mature dependence is what we call the process of growing up—or psychic growth (Clarke, 2005). Mature dependence in Fairbairn's terms means being able to treat other people as differentiated others rather than seeing them projectively or introjectively as reflections of ourselves and our significant (internalised) others.

At the heart of Fairbairn's endopsychic model and the dynamic structures that comprise it is the idea of the lost good object—Fairbairn's original pristine self and its original object—that becomes fragmented through splitting/dissociation, based in early real experience and then integrated into person-like internal objects and ego-structures, libidinal and antilibidinal, which are repressed by a central self based upon acceptable object relations. Similarly, Fairbairn's recommendations for therapy are concerned above all with healing the splits and reintegrating the disparate elements of the self through the relationship with the analyst (Fairbairn, 1958) and thus entail an approach to psychic growth that can account for the way that the central self might grow at the expense of the subsidiary (libidinal and antilibidinal) selves (Padel, 1991).

Fairbairn used Freud's topographic categories in his 1944 paper and the endopsychic model that he developed there. I looked at the possibility of making some changes to that model to consistently reflect the idea that there were three topographic levels and that the process of internalisation was based upon object relationships (Padel). In 2005 I put forward a suggestion for a development of Fairbairn's theory so that there were preconscious libidinal and antilibidinal self-object dyads alongside the ego-ideal/ideal-object dyad that Fairbairn explicitly places in the preconscious. Later in collaboration with my friend and colleague Paul Finnegan, we used this enhanced version of Fairbairn's model of endopsychic structure to look at Fairbairn's long-standing interest in multiplicity (Chapter Three) and to try to understand patients with MPD/DID that were being treated by Paul (Chapter Four).

The good object in Fairbairn's theory

I am going to revisit an old but currently unresolved debate concerning the place of the good object in Fairbairn's theory, because I have become increasingly aware of a continuing division between Fairbairn scholars on this issue. In particular I am going to look closely at Stephen

Mitchell's interpretation of the place of the good object in Fairbairn's theory, since he is one of the most influential interpreters of Fairbairn and one who has, in turn, been most deeply influenced by Fairbairn in his development of relational psychoanalysis. I am going to defend the position developed by Fairbairn in the extended footnote to his paper on hysteria (Fairbairn, 1954), where he proposes a solution to the problem of the good object in his theory, in response to both Kleinians and Winnicott and Khan (1953) in their review of his only book *Psychoanalytic Studies of the Personality* (1952).

This is still important because there is still no commonly agreed understanding of Fairbairn's "psychology of dynamic structure" and there is unlikely to be one while this problem remains unresolved. Naturally, many people believe that it has been resolved and adopt one or other version of the theory and proceed on that basis. These vary from the position that the good object is never internalised, to those who call for changes to Fairbairn's model because it is regarded as incoherent when dealing with the question of the good object; to the version that Mitchell develops, which regards Fairbairn's 1944 paper on endopsychic structure as over-schematised and which concentrates on his pre-1944 work.

Fairbairn himself referred to his whole oeuvre post-1940 as the "progressive development of a line of thought". As a consequence, Fairbairn made explicit refinements of his theory as he went along. We can take his overall and founding axiom that people are object-seeking and not pleasure-seeking as, in general, not contested among people who value and use Fairbairn's theory, and not subject to change throughout these years. We can also take his seventeen-point description of his object-relations theory of the personality published in IJPA in 1963 as his last definitive attempt to spell out the fundamentals of the views he had been developing since the late 1920s.

In order to understand Fairbairn's viewpoint and Mitchell's response we need to bear in mind the distinction Fairbairn draws between the early and the late oral phases—the only two of Abraham's developmental stages Fairbairn accepted. In the early oral phase the child will suckle or, if not interested, just turn away; while in the late oral phase the child will suckle or react aggressively by biting. It is the arrival at the second oral phase that Fairbairn believes denotes ambivalence—the coexistence of different attitudes towards the same person or object (e.g., love and hate)—so when he talks about the *internalised pre-ambivalent* object he is talking about the internalisation of the *unsatisfactory* maternal object and breast during the first oral phase. Fairbairn consistently uses the term "unsatisfying" to characterise aspects of the relationship of the child to the mother at this time in the child's development. Mitchell in his critique characterises this relationship as in some measure "gratifying" or "ungratifying". I will not dwell on the semantic differences that there are between the ideas of "satisfying" and "gratifying" but I do want to note that these are differences, which in this case do make a difference (Bateson, 1972). Mitchell, who uses "gratifying" and "ungratifying" in his 1981 paper, argues that since these particular terms already imply ambivalence Fairbairn's view is therefore confused or wrong. This criticism clearly echoes Klein's objection to Fairbairn's theory on the basis of his thinking on the good object (Klein, 1946).

Mitchell refers to Skolnick's (1998) paper on the good object to dismiss the account that Fairbairn gives of the good object but, as we will see, Mitchell's comment that criticism of Fairbairn's work "has been directed precisely at his commitment to the notion that internalisation take place, in the beginning, because early objects are 'bad' or 'unsatisfying', leaving out the ways in which 'good' experiences are taken in" (Mitchell, 2000, p. 109) is itself a flawed representation of Fairbairn's actual theory and thus open to question. In a letter to Guntrip on 30 August 1954 concerning Winnicott's attitude to his theory, Fairbairn writes:

> He seems to fasten on "the introjection of the bad object" as a particularly virulent form of heresy ... I still think I am right in claiming that it is bad experience that leads to the establishment of internal objects as differentiated structures. According to my view, good experience is of vital importance for the development of the personality; but its effects are essentially registered in satisfactory ego-development, and not in the establishment of internal objects. As it seems to me, if external relationships are satisfactory, there is no stimulus for the substitution of internal relationships for them. It is obvious, of course, that all experience is internalised. Otherwise it would not be experience, and the phenomenon of memory would be unaccountable. But such internalisation of experience is not the same thing as the introjection of objects. Unfortunately, however, Winnicott follows Melanie Klein in confusing processes which are logically distinct and speaking of them as identical; and this is really

> due in my opinion, to faulty and slovenly conceptualisation ... (Fairbairn Project, MS.50100)

As far as I can establish, neither Fairbairn nor Winnicott and Khan use the terms "gratifying" or "ungratifying"; they all use "satisfactory" and "unsatisfactory", so it is difficult to tell where this subtle shift came from but it has important consequences.

Mitchell argues that the use of the terms "gratifying" and "ungratifying" already signify ambivalence, but, as we have already seen, these were not the terms that Fairbairn used, and it is far harder to argue that the terms "satisfying" or "unsatisfying" indicate that ambivalence has already been achieved. An important and, in this case, crucial corollary of having achieved ambivalence is that the world of relationships can be divided into "good" and "bad" object relations.

In a letter to Sutherland on the 6 September 1955 (Fairbairn Project, MS.51000) concerning Balint's proposed comments on Fairbairn's paper "A Critical Evaluation of Certain Basic Psycho-Analytic Conceptions" (Fairbairn, 1956), which was later published as part of the "Notes and Comments: Criticisms of Fairbairn's Generalisations about Object-Relations" (Balint et al., 1957), Fairbairn comments:

> ... As regards the semantic excursion ... the fact remains that Freud chose the term "libido" expressly to exclude from its connotation the element of "gratification" included in the connotation of the German "Lust".

Compare this to Freud's *Three Essays on the Theory of Sexuality* (1905d), where Freud says that he uses the word "libido" (as need or desire for a sexual relationship) as a counterpart to "hunger" (as need or desire for food).

> The only appropriate word in the German language, "Lust", is unfortunately ambiguous, and is used to denote the experience both of a need and of a gratification.
> (S. E. VII, p. 135, footnote 2 [added in 1910])

Unconscious phantasy

In a recent new video entitled "The Controversial Discussions in the XXIst Century" (Palmer, 2015) involving a number of leading contemporary psychoanalysts reflecting on the original controversial discussions, Hinshelwood argues that Susan Isaacs's paper on unconscious phantasy had the following significance:

> What they were presenting in the first of these discussions was really a new form of psychoanalysis. Klein said there's a reciprocal relationship that is conceived from the beginning. Whatever instinct is, it is represented in the mind as this relationship with objects. This is an unconscious phantasy. And she said this is the most fundamental conception that we can have in psychoanalysis. The whole thing was based, as she saw it, on relationships. And this is a radical divergence in the history of psychoanalysis which comes right down from this development of child analysis in the 1920s right down to today, when it hasn't been resolved. (Palmer, 2015)

What is not said in this film, nor in the responses to the discussion of Isaacs's paper in the Freud-Klein Controversies, is that Fairbairn's paper, presented by Glover as a response to Isaacs's account of unconscious phantasy on 17 February 1943, offers a Klein-influenced account of inner reality and internal objects shorn of their dependence upon innate destructiveness and envy, or the tendency to read Original Sin back into the baby's constitution.

> ... the time is now ripe for us to replace the concept of "phantasy" by a concept of an "inner reality" peopled by the Ego and its internal objects. These internal objects should be regarded as having an organised structure, an endopsychic existence and an activity as real within the inner world as those of any objects in the outer world. (Fairbairn, 1943b, p. 294)

These internal objects are based upon the child's experience of early object relationships; they are not based upon any constitutional factors. In a letter to Fairbairn based upon the meeting where Fairbairn's paper was read by Glover, who chaired the meeting, Glover writes:

> ... you'll be interested to know that what I anticipated has happened. Brierley mentioned your paper as deriving from Klein and Klein promptly repudiated your views as deriving from hers. Just as I thought. (Fairbairn Project MS.50192, 1943)

Fairbairn accepted the relational aspects of Klein's approach but rejected the death instinct. As one of the other commentators on the video says, "Freud's position was that phantasy came about as a result of frustration, so that in the place of satisfaction, a phantasy satisfaction is put into play." This is much closer to Fairbairn's idea that unsatisfactory relations with crucial objects like parents and mother in particular lead to the internalisation of the unsatisfactory real relationships upon which his whole theory of endopsychic structure is built. There is an excellent discussion of the differences between Isaacs and Fairbairn's understanding of phantasy and internal objects in a recent paper by Ogden (2011), which he concludes with the following comments:

> Isaacs added a chapter note to the 1952 version of her paper in which she quotes Freud's comment that: "One must not take the difference between ego and id in too hard-and-fast a sense" (Freud, 1923, quoted by Isaacs, 1952, p. 120). Perhaps this represents a movement on Isaacs's part in the direction of Fairbairn's idea that the id and ego are a single entity—the subject impelled by his needs and desires. If one adopts this position, *the structural model collapses into a real internal object relationship between two unconscious sub-organizations of the self: the ego and a split-off part of the ego (the superego)*. The movement from Freud's structural model to a model of internal object relationships structured by phantasy seems to me to be a necessary implication of Isaacs's and Klein's work, but it is an implication that Isaacs seems to actively resist, perhaps for reasons having to do with the psychoanalytic politics of her time. (Ogden, 2011, pp. 939–940, emphasis added)

One conclusion to draw then is that if the internalisation of the *unsatisfying* object occurs in the first oral phase then it is indeed a *pre-ambivalent* object, as Fairbairn argues, which is thus also pre-moral as Grotstein suggests (1982).

> Fairbairn deserves the credit for having developed a concept of the schizoid self, that is, a self which experiences a split (split in this case used as an organization of fragmented bits of self) from disappointment in object relationships. Fairbairn's concept of this split self is a pre-moral one insofar as it is based upon traumatic or unempathic experience with objects, whereas Klein's conception of splitting had

to do with moral splitting, that is, that the infant attacked his objects with the force of the death instinct and split them into good and bad part objects which were then identified within split sectors of the personality. There is thus a fundamental difference of great magnitude between Klein's splitting, which is an extension of Freud's conception of splitting, on one hand, and that of Fairbairn's on the other hand, which is based on the passive helplessness of the infant. In other words, Klein's conception is one which is almost entirely based upon phantasy in the context of an internal world, whereas Fairbairn's conception is one based upon the phenomenology of experience in the external world. (Grotstein, 1982, pp. 50–51)

This reinforces Fairbairn's idea that the original defence is internalisation (incorporation), which is only later supported by the defence of splitting after ambivalence is reached, in the second oral phase, and which then allows for there to be a tripartite split internally between libidinal, antilibidinal and acceptable (ideal) object relations clusters.

Mitchell follows Klein in believing that the differentiation into good and bad objects occurs from birth and before any objects are internalised. That is, it is the already differentiated external bad object that is internalised and then split into the over-exciting (libidinal) and over-rejecting (antilibidinal) object relationships that form the core of the sub-selves. But the question of the rationale for the internalisation of the good object then arises. As we saw earlier, for Fairbairn internalisation is only originally useful if there is a problem with the relations with the object, so the good object, in so far as it is unproblematic, is never the occasion for internalisation, a view with which Lacan agrees (1988, p. 252) and which has echoes in Macmurray's view that thinking only arises when the free flow of action is interrupted unexpectedly (Macmurray, 1957), which might profitably be compared to Bion's theory of thinking (Bion, 1962).

Mitchell goes on to ask about the fate of the "moral defence", which in his account would involve internalising an external bad object relationship and concurrently internalising an external good object relationship to reinforce the repression of the internalised bad object by strengthening the ego-ideal. Whereas in Fairbairn's theory, the ambivalent relationship would be internalised and then split internally when the child takes the bad object relationship into the antilibidinal ego-object dyad and takes the good object relationship to reinforce the ideal ego-object dyad.

In the version of Fairbairn's argument I have used above, unsatisfying object relationships are internalised and then integrated along three separate lines and split into libidinal, antilibidinal, and acceptable. Once ambivalence is achieved, the basic endopsychic structure is established through the repression of the libidinal and antilibidinal object relationships (bad, over-exciting and over-rejecting relationships) by the central ego and the ideal ego-object. This ego-ideal is the transformation of the acceptable object into the ideal ego-object in the preconscious. At the time of the moral defence, object relationships with bad, but necessary, objects (e.g., parents) are first internalised and then split, the bad aspects being repressed into the libidinal and antilibidinal selves while the good aspects are used to reinforce the ideal object in the preconscious. This can be seen as the establishment of a precursor to the Freudian super-ego in that it involves the internalisation of external relations with a good object.

This account seems to me to be clear and logical and follows Fairbairn's own formulations closely and is therefore to be preferred over Mitchell's own account.

It was Padel (1985), who suggested that (tripartite) splitting *follows* internalisation so that the splitting of the unsatisfactory object relations into libidinal, antilibidinal and acceptable objects *follows* the internalisation of object relationships. This seems to be consistent with Fairbairn's own thinking. The first defence is incorporation of object relations, which is followed by the splitting of object relations as a later defence, where the object relationships are split into acceptable, libidinal and antilibidinal clusters of relations, each of which is associated with an appropriate ego and object. If this takes place in the first oral phase, the acceptable ego/object, the "main core" of the relations with the object (point 9 of his 17-point outline (Fairbairn, 1963)), constitutes the basis of the internalisation of the "good" object. In the early oral phase, however, as Fairbairn argues, the distinction between "good" and "bad" is unavailable to the neonate.

The composition of internal objects and ego-structures

Sutherland's comments "on the ego structures envisaged in the theory for the mental constitution which [Fairbairn] submitted as a substitute for Freud's" (Scharff & Birtles, 1994, p. 153), which seem to be much more organised than—Sutherland argues—appears to be the case for some patients, in particular "advanced hysterics". "The antilibidinal ego would appear to be composed of (or at any rate contain) several active sub-structures" (op. cit.). Sutherland supports his contention by citing the reversal of roles, which may occur in cases where identification with one parent in a libidinal role is accompanied by persecution on the part of the other parent. Fairbairn notes that in this case there is no question of the antilibidinal ego reversing its role, which is always that of a persecutor. "What is changed is the internal object with which the antilibidinal ego is identified" (Scharff & Birtles, 1994, p. 154). Fairbairn suggests that Sutherland's example would be better used to support the argument that it is internal objects that are loosely organised and must contain sub-structures. Fairbairn says that such a conclusion presents no difficulties for him; indeed that he agrees with it.

> Thus the internal objects which I envisage may be composed of maternal and paternal components in all proportions and in all degrees of integration; and for that matter they may undergo both disintegrative changes under pathogenic conditions and integrative changes under therapeutic conditions. I find it difficult to believe, however, that, except in cases of advanced schizophrenia, the disintegration of internal objects often reaches a point at which my differentiation between the exciting, the rejecting and the ideal objects (if only as constellations) becomes meaningless. ... the three ego structures which I describe would seem, characteristically, to be much more organised and differentiated—a phenomenon which may be attributed to the simple fact that they are ego-structures ... (op. cit., p. 154)

This description of the dynamic structures seems to me to be strongly parallel to Glover's ego-nuclei-based model of both development of the ego and the classification mental disorders, but involving ego-nuclei-based upon object relationships rather than component instincts.

Dissociation and/or repression

Fairbairn's MD thesis was on dissociation and repression and he concluded that dissociation was a special form of repression. It is worth quoting part of Fairbairn's conclusions at length. In a six point list that summarises his MD thesis, Fairbairn makes the following points.

> 1. ... dissociation should be regarded as: An active mental process, whereby unacceptable mental content or an unacceptable mental function becomes cut off from personal consciousness, without ceasing to be mental— ... if it is either irrelevant to, incompatible with or unpleasant in relation to an active interest.
> 2. Repression was found to be: An active mental process, whereby certain mental elements, the appearance of which in consciousness would cause unpleasure, are excluded from personal consciousness without ceasing to be mental.
> 3. ... it follows that repression is to be classed with dissociation of the unpleasant.
> 4. ... repression is a special form of dissociation of the unpleasant ... which occurs when the dissociated elements consist of tendencies belonging to the instinctive endowment and thus forming part of the structure of the mind itself.
> 5. This ... led to a modification of the definition of repression ... A process whereby certain mental tendencies are denied conscious expression, if their incongruity with the structure of the organised self is such that conscious expression of these tendencies would cause unpleasure.
> 6. This ... suggests that whereas the term "mental conflict" is applicable to the conditions giving rise to repression, it is not applicable to the conditions which give rise to other forms of dissociation. (Birtles & Scharff, 1994, p. 79)

It is clear that as far as Fairbairn was concerned both dissociation and repression can and do occur, and in our attempt to understand MPD/DID Paul Finnegan and myself suggest that the alter personalities that characteristically arise in these conditions are dissociated parts of (libidinal, antilibidinal or ideal egos or objects) endopsychic structures in the preconscious.

Conclusion

I have argued that Mitchell's account of Fairbairn's understanding of the good object and the ways in which it becomes established internally are vitiated by a semantic slippage between the terms "gratifying" and "satisfying", which might be blurred by common usage in the U.S. This leads him to reject Fairbairn's account of endopsychic structure as over-complex and too theoretical. Since he does not try to use this model, he contributes to the wealth of misreadings of Fairbairn theory that there have been. For Fairbairn, the developmental approach to an understanding of the growth of the ego and the mind are crucial and a link back to the early, simpler, more instinctual motivations of the child and their part in the progress towards the more nuanced, sophisticated, and relational, character of mature dependance.

I argue that Fairbairn's theory of dynamic structure and the endopsychic system of inner reality, while based in classical thinking, when understood fully is founded upon a thoroughgoing (object) relational approach, and as such it is a true and original synthesis of the two approaches.

CHAPTER EIGHT

Fairbairn's object-relations-based psychology of dynamic structure, as a synthesis of the classical (thesis) and the relational (antithesis) in psychoanalytic theory

Introduction

In recent years there has been the development of a much wider appreciation of the reality of child abuse in our society and the dissociative consequences of such events for the person in question, which has highlighted again the question of multiplicity and its understanding. In this context Jody Messler Davies (JMD) wrote a paper linking the post-classical developments in psychoanalysis, in particular the relational approach, to the pre-analytic thinking of Freud and Janet (Davies, 1996). In the course of this paper she characterised both the repression-based model of inner reality developed in classical psychoanalysis and the dissociation-based relational model of inner reality developed by relational psychoanalysis in such ways that *both* are consistent with Fairbairn's model of endopsychic structure.

I think that this is an important paper and I want to respond to it in detail, since it seems to me to be a sophisticated and nuanced response to historical developments in psychoanalytic thinking. In order to respond appropriately I will begin with a detailed review of Fairbairn's model of endopsychic structure and I will then use JMD's paper to look in some detail at the relational argument and the view of Fairbairn that she espouses. It is my intention to suggest that Fairbairn's theory is broader and more flexible than the manner in which it is used by JMD.

Fairbairn and relational thinking

Fairbairn's endopsychic model of inner reality (Fairbairn, 1944) combines both repression and dissociation and is concerned with dynamic structures, splitting, and multiplicity. It seems to me that Fairbairn's model provides a bridge between the purely repression-based classical model and the purely dissociation-based relational model and has something to offer both. While his initial development of the model was clearly intended to reinterpret Freud's model, by changing the underlying basis of that model to recognise and incorporate some of the discussion concerning repression and dissociation that had formed the topic of Fairbairn's MD thesis (Chapter One, part 1, Birtles & Scharff, 1994), it was also intended to render this systems-based model more consistent with a post-Einsteinian understanding of physics, where energy and structure are mutable under particular circumstances rather than separate as in Freud's Helmholzian model.

This model was consistent and thoroughly based upon object relationships and the internalisation of object relationships and as such follows Freud's paper on narcissism (Freud, 1914c), and it was also influenced by Melanie Klein's development of the idea of the internal object. Thus the super-ego in Freud's theory came to exemplify the idea of an active agentive internal object for both Klein and Fairbairn.

The crucial move, however, was from a libido theory based upon the pleasure principle to a theory based upon the need for relationship with an object (other). This entailed a reassessment of the reality principle, which, combined with Fairbairn's idea that the earliest situation was a schizoid situation (unlike Klein and Freud's concentration on depression), led to a thoroughgoing object-relations theory accounting for and providing different formulations to many of the classical concepts within a new systems- and information-based relational reworking of the model of inner reality.

This model came out of Fairbairn's own attempts to understand the fundamental relationship between repression and dissociation and to recognise and acknowledge the importance of trauma, and the real events of the person's life, for the constitution of their inner reality. At the time that JMD was writing her paper, Fairbairn's early and previously unpublished papers had only just been published, including his MD thesis written in 1927 on the topic of repression and dissociation. Paul Finnegan and I have published papers about the degree to which Fairbairn thought that his theory was ideally suited to understand and treat dissociation and multiple personality disorder (Chapter Three), and about using an extended version of his theory, based in my attempts to reconcile the topological categories with his endopsychic model (Clarke, 2005) to understand DID/MPD (Chapter Four).

JMD in her paper on repression and dissociation (Skolnick & Scharff, 1998) resorts to Fairbairn's earlier formulations of personifications (Fairbairn, 1931), which she sees as a precursor to his developed theory of endopsychic structure, but like Mitchell she seems to ignore or at least not use the endopsychic structure model.

Fairbairn's model was poorly received when his first and only book was published in 1952, but with the publication in 1983 of Greenberg's and Mitchell's *Object Relations in Psychoanalytic Theory*, Fairbairn theory was analysed and compared with other putative object relations theories and declared to be the most consistently object relational approach of them all. Mitchell, who went on to be one of the main developers of a relational approach, was subsequently well disposed towards Fairbairn and his theory and wrote about his theory in ways that help us to understand the nature of the theory he, Fairbairn, had developed. But there are two areas in which he was unable to follow Fairbairn, which had consequences for the relational approach then and in JMD's account. One concerns the question of the good object, which echoes an argument put forward by Kleinians against Fairbairn's theory at the time of the Controversial Discussions and is repeated by Winnicott and Khan in their review of Fairbairn's book in 1953. The other is intimately related, in that a full answer to the first question depends upon a detailed understanding of Fairbairn's own final model of inner reality, which was initially developed in his 1944 paper on endopsychic structure and refined in his subsequent papers up to his summary of his object relations approach published in the IJPA in 1963 (Fairbairn, 1963). This is the model upon which I am basing my own interpretation of Fairbairn.

Mitchell referred to Fairbairn's development of the endopsychic structure model as characteristic of his "tendency to become absorbed in schematic, intricate theoretical constructs which drift away from their clinical and developmental referents" (Mitchell, 1994, p. 80). These arguments will be explored later on, but for the moment let me just note that the criticism of the place of the good object in Fairbairn is made less clear by Mitchell, in that he imports a Kleinian use of the term "gratification" and attributes it to Fairbairn, who actually used the term "unsatisfactory" in his account of the first two oral stages of infant development. Further on in Mitchell's paper just quoted, it looks as if he is quoting from Winnicott and Kahn's critical review of Fairbairn's book when he writes, "First, if the original 'pre-ambivalent object' is internalised because it is 'in some measure gratifying and in some measure ungratifying' what is meant by ambivalence". But this is not what Winnicott and Kahn wrote. They quoted accurately Fairbairn's work where he says, "The internalization of the pre-ambivalent object would then be explained on the ground that it presented itself as unsatisfying in some measure as well as in some measure satisfying" (Winnicott & Khan quoting Fairbairn, 1953, p. 332). For its entry on "Satisfactions", the index to Mitchell and Greenberg's *Object Relations in Psychoanalytic Theory* (1983) says "see Gratification". Whether this is an example of two cultures divided by a common tongue, or not, I am not sure, but I think this difference needs to be looked at.

Parallel to this, the creation of good and bad objects in Kleinian thinking is much closer to the (current) relational understanding of the dynamics of inner reality than the necessarily mediated concepts of libidinal, antilibidinal, ideal and central egos (selves) and objects (selves) and the repressive and dissociative aspects of endopsychic structure, all of which will also have to be looked at later.

The advantages of accepting a Fairbairn-based model of inner reality over the original Freudian version of that model have been argued in many places many times over, and apart from saying that contemporary Freudians are using a model that owes much to Fairbairn's observations, vis-à-vis the underlying physical understanding of the way energy and structure interact, there is no pressing need to pursue these arguments further here.

On the other hand while the developers of the relational approach have often mentioned Fairbairn and the importance of his contribution they have not in my view fully understood what his object relational approach could do for them. Partly this is due to the fact that Fairbairn's theory has not had the sort of widespread acceptance that the Kleinian approach has had and therefore has not been developed anything like as fully, clinically, and theoretically. And second because the full object relations model with its combination of repression and dissociation—with the complex mediations of ideal, central, libidinal and antilibidinal selves and topographic categories *Cs*, *Pcs* and *Ucs*—has not lent itself to easy application, even if there are some good clinical applications of the theory (e.g., Celani, 2010).

For instance, a central and more or less completely undeveloped aspect of Fairbairn's theory to this day concerns the concept of transitional techniques, which combines developmental processes for amending and putting right earlier decisions as to which object relations repertoires you might allow yourself, with the idea of projective identification and the Freudian notion of the neuroses (phobia, paranoia, hysteria, and obsession), all of which are regarded by Fairbairn as operating at the same level and to be directly related to difficulties we have in the way we deal with objects. This is one of the areas that I would suggest might be usefully developed within a clinical framework and something that might be able to shed light on some of the complexities of object relationships and self states as developed within relational analysis.

This opens up the whole question of what self states or self-object states are as understood by relational analysis. These are clearly influenced by self-psychology and the latter certainly owes its title to Kohut, but a question that might be asked is how the relational understanding of self state or self-object differs from the active aspect of all of the components of Fairbairn's endopsychic structure. Does a specific libidinal ego or self acting in relation to an external libidinal object (self state in another person) or to an internal self state—for example, a libidinal object internalised during development and incorporated in a complex multiform matrix of similar object relations—not qualify as a self state or a self-state description of a process that might be both inter- and intrapersonal? In other words I believe that we can replace the terms self state or self-object by reference to specific dynamic locations—central ego, libidinal object, etc.—within Fairbairn's model of endopsychic structure as they interact with other such entities internally or externally.

This is where we need to return to Mitchell and his interpretation of Fairbairn's theory, and the view that he shares with Richard Rubens concerning Fairbairn's theory. Both think that the formalised endopsychic structure model is a step too far and that the 1943 paper where the development of the "moral defence" and the "ego-ideal" was described is sufficient. I believe that this is a fatal flaw in the relational approach.

What I am therefore suggesting is that Fairbairn's developed model fits the characterisation of the relational model as given by JMD but that it offers some particular advantages over the purely dissociative relational model she espouses. One advantage is that it combines repression and dissociation within its structures and dynamics. A second advantage is that it offers a developmental theory of the nature and origin of the neuroses and a way of investigating them in which the notions of projection and introjection are intrinsic. A third advantage is that the variety of places in which person-like selves might be located and operate from is widely extended but within a meta-structure that is consistent with the classical ideas that love and aggression are the key dynamic factors, and that love is the most important and the more fundamental—all within an overall framework that recognises that we are object-seeking and relating throughout our lives and that what actually happens to us, and what we make of it, is crucial both to our development and to understanding ourselves.

Overall I am suggesting that Fairbairn's object relations model offers us advantages over the classical model and the (exclusively) relational model and that it does in fact incorporate and exemplify the most important aspects of both whilst correcting the least useful aspects of each.

One question that will arise regarding my suggestion is the degree to which this alternative model based in Fairbairn's work can help the relational approach clinically. Fortunately JMD has provided a clinical vignette that lends itself to a Fairbairnian reinterpretation in ways already familiar from my and Paul Finnegan's paper on a Fairbairnian approach to MPD. I think it helps to be able to identify the different transference—countertransference configurations that JMD experiences and describes as libidinal or antilibidinal and the self that emerges in what JMD calls a "therapeutic dissociation"—which exhibits the patient's confidence in her own powers to some degree and shows she is prepared to fight her own corner. This alternative self, which is regarded by the patient as bad, is more developed than the other alters that JMD discusses. In an echo of the "moral defence", this alter has taken all of the badness that comes from her relations with others—mother, father, stepmother, grandmother—and turned it into an independent strength. It is the work that JMD and the patient do together to take the independent confidence from the alter and (re)incorporate it into the central self that both echoes Padel's (1991, pp. 600–602) description of psychic growth within Fairbairn and illustrates the usefulness of this (Fairbairnian) approach to the clinical material. Before looking in detail at JMD's paper I want to restate what I understand to be Fairbairn's psychology of dynamic structure.

An overview of Fairbairn's psychology of dynamic structure

I want to set out my interpretation of Fairbairn's psychology of dynamic structure as it is developed within his writings "... *not the elaboration of an already established point of view, but the progressive development of a line of thought* ..." (Fairbairn, 1952, p. x).

Some underlying assumptions

There are two different forms of aggression: the first is goal-seeking (or just seeking), which is present from birth, and the second is aggression, as we commonly understand it, which is reactive—a response to something that has been done or has been imagined to be done to the child. The development of the second form is the development of a notion of good or bad and coincides with the second oral phase and the development of teeth and biting.

First oral phase

The child is born as an active, realistic, creative, libidinally oriented, object-seeking, object-relating but pristine person. During the first oral phase the child has a limited repertoire of responses. It can seek with eyes and mouth for an object; it can cry if it is upset or frustrated or in pain; it can hold eye contact, smile, make noises, and respond to other stimuli by mother and others.

The basis of the process of incorporation that is fundamental to Fairbairn's idea of the development of inner reality is based in the experience of satisfaction. This process, according to Laplanche and Pontalis, is discussed as a

> type of primal experience postulated by Freud, consisting in the resolution, thanks to an external intervention, of an internal tension occasioned in the suckling by need. The image of the satisfying

> object subsequently takes on a special value in the construction of the subject's desire. This image may be recathected in the absence of the real object (hallucinatory satisfaction of the wish). And it will always guide the later search for the satisfying object. (Laplanche & Pontalis, 1973, p. 156)

In his theory, Fairbairn postulates a unique and separate process for the incorporation of relations with the other that become established in the internal world as ego-structures or internal objects—all of which are person-like active agents.

During this phase if the child finds an object that is unsatisfactory it can turn away, or refuse to suckle and protest by crying, but it cannot actively reject or attack the object. During the first oral phase a variety of object relationships with mother will become internalised. Some of these will be based upon acceptable object relations, some on over-exciting object relations and some on over-rejecting object relations.

Given Freud's description in "On Narcissism" of the internalisation of the nursing couple and the ability of the child to act from either "end" (agent/patient) of the internalised object relationship, during the early oral phase the child can respond to the mother in ways that might be rejecting of mother but the lack of motor coordination, etc. means that the ability to direct aggression against mother is very limited. Fairbairn suggests this period involves a "pre-ambivalent" object. An object that is satisfactory, or not, about which the child can do little; it can turn away from the object and it can also internalise that object relationship, but it cannot direct aggression towards the object.

Second oral phase

With the advent of the second or later oral phase and the eruption of the teeth and the greater motor control of the normally developing child, the object becomes ambivalent, according to Fairbairn. It is a good object if it is satisfying and a bad object if it is in some way unsatisfying. If it is a bad object then relations with bad objects may be invoked and it can be attacked by biting. If it is a good object then object relations can be internalised as an extension to and a deepening of the acceptable object relations. At this time where there is no clear differentiation between libidinal, antilibidinal and acceptable object relationships, any one of these object relationships might be evoked by a new experience of mother. Since mother as primary caregiver is normally the person who is going to maximally protect the child and ensure its survival, anything that might endanger or sour that relationship is potentially life-threatening for the child.

It is at this time and for survival purposes that the child dissociates libidinal and antilibidinal object relations from acceptable object relations. It is also at this time that the central self, associated with the acceptable object relations, takes over a controlling role in repressing the separate libidinal and the antilibidinal repertoires of object relations possibilities.

Having separated the acceptable object relationships from the over-exciting and over-rejecting object relations, the acceptable object relations become idealised and operate as ideal object relations, so the central self and the ideal object keep the potentially unruly or transgressive over-exciting and over-rejecting object relations under their control. This is the basic endopsychic structure, which shares aspects with Glovers's theory of ego-nuclei, where it appears to be a higher ordering of these ego-nuclei but also insists that these ego-structures will be linked to internal objects based upon object relationships. It also shares features common to both Bowlby's idea of multiple working models of mother and Stern's notion of Repeated Interactions Generalised (RIGs). Each of the six dynamic structures in Fairbairn's theory are themselves based on many examples of object relationships, leading to the view that each of these ego-object or self-object dyads is actually a composite of many different object relationships with different others that have been generalised to produce a rich complex repertoire of object relations possibilities.

It is at this time, after the development of the basic endopsychic structure, that Fairbairn introduces the idea of the moral defence. Initially (first oral phase) there was just satisfactory or unsatisfactory object relations that were being accumulated, then (second oral phase) there were good and bad object relations that were being accumulated and responded to. Then (basic endopsychic structure) there was the patterned dissociation and repression of object relations possibilities (libidinal and antilibidinal) that might put in jeopardy the crucial relationship between mother and child.

Now there arises the possibility that the mother and others treat the child badly, as its ability to understand the world and operate within it is developing. There is then a conflict between the mother as an (internal) ideal object and the (external) mother as she appears to the child who is being treated badly. In order to preserve the idea that the external mother is an ideal object the child has to take on the burden of guilt that his treatment by mother initially engenders—that is, anger directed towards her is turned against him- or herself. Guilt as anger directed towards the self or sub-selves—that is, conflict between different parts of the self—is then the mechanism for the moral defence. She hurts me, I must have deserved it, since she is an ideal (good) mother, therefore I am a bad person and I am judged as such by my ideal object. Thus my ideal object becomes my ego-ideal.

Fairbairn goes on to develop the idea that the ego-ideal and the antilibidinal self together form what Freud called the super-ego, the antilibidinal self being internalised *punitive* relations with significant others, and the ego-ideal being internalised *positive* relations with significant others.

There is then the question of the further development of the self through an increasingly wider experience of the world and the development of powers. For Fairbairn the move from infantile dependence towards mature dependence via the transitional techniques is how he understands the development of our abilities to relate more widely to others in the world. During that early period, and depending upon how we have been treated, we may have had to severely restrict our powers, our freedom to act and our repertoire of acceptable actions in order not to threaten the relationship with mother as the crucial caretaker and provider.

Part of the early processing of objects—that is, other people—involves internalising different aspects of our object relations with them as we develop and grow towards mature dependence. To become mature we have to free ourselves from our infantile identifications with others and move towards differentiated relationships free of projection and introjection. Fairbairn suggests that the neuroses are all in one way or another mired in projective and introjective relations with others. The transitional techniques are what might allow us to set ourselves free from our usually unrecognised projective and introjective entanglements with others, in particular our early objects—parents and siblings. An important function of the neuroses is to defend against the far greater disaster of psychosis. Fairbairn gives a detailed account of the characteristic way internal objects are disposed of through projection and introjection for each of the neuroses—obsession, paranoia, hysteria, and phobia. This is an hypothesis that has yet to be systematically tested.

Psychic change in Fairbairn's model can be integrative or disintegrative, but the project for therapy is to open up the closed world of the patient to relations with the (external) world, mature dependence being the ability to relate to properly differentiated other people and situations on a realistic basis in the external world, without projection and introjection.

Elsewhere (Clarke, 2005), I have suggested that in order to bring the topographical features of classical psychoanalysis into Fairbairn's model consistently, you need to introduce a structured preconscious of ideal, libidinal and antilibidinal ego-object (self-object) dyads, all of which are complexly structured. Paul Finnegan and I have used this model to suggest that there is a Fairbairnian approach to MPD/DID, which involved both repression and dissociation, along with a structured preconscious and a structured unconscious.

This model (which has been developed in the following publications: Clarke, 2006; Chapter Three; Chapter Four) relies upon both Fairbairn's original papers and Padel's approach to psychic growth and is different from the model developed by Mitchell and Rubens in that it involves the basic endopsychic structure as an explanatory framework throughout, but incorporates the work on the moral defence too. For Padel, the central self grows at the expense of the subsidiary selves by aspects of the dissociated and repressed sub-selves being worked over, transformed and reintegrated into the ideal and acceptable aspects of the central self and its ego-ideal.

At this point I think it is necessary to point to a striking parallel between Fairbairn's developmental view of the growth of self and its concomitant theory of the process of disintegration or breakdown and Glover's 1932 developmentally based classification of mental disorders. Fairbairn's model as represented in his 1941 paper, and which forms Chapter 2 of the first section of his book, is very close in structure to Glover's component instinct-based model. Glover does use all of Abraham's erogenous zones in his model, whereas Fairbairn does not use the anal and phallic but suggests that the neuroses (transitional techniques) are all alternative ways of dealing with problems of internal objects in the process of development. Since for Fairbairn instinctual impulses are the activity of objects in relationship, this suggests that underneath the object relations model lies a component instinct model that is secondary to the object relationships, short of deep regression or disintegration as in psychosis.

This model is a rational reconstruction of Freud, using object relationships and dynamic structures consistently, and can, I believe, model the classical along with the relational model offered by JMD while offering clarifications and advantages to both models.

JMD's linking of the pre-analytic with the post-classical

In the introduction to her paper, JMD wisely reminds us that "The notion of multiple self-states was born in the 19th century literature on hysteria, childhood trauma, hypnoid states and multiple personality disorder" (Davies, 1996, p. 554). She goes on to suggest that "the ways in which we understood trauma a hundred years ago were not only consistent with contemporary trauma theories, but comprise the nascent underpinnings of a model of mind more in keeping with contemporary psychoanalytic practice, most particularly with relational psychoanalysis" (ibid.). A decisive part of her argument is that Freud's rejection of the seduction hypothesis in 1897 did not just set back our understanding of the longer term consequences of childhood traumatisation but directed the attention of the psychological community away from the dissociation-based model of the mind that was beginning to take shape towards a repression-based model of mind. JMD in this paper wants to reconnect contemporary psychoanalytic theory with those early dissociation-based theories of mind, which she suggests anticipate our current understanding of fragmentation and trauma and reveal their relevance to post-classical models of mind.

At this point a look at JMD's characterisation of the classical and the relational models and how they relate to Fairbairn is fitting.

Classical

> The classical unconscious is, therefore, a repression-based model, organized around a developmental layering of fixed but discarded structures denoting the history of endogenously organized, phase-specific, object-related drives and drive derivatives. The very nature of significant objects toward whom these unconscious wishes are directed is overwhelmingly determined by the developmental progression of phase-specific drive derivatives, rather than by the

actual qualities and textures of self-object interactions. (Davies, 1996, p. 561)

Given my description of Fairbairn's theory above, I do not think it is hard to see that this could be a description of the way that the endopsychic structure operates, the differences being that the "fixed but discarded" structures are still active for Fairbairn and can take control under disintegrative circumstances, and the "object-related drives and drive derivatives" being the energetic basis of the object relations and the "phase-specific drive derivatives" operating as part of, but subsidiary to, object relations.

Relational

> As described here, the "relational unconscious" would be composed of three categories of experience: (1) object-related wishes or fantasies that become unacceptable within the context of a particular internalized, real, or fantasized self-object dyad (this aspect is closest to the classical unconscious, except that what is conscious or unconscious at any given instant will vary in accordance with what internalized self-other dyad is being evoked by the interpersonal present); (2) mutually incompatible experiences of self in relation to irreconcilable aspects of the other that cannot be maintained in simultaneous awareness (the kind of dissociation that occurs in cases of traumatic abuse might well be the prototype for this aspect of unconscious experience); and (3) aspects of self-experience that because of their idiosyncratic or extreme nature become dropped from the linguistic categorization of generalizable experience. (Davies, 1996, p. 563)

I think that this description could also be used to characterise Fairbairn's theory as I have described it earlier and that the significant differences from the classical are located in the object-relatedness of the infant and the underlying assumptions of the system where energy and structure are closely related and interchangeable as opposed to totally separate. Equally significant differences from the relational viewpoint are related to the presence of repression as the action of the central self on dissociated sub-selves. One further advantage that the Fairbairn model offers both systems is the categorisation of self-object dyads into ideal, libidinal, or antilibidinal.

While Mitchell talked about Fairbairn's theory as "between paradigms"—meaning, as far as I understand it, a bridging theory between the move from the classical to the relational—I want to assert that Fairbairn's theory is a synthesis of the classical (thesis) and the relational (antithesis) psychoanalytic paradigms and thus an advance on both. It may have taken the fuller development of the relational viewpoint to reveal the degree to which Fairbairn's theory was an improvement upon the classical theory and more flexible than the relational paradigm, which has no room for repression or for giving a precise location to and characterisation of the self-object systems that comprise it.

JMD's clinical example

Here I am looking at JMD's account of her relationship with her patient using the model developed in Chapter Three. In this particular example I am suggesting that the therapeutic dissociation that JMD encourages her patient to make is based on identifying dissociated antilibidinal object relationships in her patient and in herself.

In this section of her clinical vignette, JMD describes how the relationship between herself and her patient, Helen, took an unfamiliar turn, with the patient being unmoved by JMD's illness and Helen's "frank and undisguised rage", which seemed to come from a completely unknown part of her patient. This was a transferential process that was at the time perplexing to JMD (Davies, 1996, p. 570).

During the next session JMD and her patient explore what went on between them. JMD introduces the idea of a therapeutic dissociation, which might be rendered in Fairbairn's terms as letting the dissociated and repressed sub-self speak. In this case, given the nature of the earlier exchange it would be Helen's antilibidinal self or an aspect of it that had emerged.

By the next session her patient is full of apologies and unable to explain her behaviour and this provides JMD with the opportunity to use the dissociation-based model of mind she has been developing to encourage what she calls a therapeutic dissociation. She tells her patient that she would like to meet this previously unknown aspect of her patient and get to know her better. She guesses that this other self has been there all along and that she is a bad aspect of her patient, to which the patient readily agrees and even suggests that she is "The worst a person could ever imagine" (p. 570). JMD suggests that they invite her in and the patient's response to this is to remember an occasion when her grandmother was sick and the patient walked right over her when she was lying on the floor.

> "That's how bad she is ... that's what I thought of when you were choking and I walked right out of here! I haven't thought about that in so many years. I walked right over her frail little body." "I guess you were tired of people being sick," I suggested. "Maybe you got scared and frightened that day when my cold wouldn't go away." (ibid. pp. 570–571)

At this point the patient began to cry and the hidden part of herself is accused by the patient of wishing that her mother would die and of making both her mother and her grandmother die. This is also associated with her being hit and rejected by her father for wanting a new mother, "make sure she's a healthy one this time" (Davies, 1996, p. 571), for which she feels she was duly punished by her father, a punishment she felt she deserved. This internalisation of her father as a good object into her ego-ideal is an example of the moral defence, its purpose being to keep her dangerous antilibidinal self in check, which on the basis of this example it seems to have done successfully for a considerable time.

JMD describes a productive period of clinical work that followed and led to the patient growing by letting the antilibidinal aspects of her subsidiary self become worked over and incorporated into her central self (Davies, 1996, p. 572). This is an example of psychic growth as described by Padel (1991) and involved recuperating aspects of her relationship with her grandmother and transforming them from antilibidinal to acceptable or even ideal through the encouragement of the therapist to see these qualities differently. The transformation of the antilibidinal self depends upon a retranscription from a negative to a positive set of characteristics, which can now be accepted and become part of the repertoire of powers available to the patient.

> in allowing these fragmented and scattered images of Helen's secret and most hateful self to emerge and coalesce in the foreground of the analytic work, an opportunity arose for redefining the meaning, as well as the adaptive significance, of these parts of herself. Thus

> the "rotten core," "the evil one," "the bad seed" became known as "the fighter," "the protector," "the survivor," even "the guardian of hope." So, compassionately redefined, this persona could once again be integrated with other dimensions of the patient's personality. Her spirit, her sense of righteousness and justice, even her outrage were free to be called upon when needed, and as such could be granted a permanently important place within the patient's psychic equilibrium. (Davies, 1996, p. 572)

Thus the central self is enhanced by the recuperation of these previously dissociated and repressed powers and the ego-ideal is similarly expanded towards a more realistic assessment of the powers the person has within the world.

Conclusion

I suggest that Fairbairn's theory as a rational reconstruction of both Freud's structural model and his libido theory can be interpreted as fitting JMD's characterisation of both classical and relational approaches to psychoanalytic theory. I looked in detail at one of JMD's clinical vignettes in order to offer a Padel-inspired, Fairbairn-based interpretation of the relationship with one of her patients and the changes that it undergoes. In Chapter Two I proposed that Fairbairn's theory combines aspects of both classical and relational theory in a novel but enduring way. The parallels between Glover and Fairbairn and their developmental approaches to the growth and disintegration of the mind suggest that the object relations model sits on top of a drive-based model and that both are necessary for a proper understanding of mind. I think that there is some powerful evidence for the existence of both in human motivation in an assay of the culture that surrounds us and that during this era is in many ways shockingly open and free but always under threat.

PART V

INSTINCT, AFFECT, AND
NEUROPSYCHOANALYSIS

CHAPTER NINE

The place of instincts and affects in Fairbairn's psychology of dynamic structures

Introduction

The intention of this chapter is to show that Fairbairn never dispensed with ideas of instinct and affect but carefully placed them within an object relations context where they are a necessary and central constituent. Imagine an object relationship without affect and you have an empty formality—a habit or a dry as dust duty, a formal rather than a felt reality, the nightmare world of dystopia—where love is forbidden. Sometimes, because of the level of abstraction involved, metapsychological terms like libidinal and antilibidinal, egos and objects, can seem to be devoid of vitality, but this is the danger with all attempts to find an objective viewpoint from which to describe and understand a complex and multifaceted lived reality.

A secondary intention is to suggest that some of the recent findings within neuropsychoanalysis have strong resonances with Fairbairn's model of endopsychic structure and its development. This is far from a detailed or conclusive set of parallels, but since some at least of Freud's certainties are being questioned by these developments, so one could argue that Fairbairn's theory better fits this emerging model, which is based in affective neuroscience. This is a development that requires a lot more research, but the integration of a neuropsychoanalytic and a psychoanalytic model of mind and personality is a pressing but incomplete project. It is unfortunate that Fairbairn's theory is not better known or understood, since I believe that it has a lot to offer affective neuroscience.

Before considering Fairbairn's thoughts on instinct and affect in his mature work I want to look back to a paper he wrote in 1930, which takes a clear look at Freud's libido theory and develops an alternative based upon a viewpoint that is commensurate with that developed by Glover.

"Libido Theory Re-evaluated" (1930)

In 1930 Fairbairn wrote a long paper entitled "Libido Theory Re-evaluated", which only became public when Birtles and Scharff published it for the first time in their invaluable *From Instinct to Self*, Volume II (1994). This paper was written "to consider the meaning for psychology of two important Freudian theories, the 'Libido' Theory and the theory of the 'Pleasure Principle'" (Fairbairn, 1930, p. 115). Fairbairn intended to publish this paper as "The Libido Theory and the Theory of the Pleasure Principle Interpreted in Terms of Appetite" in the *British Journal of Medical Psychology* (Birtles & Scharff, 1994, p. 10). The paper was not actually published until long after Fairbairn's death. Richard Rubens (1996) wrote a review of Birtles and Scharff's book entitled "The Unique Origins of Fairbairn's Theories" and devoted a section to each of the three substantive pieces from the late 1920s and 1930—Fairbairn's MD thesis, his paper on the super-ego, and his paper on the libido theory, published for the first time—as the first three chapters of Birtles and Scharff's Vol II (1994).

As we have seen in previous chapters, Fairbairn's early work was crucial for the development of his later approach and is usually based upon some of those earlier papers; for example, his thoughts on dissociation and repression from his MD thesis inform the development of his endopsychic model, and his attention to his developed theories' usefulness in understanding dissociative disorders in general, including multiple personality disorder. As Rubens comments:

> Fairbairn ... saw dissociation as being relevant to the entire range of phenomena—from the most benign to the most severe; and

> this clearly foreshadows his mature interest in splitting and his insistence on the universality of schizoid mechanisms inherent in all levels of personality development. (Rubens, 1996, pp. 416–417)

The "chief interest", for Fairbairn, is that Freud's theories about libido and the pleasure principle be framed in terms that would be familiar to psychology in general so that "the truths embodied in these theories come to exercise their just influence upon psychological thought" (Fairbairn, 1930, p. 115).

Fairbairn asserts that the interest in these theories is related to their significance for problems concerning the nature and classification of the instinctive tendencies and the mode of operation of these tendencies. He suggests that the libido theory is most significant for the first group of problems and that the pleasure principle is most significant for the second group of problems. He spends the first half of his paper considering the libido theory and the second half considering the pleasure principle.

He praises the libido theory for its attempt:

> to interpret the whole field of human behaviour and character formation from a genetic standpoint and to establish fundamental principles for the understanding of both the normal and the abnormal phenomena of mental life. (Op. cit.)

Having discussed the limitations of contemporary psychological theories and the criticisms of libido theory as a form of pansexuality, Fairbairn looks at the way that Freud developed the libido theory from his original formulation of it in 1905, where he argues that Freud, from the outset, conceived of a dualism of instinctive tendencies—one based upon "the sexual processes of the organism" and the other based upon "the nutritional processes". This essential dualism of Freud's instinct theory becomes progressively clearer in his later works, where by 1910 the duality is between the two fundamental instincts—the sex instincts and the ego instincts. Fairbairn cites and quotes at length Freud's paper "On Narcissism" because it contains an admission on the part of Freud that his theory is based primarily on biological and not upon psychological considerations. The modification of the theory is continued in 1920 in *Beyond the Pleasure Principle* by the establishment of a new dualism involving the life instincts and the death instincts (Freud, 1920g, p. 48).

Fairbairn argues that, like the earlier dualism, Freud's later dualism of life and death instincts is based upon biological and not psychological considerations. Fairbairn goes on to argue that this dualism of instincts, which are both essentially biologically based, contains a contradiction:

> All instincts are essentially expressions of life. *The instincts with which an individual is endowed are simply the characteristic ways in which life manifests itself in members of the species to which it belongs.* … *All* instincts are therefore life instincts in the last resort. (Fairbairn, 1930, p. 122, Fairbairn's emphasis)

Rubens notes the fact that Fairbairn's critique of Freud's libido theory is of a dualism based upon biology not psychology and that in Fairbairn's view the so-called "death instinct" is nonsense.

> Now, it is in no way special that he rejected Freud's notion of the death instinct: virtually no significant theorist—with the very notable exception of Melanie Klein—found the death instinct a particularly compelling construct. There is, however, in what Fairbairn raised as his objection, a foreshadowing of his own eventual theory of psychic energy, which he eventually saw as standing behind the basic object-seeking behavior of human beings. (Rubens, 1996, p. 422)

Fairbairn argues that Freud did recognise an instinct of aggression but that he mistakenly identifies this with the death instinct. Fairbairn counters Freud's argument by suggesting that rather than a death instinct we can understand self-destructive tendencies as instances of aggression being deflected inwards from external objects to the ego, or parts of the endopsychic structure, a viewpoint that he incorporated into chapter three (1943) of his book. He asserts, "It seems doubtful if there is a single psychoanalytic observation at present explained in terms of the instinct of aggression" (Fairbairn, 1930, p. 127).

Fairbairn goes on to question the usefulness of a dualistic theory of instincts at all and suggests that these have the tendency to shift from psychological to philosophical and religious considerations of "cosmic forces"; something that Fairbairn is keen to avoid. So, he raises the question of converting Freud's dualism to a monism, but he recognises that reducing all instincts to libido is unsatisfactory.

Fairbairn argues that in order to satisfy psychological criteria a theory of instinct must satisfy the following demands: that it should be based upon a comprehensive survey of instinctive activity as a whole and that it should depend primarily upon strictly psychological considerations, at which point Fairbairn turns to the work of fellow Scot James Drever, the first professor of psychology at a Scottish University.

Under Drever's leadership, the psychology department expanded to include:

> Mary Collins (1895–1989) an expert on colour vision, with whom Drever collaborated on a number of books; the psychoanalyst Ronald Fairbairn (1889–1964); and John Derg Sutherland (1905–1991), future Director of the Tavistock Clinic. (See www.ourhistory.is.ed.ac.uk/index.php/Sir_James_Drever_(1873–1950))

Fairbairn's use of Drever's theory of instincts in or around 1930 runs parallel to Glover's use of Freud's libido theory to publish his theory of ego-nuclei in 1932.

Drever divides instinctive tendencies into two main groups whose labels are already familiar to us from Glover's classification of mental disorders. These are the "appetitive" and the "reactive".

> Among the appetitive tendencies hunger and the tendency to prolong or seek agreeable experiences, and among the reactive tendencies fear and play, may be taken as adequately representing the two types. (Drever, 1922, p. 51)

Fairbairn reproduces Drever's table of the appetitive and reactive tendencies and suggests some additions to the table in the form of the excretory functions as part of the appetitive instinctive tendencies. In the discussion of Drever's classification Fairbairn raise a number of questions of interest to psychoanalysis.

Drever brings under the category of instinct all classes of innate human reactions, whether associated with specific emotions or not, and he holds that emotion is not necessarily an accompaniment of instinctual activity. Drever identifies some general tendencies like play and imitation, which attach themselves to the specific ends or interests of the specific tendencies from which they derive their emotional colouring. While the general tendency of play may be recognised as having its own characteristics, it also manifests itself in activities that may be aggressive: sexual, parental, hunting, etc. This blending of instincts can also occur between specific tendencies.

> Thus, when two or more specific tendencies are evoked simultaneously by the same situation, the specific affects or emotions concerned fuse so as to produce an affective state which, while analysable into its components, is quite distinctive, and the resulting behaviour is a complication of the forms of behaviour of the instinctual tendencies in question. (Fairbairn, 1930, p. 136)

These fusion phenomena are regarded by Drever as of considerable importance for mental development and are the basis of two of Drever's seven fundamental laws of mental development—"the law of fusion of feeling and emotion" and "the law of complication of behaviour". This idea of the layering and fusion of different emotions and its link to significant development later appears in Fairbairn's discussion of the Oedipus situation (Fairbairn, 1952, pp. 122–123). Fairbairn, however, singles out as the most important feature of Drever's classification of the instincts the distinction between the appetitive and the reactive tendencies, which "demands special attention here". Fairbairn notes that:

> The situations with which the *appetitive* tendencies deal are essentially *internal*, whereas the *reactive* tendencies are concerned with situations which are essentially *external*. (Fairbairn, 1930, p. 137, Fairbairn's emphasis)

Appetitive tendencies are oriented towards the satisfaction of basic organic needs more or less regardless of external conditions, whereas reactive tendencies are directed towards external conditions and are primarily adaptive. Fairbairn notes that the appetitive and reactive tendencies differ in the kind of feeling state that accompanies their activation. Appetitive tendencies manifest in consciousness as a sort of uneasiness, which he says might best be described as a craving, and, depending upon the specific appetite, the craving will have a distinctive quality according to the particular need that demands satisfaction. Fairbairn suggests that the affective element present when the reactive tendencies are stirred is best described as "object-interest", where the character of the object-interest in each case differs according to the reactive tendency activated, so the object-interest might be "fearful, thwarting, unusual, etc." But in all cases the object-interest differs essentially from the uneasiness of appetite. Fairbairn characterises the differences between the appetitive and the reactive tendencies in the following manner.

> ... the appetitive tendencies are seen to possess the following features:
> 1. the situations which activate them are internal situations constituted by organic needs and the aim of the tendencies is to satisfy these needs
> 2. the feeling-states experienced in these situations are states of uneasiness or tension best described as cravings
> 3. the tendencies demand immediate satisfaction
>
> In the case of the reactive tendencies, on the other hand:
> 1. the stimuli to activity are provided by external situations or external objects, and the aim of the tendencies is successful adaptive behaviour in relation to these
> 2. the feeling-states experienced in these situations partake characteristically of the nature of "object-interest" rather than of uneasiness
> 3. the tendencies seek their goal by adaptive behaviour, which characteristically involves postponement of satisfaction (Fairbairn, 1930, p. 140)

Fairbairn argues that the differences between the appetitive and the reactive tendencies forcibly remind us of Freud's distinction between "the pleasure principle" and the "primary process" on the one hand and "reality principle" and the "secondary process" on the other. Fairbairn prefers Drever's terminology because it makes it possible to bring psychoanalytic findings into line with general psychology. In trying to explore the degree to which this correspondence is exact, Fairbairn introduces Stout's (1927) conception of mental levels, which he also uses in his only contribution to the Controversial Discussions, when he proposes replacing unconscious phantasy by inner reality (Fairbairn, 1943a). After some analysis Fairbairn satisfies himself that the distinction between the appetitive and the reactive tendencies does correspond to Freud's distinction between the pleasure principle and the reality principle and wonders if this distinction may also be represented in the libido theory. In approaching this question Fairbairn is reminded of the distinction between the "aim" of libido and its "object". In a passage that resonates with the parallels I have noted between Glover's classification of mental disorders and Fairbairn's model of endopsychic structure (Chapter Two above) Fairbairn writes:

> It is now held as an integral part of psychoanalytic theory that in the history of the individual the libido undergoes both a regular process of evolution as regards its object and a regular process of evolution as regards its aim; and the various symptom-complexes found in the psychoses and psycho-neuroses, as well as certain character traits and perversions, are attributed to characteristics disturbances in one or other (or both) of these evolutionary processes. (Fairbairn, 1930, p. 145)

Rubens makes some interesting remarks vis-à-vis Fairbairn's understanding of the object for Freud, accusing Fairbairn of imposing his own conception of the object on Freud.

> To begin with, Fairbairn very clearly states a misconception he obviously has of Freud's position:
>
>> What Freud (1905c) meant by the "object" of the libido is plain enough; he means an external object (usually a person) to which libido is attached and in relation to which satisfaction is sought. This being so, it is evident that the relationship of the libido to its object is essentially a phenomenon of reactive behavior; and in this object-relationship we discern above all the reactive tendency of sex (Fairbairn, 1930, p. 145).
>
> While the specific meaning of object is somewhat confused in early Freud, it is quite certain that the meaning is essentially involved with the inner, intra-psychic object. Fairbairn's reading here reflects his *own* conception of object much more than it describes Freud's. What this citation goes on to state, however, is an exact forerunner of Fairbairn's mature view: remembering that "reactive tendencies" refer (*via* Drever) to the expression of the self according to the reality principle, what we have here is an early—prior

to the influence of Melanie Klein—statement of his belief that the fundamental "drive" is that of the person *towards other people in reality*. (Rubens, 1996, pp. 425–426, Rubens's emphasis)

But if we go back to the source that Fairbairn indicates—that is, Freud's *Three Essays on the Theory of Sexuality* (1905d)—in the third paragraph of the opening section we note that Freud writes:

Let us call the person from whom sexual attraction proceeds the *sexual object* and the act toward the instinct tends the *sexual aim*. (Freud, 1905d, pp. 134–135, emphasis in original)

Fairbairn substitutes Drever's classification of instincts for Freud's instinct dualism and insists that there will be countless situations in which one or more of the reactive tendencies will be stirred in conjunction with the reactive tendency of sex and that this will lead to a "functional fusion" between them. He goes on to suggest that as functional fusion will occur between simultaneously activated instincts so the more commonly associated active instincts will form more or less permanent connections in the mental structure, and that psychoanalysis has shown that permanent connections of this sort are formed in the earliest years of life and that particular reactive tendencies become integrated with the sex instinct in a specially intimate way. He suggests that of these tendencies, the parental instinct and those of curiosity, self-display, self-abasement and aggression are the most notable. This leads Fairbairn to again look in some detail at the instinct of aggression. In his discussion of the instinct of aggression Fairbairn rehearses aspects of his later argument regarding ambivalence and aggression as borne of frustration.

If love is regarded as a phenomenon of the sex-instinct, hate must be regarded as a phenomenon of the instinct of aggression. It is because love and hate derive from separate tendencies that they are able to occur in conjunction in relation to the same object. … While the appropriate stimulus for the reactive tendency of sex is the presence of a sexual object …, the appropriate stimulus for the aggressive tendency is the presence of an obstacle … The aggressive tendency is thus liable to be activated when any other tendency is baulked or frustrated; for frustration involves the presence of an obstacle … It is in this way that the sentiments of love and hate come to be entertained for the same persons and that a state of ambivalence is constituted. (Fairbairn, 1930, p. 149)

Psychoanalytically, ambivalence originally arises from the affective relationship between the child and its parents in early years. The parents are the first objects of love but they also erect the most formidable barriers that the child encounters, in denying the child satisfaction of its longings.

Fairbairn ends his exegesis of Drever's classification of instincts in the following way:

> ... the various "aims" of the libido described by Freud are determined by specific appetitive tendencies belonging to the innate endowment of man. Similarly the "erotogenic zones" from which, according to Freud, the aims of the libido derive their characteristic colouring, are seen to correspond to what may be called "the significant zones" of the specific appetites. (Fairbairn, 1930, p. 156)

This conclusion would be developed and refined in Fairbairn's groundbreaking "psychology of dynamic structure", which was developed in a series of papers in the 1940s that comprise the first section of his only book (1952).

A pristine ego

Fairbairn's view of the ego is that it is an inherent structure, present from birth but pristine—that is, untouched by experience at that point. This is in stark contrast to the views of both Freud and Klein. In the seventeen-point description of his object relations theory of the personality that Fairbairn prepared for the IJPA in 1963, towards the end of his life, the first five points outline his overall view of an alternative architecture of the mind to Freud's.

1. An ego is present from birth.
2. Libido is a function of the ego.
3. There is no death instinct; and aggression is a reaction to frustration or deprivation.
4. Since libido is a function of the ego and aggression is a reaction to frustration or deprivation, there is no such thing as an "id".
5. The ego, and therefore libido, is fundamentally object-seeking.
(Fairbairn 1963, p. 224)

In an earlier paper, Fairbairn had looked at the differences between his own view of the ego and Freud's:

> ... it is an integral feature of Freud's description of "the ego" that this structure is essentially a defensive (and not, like my "original ego", an inherent) structure; and it would appear to follow that Freud's "ego" is founded upon a basis which is essentially psychopathological. The same consideration necessarily applies to the splitting of the "original" ego, which I have described. But it does not apply to the "original" ego itself, which is inherent according to my theory; and, according to my theory, in so far as the splitting of the "original" ego is reversed by psycho-analytical intervention, the psychopathological element in the endopsychic situation is reduced and a genuinely psychotherapeutic result is obtained—an eventuality for which there would appear to be no logical explanation in terms of Freud's theory. (Fairbairn 1958, p. 375)

I think that what is most striking about this approach, which goes back to Fairbairn's ground-breaking work of the1940s, are the parallels with at least one strand of neuropsychoanalytic thinking represented by the recent work of Jaak Panksepp and Mark Solms. The conscious bodily ego that Freud originally suggested and which is the ego that is "present from birth" in Fairbairn's theory is totally consistent with their discovery of the roots of consciousness in the brain stem and the primal emotions as intrinsic to that original "feeling being" or "emotional consciousness", which is the bedrock of the pristine self. In addition, as Panksepp clearly states, "the cortex is empty at birth" and later on "everything in the cortex is learned" (Panksepp, 2015 video on The Neuropsychoanalysis Association site). Since for both Panksepp and Solms the cortex is the site of the ego, and the cortex is essentially random access memory, then this is strong support for Fairbairn's assertions that the original ego is pristine and that our internalisation of object relationships based upon our own real experiences is the source of the multi-agent system of egos and objects—as conceived by Fairbairn—that develops and constitutes the structure activity of the cortex.

When it comes to point two of Fairbairn's account of the origins of the mind, there is some room for doubting that what he is saying is consistent with what Solms and Panksepp are saying, in particular with Solms proposal of a "Conscious Id" (2013). This "Conscious Id" is closely associated with the ego in Solms's account, which is now seen in a different light by Solms as a mechanism for automatising consciously achieved solutions to problems faced by persons in relation, and thus largely unconscious. (The unsatisfactory solutions that become automatised you might expect to be stored in a different location from those that appear to be satisfactory, thus the distinction between the automated aspects of the central ego and the subsidiary sub-selves of libidinal and antilibidinal solutions.)

Leaving aside the question of Panksepp's elaboration of the instinctive and affective underpinnings of all behaviours for a moment, Fairbairn's second point on his list—"Libido is a function of the ego"—can be interpreted as saying that we never encounter instinctive and affective phenomena directly, but only through the activity of an ego or self (or egos and selves) in a social context. The "id" that Fairbairn rejects is a set of hypostatised instincts and affects separated from a person engaged in a social world. The discovery by Panksepp and others of a number of different deep brain emotional patterns and the division of these into either "rewarding" or "punishing" affective feelings will remind us of the categorisation by Glover of basic instinctual approaches as either "libidinal" or "reactive", which appear in Fairbairn's model as "libidinal" and "antilibidinal". Panksepp says:

> It is important to note that ... what is being referred to are primary-process affective systems of the brain, which are next to impossible to study incisively in humans ... I divide the evolved brain mechanisms critical for understanding affective phenomena into a tripartite level of analysis—Primary (raw instinctual-affective), secondary (unconscious learning and memory related processing) and tertiary (higher cognitive manifestations) levels. (Panksepp, 2012)

In my view, each of the dynamic structures of Fairbairn's theory derives their energy from these sub-cortical sources. However, given Fairbairn's identification of a libidinal self based upon the internalisation of over-exciting relationships and an antilibidinal self based upon the internalisation of over-rejecting relationships you would expect to find a repository of automated solutions to particular problems based upon an (in)appropriate set of object-relations problems. Thus the libidinal self would have a preponderance of inappropriate solutions to situations involving the primal emotions: SEEKING, LUST, CARE and PLAY (these have been capitalised in keeping with Panksepp's practice), while the antilibidinal self would have a preponderance of inappropriate solutions to the primal emotions: RAGE, FEAR and PANIC. We might further propose that the libidinal might be more concerned with LUST and the antilibidinal might be more concerned with FEAR, which would marry with the general notion of libido and aggression as the primary motivating factors.

One aspect of Fairbairn's diagram, which has always worried me, but which I accounted for by suggesting that there was a considerable amount of non-repressed but nevertheless unconscious processing being done in the central ego, is the depiction of the central ego as having a considerable part of it in the preconscious and the unconscious. This would now seem to indicate that Fairbairn was aware of and accepted the need for a considerable amount of unconscious processing within the central ego. This is a view that has, only belatedly, become a cognitive scientific and neuropsychoanalytic commonplace.

Instincts and affects

Splitting

In his paper on schizoid factors in the personality (1940, pp. 9–10), Fairbairn discusses splitting of the ego from a "psychogenetic standpoint". He asserts that this means that consideration of what is involved in the development of the ego is necessary. Fairbairn mentions three functions of the ego that must be borne in mind. One is Freud's view on its adaptive function in relating "primal instinctive activity" to conditions in outer reality, particularly social conditions. Another is the integrative function of the ego, most important of which is the integration of perceptions of reality and the integration of behaviour. A third important function of the ego is the ability to discriminate between inner and outer reality. Splitting, for Fairbairn, compromises the "progressive development of all these functions" and he thus envisages a theoretical scale of integration, with a lack of integration at one end and total integration at the other, with all levels of integration in between. Fairbairn places people exhibiting schizoid tendencies on this scale with schizophrenics at the lower end, schizophrenic personalities at a higher level of integration, and schizoid characters at a still higher level of integration. He regards perfect integration with an absence of splitting only as a theoretical possibility. He suggests that keeping such a scale in mind can help us to understand how particular individuals can display some schizoid features under sufficiently extreme conditions. He points to differences in the degree to which people are likely to display such features, some responding to the readjustments attendant upon "adolescence, marriage or joining the army in wartime", whereas others may display such features under everyday circumstances. The spine of this model is consistent with the levels of integration of ego-nuclei in Glover's model (1932) (See Chapter Two above).

Impulses

In a section on impulse psychology and its limitations (Fairbairn, 1952, pp. 84–85), Fairbairn says that he is sceptical of "the explanatory value of all theories of instinct in which the instincts are treated as existing per se" (p. 84). He says that this is particularly true in clinical therapeutic work, since revealing the impulses is one thing but doing something about them quite another. What the patient does with his impulses is "clearly a problem of object-relationships" (ibid.) but it is equally a "problem of his own personality" (p. 84). But problems of personality are a matter of "the relationships of various parts of the ego to internalised objects and to one another as objects" (pp. 84–85). Consequently, impulses cannot be considered *"apart from the endopsychic structures which they energize and the object-relationships which they enable these structures to establish"* (p. 85, emphasis added.). So it follows that *"'instincts' cannot profitably be considered as anything more than forms of energy which constitute the dynamic of such endopsychic structures"* (ibid., emphasis added.). On the basis of his analysis of patients with schizoid tendencies, Fairbairn argues that the analysis of impulses *apart* from the structures they energise is a particularly sterile procedure. He cites a clinical example of a patient who was able to release a flood of associations "in the form of oral-sadistic phantasies" (p. 85) without any movement in the direction of greater integration or significant therapeutic development. Fairbairn's explanation of this process is that the central ego does not participate in these phantasies except as "a recording agent" (ibid.). This is a process that he terms a "masterpiece of defensive technique" (p. 85) and characteristic of schizoid individuals when the analyst's interpretations are couched too much in terms of impulses. This allows the patient to evade the central therapeutic problem of "how to release those dynamic charges known as 'impulses' in the context of reality" (ibid.), which Fairbairn says is clearly a problem of object-relationships within the social order.

Ego-nuclei
(See also Chapter Two comparing Fairbairn with Glover)

In 1941 Fairbairn published his paper offering a revised psychopathology of the psychoses and psychoneuroses in the *International Journal of Psychoanalysis* (1941). In the introduction to that paper he made the following comments on Glover's ego-nuclei hypothesis and the paper in which it was first mooted.

> As has been well described by Edward Glover (1932, J. Ment. Sci., 78, 819–842), the ego is gradually built up in the course of development from a number of primitive ego-nuclei: and we must believe that these ego-nuclei are themselves the product of a process of integration. The formation of the component nuclei may be conceived as a process of localized psychical crystallization occurring not only within zonal, but also within various other functional distributions. Thus there will arise within the psyche, not only e.g. oral, anal and genital nuclei, but also male and female, active and passive, loving and hating, giving and taking nuclei, as well as the nuclei of internal persecutors and judges (super-ego nuclei). We may further conceive that it is the overlapping and interlacing of these various nuclei and classes of nuclei that form the basis of that particular process of integration, which results in the formation of the ego. Schizoid states must, accordingly, be regarded as occurring characteristically in individuals in whom this process of integration has never been satisfactorily realized, and in whom a regressive disintegration of the ego has occurred. (Fairbairn, 1941, p. 251)

(This section of Fairbairn's paper was excluded when the paper was included "with minor amendments", as Chapter 2, in his book.)

Fairbairn goes on to consider Freud's libido theory and its extension by Abraham to include a theory of erogenous zones.

> Abraham, of course, allotted to each of the more significant libidinal zones a special place in psychogenetic development and postulated a series of phases of development, each characterized by the dominance of a specific zone; and, in accordance with this scheme, each of the classical psychoses and psychoneuroses came to be attributed to a fixation at a specific phase. (Fairbairn, 1941, p. 252)

Fairbairn argues for the cogency of considering the two oral phases as being correct but questions the correctness of subsequent phases—for example, the two anal phases and the early genital or phallic phase. Fairbairn writes:

> There can be no question of the correctness of relating schizoid conditions to a fixation in the early oral (*incorporative and pre-ambivalent*) phase characterized by the dominance of sucking. Nor, for that matter, can there be any doubt about the correctness of attributing manic-depressive conditions to a fixation in the later oral (*ambivalent*) phase characterized by the emergence of biting. *For the dominant ego-nuclei in the schizoid and the manic-depressive are found to conform in character to these respective attributions.* (Fairbairn 1941, p. 252, my emphasis)

When Fairbairn reproduced the paper in his book it was modified to read as follows:

> There can be no question of the correctness of relating schizoid conditions to a fixation in the earlier oral phase characterized by the dominance of sucking. Nor, for that matter, can there be any doubt about the correctness of attributing manic-depressive conditions to a fixation in the later oral phase characterized by the emergence of biting. (Fairbairn, 1952, p. 29)

The difference between these two quotations is worth discussing for two reasons. The first is that the distinction between the pre-ambivalent and the ambivalent and their intimate association with the early and later oral phases is clearly already present in 1941 and not part of his later response to criticism of his account of the origins of the good object. The second is that the use of the term ego-nuclei is dropped in the later quotation.

The importance of the early oral phase and pre-ambivalence is only fully developed later on when Fairbairn is having to defend his ideas of psychic development against the Kleinians and others, including Winnicott, who do not recognise this distinction, which is crucial to the discussion of the origin and the place of the good object. This is also one of Mitchell's major criticisms of Fairbairn (see Chapter Seven).

The question of Fairbairn's rationale in dropping the term ego-nuclei as part of his critique of the libido theory may become clearer as we look in greater detail at his later developments of his alternative theory. Given that Glover had left the British Psychoanalytic Association by the time Fairbairn's book was published, Fairbairn might have thought it tactically sensible to differentiate his use of Glover's developmental schema from any association with Glover. Glover did accept Abraham's schema and thus had no argument with the anal and the phallic phases, which Glover included in his original diagram (Glover, 1932), and which he continued to use until 1968 (Glover, 1968) at least.

Fairbairn in the meantime had raised serious objections to the whole theory of erotogenic zones and the developmental argument concerning their specifying a level of integration. Fairbairn's main argument against the erotogenic zones that Abraham proposes is that whilst the first two oral phases and the last genital phase have a natural, biological object (e.g., the breast or mother initially, and a sexual partner in relation to the latter), the anal and phallic phases have no natural, biological object. For Fairbairn what unites them is that they are a way of dealing with incorporated objects.

> The conception of fundamental erotogenic zones constitutes an unsatisfactory basis for any theory of libidinal development because it is based upon a failure to recognize that the function of libidinal pleasure is essentially to provide a sign-post to the object.... The conception of erotogenic zones is itself based upon the phenomenon of autoerotism and has arisen largely owing to a mistaken interpretation of the real significance of this phenomenon. Autoerotism is essentially a technique whereby the individual seeks not only to provide for himself what he cannot obtain from the object, but to provide for himself an object which he cannot obtain.... The significance of the anal and phallic attitudes lies in the fact that they represent the libidinal aspects of techniques for dealing with objects which have been incorporated. It must always be borne in mind, however, that it is not the libidinal attitude which determines the object-relationship, but the object-relationship which determines the libidinal attitude. (Fairbairn, 1952, pp. 33–34)

Fairbairn proposes a developmental schema that starts with infantile dependence, passes through a transitional phase, and ends with mature dependence. It is within the transitional phase that the neurotic aspects of the person manifest themselves.

> ... my own findings leave me in equally little doubt that the *paranoid*, *obsessional*, and *hysterical* states—to which may be added the *phobic* state—essentially represent, not the products of fixations at specific libidinal phases, but simply *a variety of techniques employed to defend the ego against the effects of conflicts of an oral origin*. The conviction that this is so is supported by two facts: (a) that the analysis of paranoid, obsessional, hysterical, and phobic symptoms invariably reveals the presence of an underlying oral conflict, and (b) that paranoid, obsessional, hysterical, and phobic symptoms are such common accompaniments and precursors of schizoid and depressive states. (Fairbairn, 1952, p. 30, emphasis in original)

While Glover used Abraham's suggestions regarding stages of libidinal development, Fairbairn was looking at the process of moving from infantile dependence to mature dependence as being more or less on one level, with the different techniques protecting the person from the worse fate of becoming psychotic.

Object relationships

Fairbairn moved to develop his theory in terms of object relationships rather than ego-nuclei or structures that were explicitly based upon integrated ensembles of ego-nuclei, but I want to suggest that it was as integrated ensembles of ego-nuclei that he saw the libidinal and antilibidinal, the central and the ideal egos, and objects of his 1944 endopsychic structure—a system of integrated structures that could fall apart (disintegrate, deteriorate) under (internal or external) stress. There is one place in his 1944 paper in which Fairbairn slips back into the use of (ego) nuclei and that is in his discussion of the Oedipus situation where he writes:

> Once the Oedipus situation comes to be regarded as essentially an internal situation, it is not difficult to see that the maternal components of both the internal objects have, so to speak, a great initial

advantage over the paternal components; and this, of course, applies to children of both sexes. The strong position of the maternal components is, of course, due to the fact that the nuclei of both the internal objects are derivatives of the original ambivalent mother and her ambivalent breasts. In conformity with this fact, *a sufficiently deep analysis of the Oedipus situation invariably reveals that this situation is built up around the figures of an internal exciting mother and an internal rejecting mother* ... thus, for all practical purposes, [the child] comes to equate one parental object with the exciting object, and the other with the rejecting object; and by so doing *the child constitutes the Oedipus situation for himself*. Ambivalence to both parents persists, however, in the background; and at rock bottom both the exciting object and the rejecting object remain what they originally were, viz. figures of his mother. (Fairbairn, 1952, pp. 123–124, emphasis in original)

There are other areas where the ego-nuclei approach seems essential to an understanding of what Fairbairn is arguing. One place that this seems to be obvious is in his distinction between the reality principle and the pleasure principle. This seems to me to point towards a recognition and acceptance of the fact that the object relationship is not just a relationship between a subject and an object but an affective relationship between the two and that where the affective aspect of the object relationship is what dominates then this is the deterioration of an appropriate affective relationship with an object—the object matters less, the affect is all, like the thumb-sucking example that Fairbairn discusses in his 1941 paper where thumb-sucking represents a technique for dealing with an unsatisfactory object relationship.

from the point of view of object-relationship psychology, explicit pleasure-seeking represents a deterioration of behaviour. I speak here of a "deterioration", rather than of a "regression", behaviour because, if object-seeking is primary, pleasure-seeking can hardly be described as "regressive", but is more appropriately described as partaking of the nature of deterioration. Explicit pleasure-seeking has as its essential aim the relieving of the tension of libidinal need for the mere sake of relieving this tension. Such a process does, of course, occur commonly enough; but, since libidinal need is object-need, simple tension-relieving implies some failure of object-relationships. The fact is that simple tension-relieving is really a safety-valve process. It is thus, not a means of achieving libidinal aims, but a means of mitigating the failure of these aims. (Fairbairn, 1952, pp. 139–140)

I think that when Fairbairn discusses the composite nature of internal objects and ego-structures (Fairbairn, 1952, pp. 131–132) we are also implicitly made aware of the possibility that these are the synthesis of a number of lower level ego-nuclei. Under stress these synthesised egos and objects can deteriorate and fragment, resulting in a lot more uncontained affect internally that is usually discharged externally. From this perspective we can see that the primary process is when affect takes precedence over the relation to the object, and secondary process is when the relation to the object contains and shapes the affect. In terms of Fairbairn's own model, the (unconscious) subsidiary selves are more primitive because they are based upon internalisations of relationships early in the child's life where affect dominates the relation to the object. The secondary process is therefore based upon object relationships in which the relation to the object contains and shapes the affect. So what characterises the central and ideal selves is the fact that the relationship to the object contains and gives form to the affect.

This is even more clearly the case with Panksepp's diagram of a hierarchy of processes (Panksepp & Panksepp, 2013), his "Two-way or circular causation". In this diagram I would place the ego-nuclei at the "secondary-process" level and dynamic structures and object relationships at the tertiary level.

This also seems to resonate with Solms's conjecture concerning the processes involved in therapy where he says:

> The therapeutic task of psychoanalysis, then, would still be to undo repressions (to allow the associative links to regain episodic status), in order to enable the reflexive subject to properly master the object-relations they represent and generate executive programs more adequate to the task, so that they may then be legitimately automatized. (Solms, 2013, p. 17)

Conclusion

I hope that I have demonstrated that Fairbairn's object relations theory does include an essential affective core that is only accessible through the

THE PLACE OF INSTINCTS AND AFFECTS IN FAIRBAIRN'S PSYCHOLOGY   203

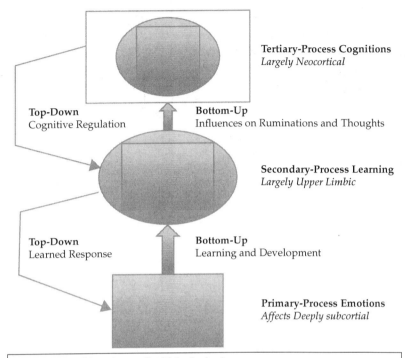

Figure 9.1 Panksepp's diagram

object relationships that the person is involved in and the multi-agent object relations base of the self, as an ensemble of egos and objects in relationship, many of which are split off from conscious inspection and in some cases control and form powerful alternative selves that can act independently to the concern and confusion of the person involved.

I have tried to show how these dynamic structures are the synthesis of previous experiences and can lead to high levels of integration and synthesis of the original lower level object relationships that Glover identifies as ego-nuclei.

Primary-process activity is directed by the primal emotions and leads to a simpler, more basic but more demanding and extreme all or nothing sort of experience that become instantiated as ego-nuclei. Secondary-process activity is the process whereby the object relationships begin to both contain and shape these primitive emotions into ego-directed activity. Tertiary-level processing involves the complex development of object relationships and sophisticated predictions of how the world will behave and what you need to do in order to realise your goals.

While the apparent "flatness" of the cortex as random access memory lends itself to the idea of a simple holistic self, the reality of clinical and other experience and the ability to repress and dissociate unacceptable aspects of the world and the self suggests that as in the use of computers to run multi-agent systems the cortex can support multiple self interpretations whose logical far point would include cases of multiple personality.

Mark Solms suggests that repressions are often of inadequately developed solutions to a problem and it may be that the libidinal and antilibidinal sub-selves that Fairbairn argues for are themselves the repository of such unsuccessful accommodations to reality, as Fairbairn writes in his paper on Ernst Kris's approach to art using classical language.

> According to the principle of dynamic structure, it is not a case of a structural ego being differentiated under the pressure of the impact of external reality out of an original id which is relatively formless, so much as of an id being a structure with primitive characteristics which is differentiated from an original (and relatively primitive) ego-structure under the influence of repression: and it can be seen that once such a differentiation has occurred, the repressed id-structure will retain primitive features (and acquire exaggerations of such features under the influence of repression), while that part of the ego which remains conscious and in touch with external reality will be free to develop under the influence of relationships with external objects ... The primary process will present itself as a characteristic feature of the activity of the repressed id-structure, and the secondary process as a characteristic feature of the activity of the conscious ego-structure; and the nature of artistic activity will then come to be described, not as an ego-controlled regression

to the level of primary process but rather as an attempt to reconcile the primitive expression of a repressed id-structure with the requirements of a conscious ego-structure oriented towards external objects in a social milieu. (Fairbairn, 1953, p. 429)

It seems to me that the project of finding ways to relate the object relational and ego-nucleic understanding with the neuropsychoanalytic is going to have to find the equivalent of an extended haptonomic (www.haptonomie.org/en/) understanding of the embedded nature of the affects within a complex relational, sensory manifold.

CODA

CHAPTER TEN

Thinking through Fairbairn redux

I have continued my investigations of the relationship between Fairbairn's theory and his Scottish contemporaries and suggested that Fairbairn's commitment to the view that the child is originally object-seeking, and not pleasure-seeking as Freud suggested, is based in part on the influence of Suttie (Chapter One). Early infant needs are all-at-once, basic needs for company, sustenance, comfort and security, for which more or less continuous close contact with the mother or a similar caregiver is required over a long period of time. Comparison with primate and tribal societies demonstrates that this process takes years rather than months. We are adaptable, and children are adaptable, but adaptation to less than optimal conditions can lead to changes in the way we relate and in our ability to relate.

I have also suggested that Fairbairn's theory, which in my view has been misinterpreted as being a purely relational theory—or at least on the way to being a purely relational theory—is a bio-psycho-social theory deeply influenced by Glover's theory of ego-nuclei (Chapter Two), a concept that was also used by Winnicott to model primitive emotional development (Winnicott, 1975, pp. 221–228). I have suggested that a full understanding of Fairbairn means recognising the degree to which his object relations theory is built upon an ego-nuclei theory akin to that of Glover. Part of the process of recognising that Fairbairn was more influenced by Glover than anyone had imagined came out of my attempt to make sense of Fairbairn's inclusion of Freud's topographic categories within his object relations model. As soon as one starts to look at the combination of the relational with the topographical one realises that Freud's structural model is open to criticism and conjecture. I developed a model with an expanded preconscious based on Fairbairn's original diagram but incorporating the topographical categories in a consistent way. This led to the development of a model that offered some insight into the underlying mechanisms of dissociative disorders (DID); including multiple personality disorder (MPD). When I came to work with Paul Finnegan, despite having read Fairbairn's work many times, I was surprised to realise that Fairbairn had been arguing consistently throughout his work for the usefulness of his model to understanding dissociation and dissociative disorders like MPD/DID. The model that Paul Finnegan and I developed, based upon the extension of Fairbairn's model to include the preconscious (Clarke, 2005), seemed to be capable of explaining some of the common experiences of MPD/DID and offered a roadmap for disentangling the many and various "alters" that can arise as well as suggesting ways of treating these "split off" persona (Chapters Three and Four).

I have been interested in film for as long as I can remember and the approach to dream and phantasy that Fairbairn developed (Fairbairn, 1952, p. 99) seemed to offer an approach to dramatic narrative as a whole that was both psychoanalytically based and also capable of treating the personified figures of dramatic narratives at two different levels—as actors in a drama and dynamic structures in the inner reality of an observer. Fairbairn's underutilised theory of art with its ideas of under- and over-symbolisation seems to me to open a way to understanding value within the work of art (Chapters Five and Six).

Some of the most important supporters of Fairbairn's work and approach have been people who have contributed to the relational approach to psychoanalysis, but, as I argue, this is at some cost to a full understanding of Fairbairn. My argument with relational psychoanalysis has centred on Fairbairn's account of the early development of the self and on the usefulness of his attempt to capture his "psychology of dynamic structure" in a diagram. I think that when his model is expanded to explicitly include the preconscious, and its similarity to Glover's ego-nuclei hypothesis is also recognised, we are approaching a model in which his assertion that unconscious phantasy should be replaced by an inner reality comprising the ego and its internal objects can begin to be appreciated as a possible road untravelled from the Controversial Discussions (Chapters Seven and Eight).

It is the use of this model—a model that has grown out of Fairbairn's often obscured engagement with his Scottish contemporaries—to help understand MPD/DID, film, relationality and the nature of unconscious phantasy that offers the hope of developing an ego-nuclei-based object relations theory. In 1943, when Fairbairn made his only intervention in the Controversial Discussions, there was an opportunity to develop an approach that was a synthesis of the classical and relational and is represented by the synthesis of Glover and Fairbairn. But, "history is written by the victors", which in this case were the Kleinians.

Fairbairn's early thoughts on dissociation and repression, the super-ego and libido theory were all important for the theory that he eventually developed, which does have a coherent place for instincts, relationships, ego-nuclei and object relations and can be seen as a precursor to the neuropsychoanalytic model of mind as it is being developed by Mark Solms and Jaak Panksepp (Chapter Nine).

I think that the Fairbairn-influenced model I have developed does provide a flexible and comprehensive tool for the analysis of many different phenomena that are of interest to psychoanalysis. One of these is an understanding of the so-called "imaginary companion", which clearly has some dissociative components to it but is usually not a product of trauma and abuse as so many of the other alters of MPD/DID are.

In his influential paper on the imaginary companion Sperling offers the following—where Rudyman is the imaginary companion of his patient Rudy:

> The phenomenon of Rudyman demonstrates how the ego-ideal formation is used as an ego defense. By creating the illusion of Rudyman, Rudy preserves the pride in his omnipotence, while at the same time yielding to the demands of the outside world. This prestage of his superego as well as the real superego which Rudy established in his sixth year, after the passing of his Oedipus complex, made it possible for him to bear disapproval and ridicule without losing his self-esteem and without becoming dependent on other people's opinions, because, in these cases, Rudyman (and later his superego) told him: "You are a good boy". (Sperling, 1954, p. 258)

I think that the phenomenon of splits occurring in the ego-ideal/ideal ego can account for this phenomenon and represents a creative use of defensive dissociation.

It is important, I think, to recognise the fundamental differences that there are between Fairbairn's approach and that of Freud and Klein in particular. Fairbairn's view is of a tragic universe rather than a guilty one. We do not arrive here burdened by an excessive and inordinate innate propensity for envy, guilt, and aggression—these are developed through our relationships with our parents and our families, our class and the society and culture we are born into. The process of development of our selves is, at best, one of a continuing synthesis of the experiences and relationships we have into a more and more sophisticated, refined and realistic understanding of the world and our place in it. But, through accidents of fate, our ability to produce more sophisticated syntheses of our experience and relationships can be interrupted, baulked, impeded, and although we continue to try to "make the best of what we have been made of" we may fall short. This is not, however, a foregone conclusion. A closely related and pressing area of investigation in an era of "repressive desublimation" (Marcuse, 1964, pp. 58–76) is an understanding of the ways in which we have all become "murderers and prostitutes" (Laing, 1967, p. 11) within an amoral globalised system of market production in which our personal lives and values, insofar as they can be adequately distinguished from the dominant relations of production, are a poor second to our value as insatiable consumers, or, orally dominated, pleasure-seeking infants, trying to compensate for the catastrophe of our failed object relationships.

Thinking *through* Fairbairn's theory has led me to recognise and develop connections between Fairbairn's theory and the theories of his Scottish contemporaries like Suttie and Glover, and to suggest amendments to Fairbairn's theory that make it a synthesis of classical and relational approaches and gives the lie to those who want to argue that Fairbairn was on his way to becoming a purely relational theorist.

Thinking through Fairbairn's theory has led me to consider development, dissociation, trauma and film in a different way under the influence of Fairbairn's idea that unconscious phantasy is better understood as the activity of a complex multi-agent endopsychic structure.

The developed model, based in a synthesis of the work of both Fairbairn and Glover, recommends itself to me as a potential starting place for the integration of both psychoanalytic and neuropsychoanalytic approaches to understanding the mind.

REFERENCES

Akhtar, S. (1999). The distinction between needs and wishes for psychoanalysis. *Journal of the American Psychoanalytic Association, 47*: 113–151.
Alford, C. F. (1988). *Narcissism: Socrates, the Frankfurt School and Psychoanalytic Theory*. London: YUP.
Bacal, H. A. (1987). British object-relations theorists and self psychologists. *International Journal of Psychoanalysis, 68*: 81–98.
Bainbridge, C. (2003). Reconstructing memories of masculine subjectivity in Memento: Narrative form and the fiction of the self. Twentieth International Conference on Literature and Psychoanalysis, Greenwich, London, UK, July 2003, 47–52. www.clas.ufl.edu/ipsa/2003/litpsych-paperjuly2003.html (last accessed 11 May 2017).
Balint, M., Foulkes, S. H., Sutherland, J. D., & Fairbairn, W. R. D. (1957). Notes and comments: Criticisms of Fairbairn's generalisations about object-relations. *The British Journal for the Philosophy of Science, 7(28)*: 323–338. In: D. E. Scharff & E. F. Birtles (Eds.), *From Instinct to Self: Selected Papers of W. R. D. Fairbairn, Volume I: Clinical and Theoretical Papers* (chapter 8). Northvale, NJ: Jason Aronson, 1994.
Bateson, G. (1972). *Steps to an Ecology of Mind*. London: Paladin.
Bateson, G. (1979). *Mind and Nature: A Necessary Unity*. London: E. P. Dutton.

Beattie, H. J. (2003). The repression and return of bad objects: W. R. D. Fairbairn and the historical roots of theory. *International Journal of Psychoanalysis*, *84*: 1171–1187.

Bhaskar, R. (1978). *The Possibility of Naturalism*. London: Routledge.

Bick, E. (1968). The experience of the *skin* in early object-relations. *International Journal of Psychoanalysis*, *49*: 484–486.

Bion, W. R. (1962). The psycho-analytic study of thinking. *International Journal of Psychoanalysis*, *43*: 306–310.

Birtles, E. F., & Scharff, D. E. (Eds.) (1994). *From Instinct to Self: Selected Papers of W. R. D. Fairbairn, Volume II: Applications and Early Contributions*. Northvale, NJ: Jason Aronson.

Bohleber, W. (2010). *Destructiveness, Intersubjectivity and Trauma*. London: Karnac.

Bowlby, J. (1960). Separation anxiety. *International Journal of Psychoanalysis*, *41*: 89–113.

Bowlby, J. (1988). Foreword. In: I. D. Suttie, *The Origins of Love and Hate*. London: Free Association.

Brenner, I. (2001). *Dissociation of Trauma: Theory, Phenomenology and Technique*. Madison, Connecticut: International Universities Press.

Brierley, M. (1944). Notes on metapsychology as process theory. *International Journal of Psychoanalysis*, *25*: 97–106.

Buckland, W. (2009). *Puzzle Films: Complex Storytelling in Contemporary Cinema*. London: Wiley.

Burgoyne, B. (Ed.) (2000). *Drawing the Soul: Schemas and Models in Psychoanalysis*. London: Karnac.

Celani, D. (2010). *Fairbairn's Object Relations Theory in the Clinical Setting*. New York: Columbia University Press.

Clarke, G. (1994). Notes towards an object-relations approach to cinema. *Free Associations*, *4*: 369–390.

Clarke, G. S. (2003a). L.A. confidential: Object relations and psychic growth. *British Journal of Psychotherapy*, *19*: 379–385.

Clarke, G. S. (2003b). Fairbairn and Macmurray: psychoanalytic studies and critical realism. *Journal of Critical Realism*, *2*(1): 7–36.

Clarke, G. S. (2005). The preconscious and psychic change in Fairbairn's model of mind. *International Journal of Psychoanalysis*, *86*: 61–77.

Clarke, G. S. (2006). *Personal Relations Theory, Fairbairn, Macmurray and Suttie*. London: Routledge.

Clarke, G. S. (2008a). The internal conversation: A personal relations theory perspective. *Journal of Critical Realism*, *7*(1): 57–82.

Clarke, G. S. (2008b). Notes on the origins of "Personal Relations Theory" in aspects of social thinking of the Scottish Enlightenment. *Psychoanalysis, Culture & Society*, *13*: 325–334.

Clarke, G. S. (2011). Suttie's influence on Fairbairn's object relations theory. *Journal of the American Psychoanalytic Association, 59*: 939–959.

Clarke, G. S. (2012). Failures of the "moral defence" in the films *Shutter Island, Inception and Memento*: Narcissism or schizoid personality disorder? *The International Journal of Psychoanalysis, 93*: 203–218.

Clarke, G. S., & Finnegan, P. (2010). On: Fairbairn and dynamic structure. *International Journal of Psychoanalysis, 91*: 1001–1002.

Clarke, G. S., & Finnegan, P. (2011). Fairbairn's thinking on dissociative identity disorder and the development of his mature theory. *Attachment: New Directions in Psychotherapy and Relational Psychoanalysis, 5*: 131–153.

Clarke, G. S., & Scharff, D. E. (Eds.) (2014). *Fairbairn and the Object Relations Tradition*. London: Karnac.

Davidson, D. (1982). Paradoxes of irrationality. In: R. Wollheim, J. Hopkins (Eds.), *Philosophical Essays on Freud* (pp. 289–305). Cambridge, MA: Cambridge University Press.

Davies, J. M. (1996). Linking the "Pre-Analytic" with the postclassical: Integration, dissociation, and the multiplicity of unconscious process. *Contemporary Psychoanalysis, 32*: 553–576.

Davies, J. M., & Frawley, M. G. (1992a). Dissociative processes and transference-countertransference paradigms in the psychoanalytically oriented treatment of adult survivors of childhood sexual abuse. *Psychoanalytic Dialogues, 2*: 5–36.

Davies, J. M., & Frawley, M. G. (1992b). Reply to Gabbard, Shengold and Grotstein. *Psychoanalytic Dialogues, 2*: 77–96.

Drever, J. (1922). *An Introduction to the Psychology of Education*. London: Edward Arnold and Co.

Ellenberger, H. F. (1970). *The Discovery of the Unconscious: The History and Evolution of Dynamic Psychiatry*. London: Basic.

Faimberg, H. (2007). A plea for a broader concept of Nachträglichkeit. *Psychoanalytic Quarterly, 76*: 1221–1240.

Fairbairn Project. A joint project between the National Library of Scotland and the University of Edinburgh to classify all of Fairbairn's extant papers including his library. Manuscript numbers refer to online catalogue at www.fairbairn.ac.uk.

Fairbairn, W. R. D. (1927). Notes on the religious phantasies of a female patient. In: *Psychoanalytic Studies of the Personality* (pp. 183–196). London: Tavistock, 1952.

Fairbairn, W. R. D. (1929a). The superego. In: E. F. Birtles & D. E. Scharff (Eds.), *From Instinct to Self: Selected Papers of W. R. D. Fairbairn, Volume II: Applications and Early Contributions* (pp. 80–114). Northvale, NJ: Jason Aronson, 1994.

Fairbairn, W. R. D. (1929b). Dissociation and repression. In: E. F. Birtles & D. E. Scharff (Eds.), *From Instinct to Self: Selected Papers of W. R. D. Fairbairn,*

Volume II: Applications and Early Contributions (pp. 13–79). Northvale, NJ: Jason Aronson, 1994.

Fairbairn, W. R. D. (1930). Libido theory re-evaluated. In: E. F. Birtles & D. E. Scharff (Eds.), *From Instinct to Self: Selected Papers of W. R. D. Fairbairn, Volume II: Applications and Early Contributions* (pp. 115–156). Northvale, NJ: Jason Aronson, 1994.

Fairbairn, W. R. D. (1931). Features in the analysis of a patient with a physical genital abnormality. In: *Psychoanalytic Studies of the Personality* (pp. 197–222). London: Tavistock, 1952.

Fairbairn, W. R. D. (1938a). Prolegomena to a psychology of art. *British Journal of Psychology, 28*: 288–303. In: E. F. Birtles & D. E. Scharff (Eds.), *From Instinct to Self: Selected Papers of W. R. D. Fairbairn, Volume II: Applications and Early Contributions* (pp. 381–396). Northvale, NJ: Jason Aronson, 1994.

Fairbairn, W. R. D. (1938b). The ultimate basis of aesthetic experience. *British Journal of Psychology, 29*: 167–181. In: E. F. Birtles & D. E. Scharff (Eds.), *From Instinct to Self: Selected Papers of W. R. D. Fairbairn, Volume II: Applications and Early Contributions* (pp. 397–409). Northvale, NJ: Jason Aronson, 1994.

Fairbairn, W. R. D. (1940). Schizoid factors in the personality. In: *Psychoanalytic Studies of the Personality* (pp. 3–27). London: Tavistock, 1952.

Fairbairn, W. R. D. (1941). A revised psychopathology of the psychoses and psychoneuroses. *International Journal of Psychoanalysis, 22*(3, 4): 250–279. In: *Psychoanalytic Studies of the Personality* (pp. 28–58). London: Tavistock, 1952.

Fairbairn, W. R. D. (1943a). The repression and the return of bad objects (with special reference to the "war neuroses"). *British Journal of Medical Psychology, 19*: 327–341. In: *Psychoanalytic Studies of the Personality* (pp. 59–81). London: Tavistock, 1952.

Fairbairn, W. R. D. (1943b). Phantasy and inner reality (untitled contribution to the "Controversial Discussions". Read by Dr Edward Glover at the British Psychoanalytical Society on 17 February 1943). In: E. F. Birtles & D. E. Scharff (Eds.), *From Instinct to Self: Selected Papers of W. R. D. Fairbairn, Volume II: Applications and Early Contributions* (pp. 293–294). Northvale, NJ: Jason Aronson, 1994.

Fairbairn, W. R. D. (1944). Endopsychic structure considered in terms of object-relationships. *International Journal of Psychoanalysis, 25*: 70–92. In: *Psychoanalytic Studies of the Personality* (pp. 82–136). London: Tavistock, 1952.

Fairbairn, W. R. D. (1946). Object-relationships and dynamic structure. *International Journal of Psychoanalysis, 27*: 30–37. In: *Psychoanalytic Studies of the Personality* (pp. 137–151). London: Tavistock, 1952.

Fairbairn, W. R. D. (1949). Steps in the development of an object-relations theory of the personality. In: *Psychoanalytic Studies of the Personality* (pp. 152–161). London: Tavistock, 1952.

Fairbairn, W. R. D. (1952). *Psychoanalytic Studies of the Personality.* London: Tavistock.

Fairbairn, W. R. D. (1953). Critical notice: *Psychoanalytic Explorations in Art* by Ernst Kris (1952). *British Journal of Medical Psychology*, 26: 164–169. In: E. F. Birtles & D. E. Scharff (Eds.), *From Instinct to Self: Selected Papers of W. R. D. Fairbairn, Volume II: Applications and Early Contributions* (pp. 423–432). Northvale, NJ: Jason Aronson, 1994.

Fairbairn, W. R. D. (1954). Observations on the nature of hysterical states. *British Journal of Medical Psychology*, 27(3): 105–125. In: D. E. Scharff & E. F. Birtles (Eds.), *From Instinct to Self: Selected Papers of W. R. D. Fairbairn, Volume I: Clinical and Theoretical Papers* (pp. 13–40). Northvale, NJ: Jason Aronson, 1994.

Fairbairn, W. R. D. (1956). A critical evaluation of certain basic psycho-analytic conceptions. *British Journal for the Philosophy of Science,* 7 (25): 49–60. In: D. E. Scharff & E. F. Birtles (Eds.), *From Instinct to Self: Selected Papers of W. R. D. Fairbairn, Volume I: Clinical and Theoretical Papers* (Chapter 7). London: Jason Aronson, 1994.

Fairbairn, W. R. D. (1958). On the nature and aims of psycho-analytical treatment. *International Journal of Psychoanalysis*, 39(5): 374–385. In: D. E. Scharff & E. F. Birtles (Eds.), *From Instinct to Self: Selected Papers of W. R. D. Fairbairn, Volume I: Clinical and Theoretical Papers* (pp. 74–92). Northvale, NJ: Jason Aronson, 1994.

Fairbairn, W. R. D. (1959). Selected contributions to psycho-analysis, by John Rickman. International Psycho-Analytical Library, No. 52. *International Journal of Psychoanalysis*, 40: 341–342.

Fairbairn, W. R. D. (1963). Synopsis of an object-relations theory of the personality. *International Journal of Psychoanalysis*, 44: 224–225. In: D. E. Scharff & E. F. Birtles (Eds.), *From Instinct to Self: Selected Papers of W. R. D. Fairbairn, Volume I: Clinical and Theoretical Papers* (pp. 155–156). Northvale, NJ: Jason Aronson, 1994.

Ferenczi, S. (1928). The elasticity of psycho-analytical technique. In *Final Contributions to the Problems and Methods of Psycho-analysis*. London: Karnac, 1955.

Ferenczi, S. (1949). Confusion of the tongues between the adults and the child—(The language of tenderness and passion.). *International Journal of Psychoanalysis, 30:* 225–230.

Ferenczi, S., Simmel, E., Abraham, K., Jones, E., & Freud, S. (1920). *On Psychoanalysis and the War Neuroses.* London: International Psychoanalytic Press.

Finnegan, P., & Clarke, G. S. (2010). A Fairbairnian perspective on failure in the analysis of the Wolf Man. Unpublished paper presented at the fifth joint international conference Edinburgh 6–8 Aug 2010. Failure: Psychoanalytic Explorations.

Finnegan, P., & Clarke, G. S. (2012). Evelyn's PhD in Wellness—A Fairbairnian understanding of the therapeutic relationship with a woman with dissociative identity disorder. *ATTACHMENT: New Directions in Psychotherapy and Relational Psychoanalysis*, 6: 50–68.

Freud, S. (1893a). On the psychical mechanism of hysterical phenomena. S. E., 2. London: Hogarth.

Freud, S. (1905d). *Three Essays on the Theory of Sexuality.* S. E., 7. London: Hogarth.

Freud, S. (1914c). On narcissism: An introduction. S. E., 4: 30–59. London: Hogarth.

Freud, S. (1914d). On the history of the psycho-analytic movement. S. E., 14. London: Hogarth.

Freud, S. (1915e). The unconscious. S. E., 14. London: Hogarth.

Freud, S. (1920g). *Beyond the Pleasure Principle.* S. E., 18. London: Hogarth.

Freud, S. (1923b). *The Ego and the Id.* S. E., 19. London: Hogarth.

Freud, S., & Breuer, J. (1895d). *Studies on Hysteria.* S. E., 2. London: Hogarth. [Reprinted London: Penguin Books, 2004].

Gardener, H. (1983). *Frames of Mind: The Theory of Multiple Intelligences.* London: Basic.

Gerson, G. (2004). Object relations psychoanalysis as political theory. *Political Psychology*, 25(5): 769–794.

Gerson, G. (2009). Culture and ideology in Ian Suttie's theory of mind. *History of Psychology*, 12(1): 19–40.

Glover, E. (1932). A psycho-analytic approach to the classification of mental disorders. *British Journal of Psychiatry*, 78: 819–842.

Glover, E. (1938). The concept of dissociation. *International Journal of Psychoanalysis*, Vol XXIV, pts 1–2, 1943.

Glover, E. (1956). *On the Early Development of Mind.* London: Imago.

Glover, E. (1968). *The Birth of the Ego.* London: George Allan and Unwin.

Greenberg, J. R., & Mitchell, S. A. (1983). *Object Relations in Psychoanalytic Theory.* London: Harvard University Press.

Grotstein, J. S. (1982). Newer perspectives in object relations theory. *Contemporary Psychoanalysis*, 18: 43–91.

Grotstein, J. S. (1991). [Review.] Hughes, J. M., *Reshaping the Psychoanalytic Domain: The Work of Melanie Klein, W. R. D. Fairbairn, and D. W. Winnicott. Psychoanalytic Quarterly*, 60: 136–140.

Grotstein, J. S. (1992). Commentary on "Dissociative Processes and Transference-Countertransference Paradigms ..." by Jody Messler Davies & Mary Gail Frawley. *Psychoanalytic Dialogues*, 2: 61–76.

Grotstein, J. S. (1994a). Endopsychic structure and the cartography of the inner world: Six endopsychic characters in search of an author. In: J. S. Grotstein & D. B. Rinsley (Eds.), *Fairbairn and the Origins of Object Relations Theory* (pp. 174–194). New York: Guilford.

Grotstein, J. S. (1994b). Notes on Fairbairn's metapsychology. In: J. S. Grotstein & D. B. Rinsley (Eds.), *Fairbairn and the Origins of Object Relations Theory* (pp. 112–142). New York: Guilford.

Grotstein, J. S. (1998). A comparison of Fairbairn's endopsychic structure and Klein's internal world. In: N. J. Skolnick & D. E. Scharff (Eds.), *Fairbairn Then and Now* (pp. 71–98). London: Analytic Press.

Guntrip, H. (1971). *Psychoanalytic Theory, Therapy and the Self*. New York: Basic.

Harrow, J. A. (1998). The Scottish connection—Suttie-Fairbairn-Sutherland: A quiet revolution. In: Skolnich & Scharff (Eds.), *Fairbairn, Then and Now* (pp. 3–16). London: The Analytic Press.

Hart, B. (1926). The concept of dissociation. *British Journal of Medical Psychology*, 6(4): 241–263.

Hoffman, M. (2004). From enemy combatant to strange bedfellows. *Psychoanalytic Dialogues*, 14: 769–804.

Hughes, J. M. (1989). *Reshaping the Psychoanalytic Domain: The Work of Melanie Klein, W. R. D. Fairbairn, and D. W. Winnicott*. London: University of California Press. [reprinted 1990].

Kernberg, O. (1981). *Internal World and External Reality*. London: Jason Aronson.

Kernberg, O. (1984). *Object Relations and Clinical Psychoanalysis*. London: Jason Aronson.

King, P., & Steiner, R. (1991). *The Freud–Klein Controversies 1941–45*. New Library of Psychoanalysis, 11: 1–942. London and New York: Tavistock/Routledge.

Kirkwood, C. (2005). The persons-in-relation perspective. In: J. S. Scharff & D. E. Scharff (Eds.), *The Legacy of Fairbairn and Sutherland* (pp. 19–38). London: Routledge.

Klein, A. (2001). Everything you wanted to know about *Memento*, 28 June 2001. www.salon.com/2001/06/28/memento_analysis/ (last accessed 11 May 2017).

Klein, M. (1946). Notes on some schizoid mechanisms. *International Journal of Psychoanalysis*, 27: 99–110.

Kohon, G. (Ed.) (1986). *The British School of Psychoanalysis: The Independent Tradition*. London: Free Association.

Lacan, J. (1988). *The Seminar of Jacques Lacan, Book II*. London and New York: W. W. Norton.

Laing, R. D. (1965). *The Divided Self*. London: Pelican.

Laing, R. D. (1967). *The Politics of Experience*. London: Penguin.

Laplanche, J., & Pontalis, J. B. (1973). *The Language of Psychoanalysis*. London: The Hogarth Press and the Institute of Psycho-Analysis.

MacGregor, M. W. (1996). Multiple personality disorder: Etiology, treatment, and treatment techniques from a psychodynamic perspective. Psychoanalytic Psychology, 13: 389–402.

Macmurray, J. (1957). *The Self as Agent*. London: Faber and Faber.

Macmurray, J. (1961). *Persons in Relation*. London: Faber and Faber.

Marcuse, H. (1964). *One-Dimensional Man*. Boston: Beacon.

Migone, P. (1994). The problem of "real" trauma and the future of psychoanalysis. *International Forum for Psychoanalysis*, 3: 89–95.

Miller, G. (2007). A wall of ideas: The "taboo on tenderness" in theory and culture. *New Literary History*, 38(4): 667–681.

Miller, G. (2008a). Why Scottish personal relations theory matters ... politically. *Scottish Affairs*, 62: 47–62.

Miller, G. (2008b). Scottish psychoanalysis: A rational religion. *Journal of the History of the Behavioral Sciences*, 44(1): 38–59.

Mills, J. (2005). A critique of relational psychoanalysis. *Psychoanalytic Psychology*, 22: 155–188.

Mitchell, S. A. (1994). The origin and nature of the "object" in the theories of Klein and Fairbairn. In: J. S. Grotstein & D. B. Rinsley (Eds.), *Fairbairn and the Origins of Object Relations* (pp. 66–87, Chapter 5). London: Free Association.

Mitchell, S. A. (2000). *Relationality: From Attachment to Intersubjectivity*. London: Routledge.

Nietzsche, F. (1968). Expeditions of an untimely man, 51. In: R. J. Hollingdale (Trans.), *Twilight of the Idols* [1889] (p. 104).

Noir Network. (2011). Précis of 'Memento: An analysis of the presented amnesia'. (Elizabeth Woodruff, 2009). http://noirnetwork.blogspot.co.uk/2011/05/annotated-bibliography.html (last accessed 11 May 2017).

Ogden, T. (2002). A new reading of the origins of object-relations theory. *International Journal of Psychoanalysis*, 83: 767–782.

Ogden, T. H. (2010a). Why read Fairbairn? *International Journal of Psychoanalysis*, 91: 101–118.

Ogden, T. H. (2010b). On: The comments of Dr. Graham Clarke and Dr. Paul Finnegan. *The International Journal of Psychoanalysis*, 91: 1002–1003.

Ogden, T. H. (2011). Reading Susan Isaacs: Toward a radically revised theory of thinking. *The International Journal of Psychoanalysis*, 92: 925–942.

Padel, J. (1985). Ego in current thinking. *International Review of Psycho-Analysis*, 12: 273–283.

Padel, J. (1991). Fairbairn's thought on the relationship of inner and outer worlds. *Free Associations*, 2(24): 589–615.

Palmer, S. (2015). The Controversial Discussions in the XXIst century. PEP-Web video.
Panksepp, J. (2012). Subcortical sources of our cross-species emotional feelings and psychiatric implications. http://emotionresearcher.com/the-emotional-brain/panksepp (last accessed 1 August 2016).
Panksepp, J. (2015). Human brain evolution, video of presentation at Arnold Pfeffer Center for Neuropsychoanalysis of the New York Psychoanalytic Institute, 2 May. https://npsa-association.org/videos/human-brain-evolution-jaak-panksepp/
Panksepp, J., & Panksepp, J. (2013). Towards a cross-species understanding of empathy. www.ncbi.nlm.nih.gov/pmc/articles/PMC3839944/ (last accessed 11 May 2017).
Pereira, F., & Scharff, D. (Eds.) (1989). *Fairbairn and Relational Theory*. London: Jason Aronson. [reprinted 2002].
Rank, O., & Ferenczi, S. (1925). *The Development of Psychoanalysis*. New York: Nervous and Mental Disease Publishing Company.
Rayner, E. (1990). *The Independent Mind in British Psychoanalysis*. London: Free Association.
Read, H. (1951). Psycho-Analysis and the problem of aesthetic value. *The International Journal of Psychoanalysis, 32*: 73–82.
Rickman, J. (1957). X: On the nature of ugliness and the creative impulse (Marginalia Psychoanalytica. II) (1940). *The International Psycho-Analytical Library*, www.pep-web.org.serlib0.essex.ac.uk/search.php?volume=52&journal=ipl,%2068–89.
Rivers, W. H. R. (1919). The repression of war experience. *Lancet XCVI*, 513–533.
Roazen, P. (2000). *Edward Glover and the Struggle over Klein*. New York: Other Press.
Robbins, M. (1994). A Fairbairnian Object Relations Perspective on Self Psychology. In: J. S. Grotstein & D. B. Rinsley (Eds.), *Fairbairn and the origins of object relations*. London: Free Association.
Rubens, R. L. (1984). The meaning of structure in Fairbairn. *International Review of Psycho-Analysis, 11*: 429–440.
Rubens, R. L. (1996). Review essay: The unique origins of Fairbairn's theories. *Psychoanalytic Dialogues, 6*(3): 413–435.
Rudnytsky, P. L. (1992). A psychoanalytic weltanshauung. *Psychoanalytic Review, 79*: 289–305.
Rutherford, A. (2003). Cinema and embodied affect. http://sensesofcinema.com/2003/feature-articles/embodied_affect/ (last accessed 27 May 2016).
Scharff, D. E., & Birtles, E. F. (1997). From instinct to self: The evolution and implications of W. R. D. Fairbairn's theory of object relations. *International Journal of Psychoanalysis, 78*(6): 1085–1103.

Segal, H. (1999). Psychoanalysis, dreams, history. http://psychoanalysis.org.uk/articles/psychoanalysis-dreams-history-an-interview-with-hanna-segal-daniel-pick-and-lyndal-roper

Skolnick, N. (2006). What's a good object to do. *Psychoanalytic Dialogues*, 16: 1–27.

Skolnick, N. J. (1998). The good the bad and the ambivalent. In: N. J. Skolnick & D. E. Scharff (Eds.), *Fairbairn Then and Now* (Chapter 8). Hillsdale, NJ: Analytic Press.

Skolnick, N. J., & Scharff, D. E. (Eds.) (1998). *Fairbairn Then and Now*. Hillsdale, NJ: Analytic Press.

Solms, M. (2013). The conscious Id. *Neuropsychoanalysis*, 15(1): 5–19.

Sperling, O. E. (1954). An imaginary companion, representing a prestage of the superego. *The Psychoanalytic Study of the Child*, 9: 252–258.

Starfield, P. (2002). Memento: In search of remembrance. *Cinema and Brain Journal of Neuro-Aesthetic Theory*, 2. www.artbrain.org/memento-in-search-of-remembrance/ (last accessed 11 May 2017).

Stout, G. F. (1927). *The Groundwork of Psychology*. London: W.B. Clive.

Summers, F. (1994). *Object Relations Theories and Psychopathology*. London: Routledge.

Sutherland, J. D. (1989). *Fairbairn's Journey into the Interior*. London: Free Association.

Suttie, I. D. (1935). *The Origins of Love and Hate*. London: Kegan Paul, Trench Tubner and Co.

Swift, J. (1729). *A Modest Proposal*. [Reprinted London: Penguin Classics, 2015].

Symington, N. (1986). *The Analytic Experience*. London: Free Association.

Tolmacz, R. (2006). Concern: A comparative look. *Psychoanalytic Psychology*, 23: 143–158.

Van der Hart, O., & Steele, K. (1997). Time distortions in dissociative identity disorder: Janetian concepts and treatment. *Dissociation*, 10(2): 91–103. www.trauma-pages.com/a/vdhart-97.php (last accessed 15 October 2016).

Wallerstein, R. S. (1988). One psychoanalysis or many. *International Journal of Psychoanalysis*, 69: 5–21.

Walsh, M. N. (1973). The scientific works of Edward Glover. *The International Journal of Psychoanalysis*, 54: 95–102.

Winnicott, D. W. (1953). Transitional objects and transitional phenomenon—A study of the first not-me possession. *International Journal of Psychoanalysis*, 34: 89–97.

Winnicott, D. W. (1975). Through paediatrics to psycho-analysis: The international psycho-analytical library, *100*: 1–325. London: The Hogarth Press.

Winnicott, D. W., & Khan, M. R. (1953). Psychoanalytic studies of the personality: By W. Ronald D. Fairbairn. *International Journal of Psychoanalysis, 34*: 329–333.

Žižek, S. (2015). Slavoj Žižek: Is Hegel dead—or are we dead in the eyes of Hegel? A Hegelian view of the present age. www.youtube.com/watch?v=rHP1OwivAL0 (last accessed 2 January 2017).

INDEX

affect, 183. *See also* instinct
   impulses, 196
   object relationship without, 183
   splitting, 195–196
affective relationship between child and parents, 192
aggression, 10–11
   Fairbairn's Freudian views on, 7–8
Akhtar, S., 6
Alford, C. F., 114
alter personalities, 69–70, 73, 74, 87. *See also* dissociative identity disorder (DID)
   "Christine", 81, 87
   communication between, 83
   dissociated, 89–90
   ego, 83–84, 100
   as endopsychic structures, 89
   "father", 77–78
   "Georgina", 78–79, 80, 84, 85
   "Geraldine", 82, 84, 85
   "Helen", 80, 87
   ideal ego alters, 88
   identification as aspect of psychic growth, 83
   libidinal and antilibidinal ego, 83, 85, 87, 89
   "Linda", 80, 81, 87
   mapping of, 71
   Martha, 76–77, 83, 87
   "Mary", 81, 87
   "mother", 79, 80, 87
   Mrs R, 79, 80, 84, 87
   paternal seduction, 79
   relationships between, 73, 86
   "Robert", 80, 84, 87
   "Sammy Jankis", 108
   "Sandra", 81, 87
   "Sara", 78, 81, 84
   sexual abuse possibility, 78
   taking control of consciousness, 89
   in transferences and countertransferences prior to presentation, 88
   to understand, 83
   of young adults, 87

226   INDEX

anterograde amnesia, 107
antilibidinal ego alters, 89, 161
antilibidinal self, 122
anxiety, separation, 87–88
appetitive tendencies, 188
    vs. reactive tendencies, 189
attachment to internalised bad
    objects, 110

Bacal, H. A., 6
bad internalised object, 104, 105, 106
    attachment to, 110
    guilt as defence against
        release of, 98
    libidinal projection, 101
badness, unconditional, 111
Bainbridge, C., 107, 108
Balint, M., 156
Bateson, G., 152, 155
Beattie, H. J., 6
Bick, E., 110
Bion, W. R., 159
Birtles, E. F., 7, 10, 16, 26, 38, 68, 131,
    134, 135, 160, 166, 184
Bohleber, W., 137
Bowlby, J., xxv, 6, 173
    and Suttie, 8
Brenner, I., 60
    "self-state" dreams, 60–61
Breuer, J., 52
Brierley, M., xxvii
British Psychoanalytic Society (BPS), 4
Buckland, W., 119
Burgoyne, B., xxiv

Celani, D., 169
central self, 98
challenges to Freud's theory, 133
Clarke, G. S., xxvi, xxvii, xxix, 8, 23, 31,
    32, 44, 51, 65, 82, 89, 114, 120,
    134, 151, 152, 153, 175
Collins, M., 187
communication between alters, 83
conception of mental levels, 189
concept of "phantasy", 59
conscious bodily ego, 193

conscious Id, 193
consciousness
    alters taking control of, 89
    moving in levels of, 104
Controversial Discussions, 59–60, 211.
    See also dissociative identity
    disorder (DID)

Davidson, D., 53
Davies, J. M., 24, 90, 133, 165, 176,
    177, 178, 179–180
death camp imagery, 112
death instinct, 14–15, 186
defense, dissociation as, 90
defensive vertical splitting of ego, 90
deferred action, 136–137. *See also*
    puzzle films
delusional role, psychotherapeutic
    approach to act out, 100
disillusion, 15, 114. *See also*
    moral defence
    consequences for internal dynamics
        of child, 115
    mother's attempts to disillusion the
        child, 17, 115
dissociation, 52, 53–55, 126, 133, 184.
    See also dissociative identity
    disorder (DID)
    alters, 89–90
    and/or repression, 161–162
    as defence, 90
    as preservation of internal world,
        90–91
dissociative identity disorder (DID),
    51, 71–72, 73, 210. *See also*
    dissociation
    alter personalities, 69–70
    clinical case, 56–58
    concept of "phantasy", 59
    Controversial Discussions, 59–60
    dynamic structure, 61–62
    endopsychic structure, 60–61, 67
    Fairbairnian perspective on MPD,
        68–71
    Fairbairn's original diagram, 64
    Fairbairn's revision of Freud, 64–68

Fairbairn's thinking about multiple personality, 52–53
functioning structural constellations, 56
hysterical states, 62–64
impulses, 60
internal objects as composite structures, 68
mature model, 58
modification to Fairbairn's model of inner reality, 65
narcissism, 63
object relations, 61, 63
Padel's model, 65
personality clusters, 69
personification, 56–57
preconscious, 66
repression, 52, 53–55
schizoid factors, 58–59
"self-state" dreams, 60–61
splitting of ego, 62, 69
superego, 55–56
synopsis of development of Fairbairn's views, 61–62
theory of dreams, 60
topographical theory, 65, 67
trauma-induced vertical splitting, 70
tripartite division of mind, 56
dissociative identity disorder patient Evelyn, 74
alter Christine in, 81, 87
alter father in, 77–78
alter Georgina in, 78–79, 80, 84, 85
alter Geraldine in, 82, 84, 85
alter Helen in, 80, 87
alter Linda in, 80, 81, 87
alter Martha in, 76–77, 83, 87
alter Mary in, 81, 87
alter mother in, 79, 80, 87
alter Mrs R in, 79, 80, 84, 87
alter Robert in, 80, 84, 87
alter Sandra in, 81, 87
alter Sara in, 78, 81, 84
childhood of, 74
marital difficulties of, 74
oscillating transferences, 75
paternal seduction, 79
progress in, 92
rage of, 75, 76–77
reconciliation with daughter, 93
re-enactment of first two years of life, 76
sexual abuse possibility, 78
symptoms in, 87
therapy session, 74–75
distortions in time, 134. *See also* puzzle films
based upon dissociation, 135
deferred action, 136–137
realization, 135
trauma, 137–138
dream
as depiction of self states in internal world, 109
self-state, 60–61
space sharing, 103, 104–105
theory of, 60
wish-fulfilling aspects of, 109
Drever, J., 187
theory of instincts, 187–188
dualism of life and death instincts, 186
dynamic structures, 61–62, 204. *See also* dissociative identity disorder (DID)
and Glover's ego-nuclei-based model, 161
trauma-induced vertical splitting of, 70

early infant needs, 209
early oral phase and pre-ambivalence, 198
ego, 38
conscious bodily ego, 193
Conscious Id, 193
Fairbairn and Freud view of, 193
functions of, 195
Libido as function of, 194
and object splitting, 44
pristine, 192–195
splitting of, 62, 69, 195

ego-ideal, 16, 113, 160
ego-nuclei, xxix, 27, 31, 38, 197–200
　Abraham's theory of erogenous zones, 197, 199
　developmental theory of, 31
　early oral phase and pre-ambivalence, 198
　hypothesis, 197–200
　infantile dependence to mature dependence, 200
　libidinal primacies and, 36
Eliot, T. S., 125
Ellenberger, H. F., 69
embodied affect in film theory, 143. *See also* puzzle films
endopsychic model of inner reality, 166, 168
　rejection by Mitchell, 150
endopsychic structure, 60–61, 67, 91–92. *See also* dissociative identity disorder (DID)
　development of, 45, 68
　diagram of, 51
　duplication of, 69, 71
　model of, 24, 121, 149, 167–168
　trauma-induced vertical splitting and duplication of, 71
　vertical splitting of, 86
environment mother, 18–19
erogenous zones, theory of, 197, 199
essential dualism of Freud's instinct theory, 185
externalised internal object relations, 73

Faimberg, H., 136–137
Fairbairn-based object relations approach, 120. *See also* puzzle films
　antilibidinal self, 122
　dramatic narrative on film, 124
　Fairbairn's original diagram, 122
　model of endopsychic structure, 121
　over- and under-symbolisation in cinema, 123

　psychoanalytic approach to dreams, 123
　relationship between phantasy and desire, 123–124
　theory of art, 123
Fairbairn-influenced model, 211
Fairbairn's model, alternative version of, 82. *See* dissociative identity disorder patient Evelyn; Fairbairn's model of endopsychic structure
　alter and ego, 83–84
　alters in transferences and countertransferences prior to presentation, 88
　alters of young adults, 87
　alters taking control of consciousness, 89
　dissociated alters, 89–90
　dissociation as defence, 90
　endopsychic structure, 89, 91–92
　ideal ego alters, 88
　libidinal and antilibidinal ego alters, 83, 85, 87, 89
　object relations, 83
　psychic death, 85
　relationship between alters, 86
　separation anxiety, 87–88
　to understand alters, 83
　vertical split, 86, 91
Fairbairn's model of endopsychic structure, xxvii, 73
　alter identification as aspect of psychic growth, 83
　alter personalities, 73
　comments on question of instincts vs. object relationships, 38–39
　communication between alters, 83
　critique of libido theory, 23
　development of endopsychic structure, 45, 167–168
　development of object-relationships, 27
　dissociation, 184
　early splitting of ego and object, 44

INDEX   229

endopsychic model of inner reality, 65, 166, 168
endopsychic structure, 24, 68, 121
fundamental assumption, 24–25
Grotstein's, 91–92
internalization, 159
libidinal and antilibidinal alters, 82
modification to model of inner reality, 65
psychic growth, 73
relationships between alter personalities, 73
transference-countertransference dynamics of externalised internal object relations, 73
Fairbairn's object relations theory, 97. *See also* Fairbairn's psychology of dynamic structure
-based psychology of dynamic structure, 165, 180
Fairbairn and relational thinking, 166–171
JMDavies' clinical example, 178–180
JMDavies' linking of pre-analytic with post-classical, 176–178
object relations model, 170
self states and self-object states, 169
Fairbairn's original diagram, 64
Fairbairn's post-1940 theory vs. Suttie's theory, 9
Fairbairn's psychology of dynamic structure, 147, 162–163, 171. *See also* affect; ego; instinct; interpretation of Fairbairn's "psychology of dynamic structure"; Libido theory re-evaluated
acceptable object relationships, 173
antilibidinal ego, 161
component instinct-based model, 175–176
dissociation and/or repression, 161–162
dynamic structures and Glover's ego-nuclei-based model, 161

endopsychic structure model, 149
Fairbairn's theory, 150–151
first oral phase, 171–172
good object in Fairbairn's theory, 153–156
impulses and object relationships, 149
internal objects and ego-structures, 160–161
internalised pre-ambivalent object, 154–155
Mitchell's view of Fairbairn's theory, 148
neuroses, 174
post-1943 basic endopsychic model rejection by Mitchell, 150
psychic change in Fairbairn's model, 175
second oral phase, 172–176
self and society, 151–153
super-ego, 174
theory of potential powers, 152
unconscious phantasy, 156–160
underlying assumptions, 171
Fairbairn, W. R. D., xxv, 84, 85, 90, 101, 108, 109, 110, 112, 113, 117, 156, 187. *See also* dissociative identity disorder (DID)
object relations approach to puzzle films, 120–125
comparison of Suttie's with Fairbairn's post-1940 theory, 9
contemporaries, xxv, 53
early infant needs, 209
and Freud, 190–191
Freud's structural model, 60, 61
and Freud's view of ego, 193
and Glover, 133–134, 209–210
Glover and ego-nuclei, 27
infantile dependence to mature dependence, 200
Klein on papers by, 30–31
lack of reference to Suttie, 7
libidinal primacies and ego-nuclei, 36
mature position on aggression, 11

maturity, xxxi
on MPD, 68–71
about multiple personality, 52–53
nature of object relationships characteristic, 37
object relationship development, 32
object relations theory, xxix, 7, 24, 25
about Oedipus situation, 12
Oedipus situation, 66, 200–201
original diagram, xxvii, 64, 122
perspective on MPD, 68–71
phantasy, 120
preconscious, 66
principle of optimal synthesis, 130
psychoanalytic approach to dreams, 123
relationship between Glover and, 23
representation of object relationship, 42
revision of Freud, 64–68
schizoid position, 30
structural theory, 7
Suttie and, 6–9
theories of, xxvi–xxvii, xxviii, xxix, xxx, 32, 150–151, 209
theory of art, 123
theory of dreams, 60
on theory of erotogenic zones, 199
therapeutic relationship with DID woman, 73
transitional stage in Fairbairn's theory, 32
unconscious phantasy and inner reality, 26
viewpoint and Mitchell's response, 154–155
Ferenczi, S., 5, 114, 133, 136
film, xxviii–xxix
Finnegan, P., xxvii, 24, 73, 134, 167
forgetting as to expiate guilt, 112
Foulkes, S. H., 156
Freud, A., 59
Freud, S., 52, 56, 101, 113
    challenges to theory of, 133
    dualism of instinct theory, 185
    dualism of life and death instincts, 186
    ego, 193
    Fairbairn and, 190
    Fairbairn's revision of, 64–68
    and Fairbairn view of ego, 193
    functional fusion, 191
    functioning structural constellations, 56
    hysteria, rehabilitation, 132
    hysterical phenomena, 63
    impulses, 60
    libido theory, 185
    narcissism, 63
    structural model, 60, 61
    super-ego, 98
    topographical theory, 65, 67
    topographic categories, 82, 114
    tripartite division of mind, 56

Gerson, G., 7
Glover, E., xxv, 133, 151
    developmentally based schema for mental disorder classification, 32
    developmental theory of ego-nuclei, 31
    ego-nuclei model, xxvii, 27, 38, 197–200
    Fairbairn and, 133–134, 209–210
    libidinal primacies and ego-nuclei, 36
    object relations approach and component-instinct based approach, 25
    popularity, 25
    "primary functional phase", 24–25
    relationship between Fairbairn and, 23
    theory of ego-nuclei, 209
    transitional states, 32, 40
good object
    in Fairbairn's theory, 153–156
    normal development of, 111
Greenberg, J. R., xxix, 7, 114, 147, 148

Grotstein, J. S., 3, 91, 92, 158–159
guilt
    as defence against release of bad objects, 98
    forgetting as to expiate, 112
    as main dynamic, 112
    as resistance in psychotherapy, 99
Guntrip, H., 3

haptonomy, 48
Harrow, J. A., 3
Hart, B., 53
Hart, Van der, 124, 134, 135
Hinshelwood, 157
Hoffman, M., 6
Hughes, J. M., 7
Hutchinson, 107, 108
hysteria, 62–64. *See also* dissociative identity disorder (DID)
    amnesia, 108, 109
    as defence, 109
    psychopathological defence, 98
    states, 62–64
    to understand psychopathology, 108
hysterics, advanced, 68, 161

Ideal ego alters, 88
ideal object, 111
ideal self, preconscious, 98
impulses, 60, 196
    death, 186
    Drever's theory of instincts, 187–188
    fusion phenomena, 188
    instinctive tendencies, 187
    problems of personality, 196
Inception, the film, 103, 112. *See also* Memento, the film; moral defence; Shutter Island, the film
    bad internalised object, 104, 105, 106
    disillusion in, 115
    libidinal cathexis, 105
    moving in levels of consciousness, 104
    progressive slowing time in dreamtime, 104
    projection based on memory, 105
    sharing subconscious dream spaces, 103, 104–105
    space and time, 105–106
    story of, 104, 105
    to work on someone's mind, 103
infantile dependence to mature dependence, 200
inner reality, modification to Fairbairn's model of, 65
instinct, 183. *See also* affect; Libido theory re-evaluated
    aggression, 191
    -based model, 175–176
    death, 186
    Drever's theory of instincts, 187–188
    dualism of, 186
    fundamental, 185
    fusion phenomena, 188
    impulses, 196
    instinctive tendencies, 187
    sex, 191
    splitting, 195–196
instinctive tendencies, 187
internal dynamics of child, consequences for, 115
internal objects, 157
    as composite structures, 68
    and ego-structures, 160–161
    good object as defence, 110
    libidinal bad object projection, 101
    pre-ambivalent object, 154–155
International Journal of Psycho-Analysis (IJPA), 27
interpretation of Fairbairn's "psychology of dynamic structure", xxv
    film, xxviii–xxix
    instinct, affect, and neuropsychoanalysis, xxx–xxxii
    multiple personality disorder, xxvii–xxviii

232   INDEX

primitive affect-driven searches for adequate objects, xxxi–xxxii
relationality, xxix–xxx
Scottish contemporaries, xxvii
Isaacs, S., xx, xxii, 59, 60, 120, 121, 157, 158

Jacket, The, 126, 127, 138–142. *See also* puzzle films
analysis of, 138–142
lead character, 138
story and interpretation, 139–141
subplot, 140
time travel, 138
trajectory of, 141
Janet, P., 62
concept of time and feelings of reality, 134
extreme manifestations as dissociation phenomena, 61
hysterical states, 62
manifesting dissociative phenomena, 59
Jody Messler Davies (JMD), 165. *See also* Fairbairn's psychology of dynamic structure
characterisation of classical models, 176–178
clinical example, 178–180
linking of pre-analytic with post-classical, 176–178

Kernberg, O., 7
Khan, M. R., 147, 154, 168
King, P., 26, 59, 60, 120
Kirkwood, C., 3
Klein, A., 5, 107, 108, 154, 155
remarks on recent papers by Fairbairn, 30–31
splitting, 159
unconscious phantasy, 121
Klein, M., xvii, xxi, xxii, xxv, xxvii, 59, 108
Kohon, G., 4

Lacan, J., 113, 159, 212
Laing, R. D., 212

Laplanche, J., 123–124, 132, 136, 171–172
libidinal and antilibidinal alters, 82, 83, 85, 87
libidinal cathexis, 105
libidinal ego alters, 89
libidinal primacies and ego-nuclei, 36
Libido theory, 9–10, 185
criticisms of, 23, 185
libido as function of ago, 194
Libido theory re-evaluated, 184. *See also* instinct
affective relationship between child and parents, 192
appetitive tendencies, 188
appetitive vs. reactive tendencies, 189
conception of mental levels, 189
criticisms of libido theory, 185
Drever's theory of instincts, 187–188
dualism of life and death instincts, 186
essential dualism of Freud's instinct theory, 185
Fairbairn and Freud, 190–191
functional fusion, 191
reactive tendencies, 188

MacGregor, M. W., 69, 71
Macmurray, J., xxv, 8, 112, 114, 148, 151, 159
Marcuse, H., 212
mature theory, 58. *See also* dissociative identity disorder (DID)
McDougall, 53
Memento, the film, 106. *See also* Inception, the film; moral defence; Shutter Island, the film
alter "Sammy Jankis", 108
anterograde amnesia, 107
disillusion in, 115
dreams as depictions of self states in internal world, 109
forgetting to expiate guilt, 112

Freudian theory in, 110
hysteria as defence, 109
hysteria to understand
 psychopathology, 108
hysterical amnesia, 108, 109
moral defence to provide defence
 against internalised bad
 objects, 110
paranoid-schizoid position,
 108–109
projecting bad objects onto others,
 109
two narrative threads, 106, 107
wish-fulfilling aspects of dreams,
 109
memory based projection, 105
memory excision, 112
mental disorder classification, 32
metapsychological terms, 183
Migone, P., 7
Miller, G., 7
mind
 tripartite division of, 56
 working on someone's, 103
Mitchell, S. A., xxix, 7, 24, 66, 133,
 147, 148, 175
 endopsychic structure model, 149,
  167–168
 good object in Fairbairn's theory, 154
 post-1943 endopsychic model
  rejection, 150
 view of Fairbairn's theory, 148
model of endopsychic structure, 121
moral defence, 15–16, 97, 98, 102,
 116–117. *See also* Inception,
 the film; Memento, the film;
 Shutter Island, the film
 guilt as defence against release of
  bad objects, 98
 guilt as resistance in
  psychotherapy, 99
 paranoid-schizoid position, 102
 preconscious ideal self, 98
 psychopathological defences, 98
 unable to recognise shortcomings,
  102

moral defence, failures of, 97. *See also*
 Inception, the film; Memento,
 the film; moral defence;
 Shutter Island, the film
 as defence, 109, 110
 guilt as main dynamic, 112
 ideal object, 111
 narcissism, 111
 significant others, 111
 unconditional badness, 111
 unrealistic responses to
  disillusionment, 112
multiple personality disorder (MPD),
 xxvii–xxviii, 44, 51, 210.
 See also dissociative identity
 disorder (DID)
 perspective on, 68–71
multiple personality, Fairbairn's
 thinking about, 52–53

narcissism, 63, 111, 112–113. *See also*
 moral defence
neuroses, 169, 174
Nietzsche, F., xvi
Nolan, 99, 106

object relations, 61, 83
 model, 170
 theory, xxix, 7, 24, 114
object relations approach, 25. *See also*
 moral defence
 ego-ideal, 113
 narcissism, 112–113
 object relations theory, 114
 punitive super-ego, 113
 to puzzle films, 120–125
 schizoid split as emotional
  disorder, 114
object relationship, 63, 121, 200–202
 acceptable, 173
 without affect, 183
 characteristic of four techniques, 37
 development of, 27, 32
 Oedipus situation, 200–201
 Panksepp's diagram, 203
 representation of, 42

obsessional psychopathological defence, 98
Occurrence at Owl Creek Bridge, An, 125, 127. *See also* puzzle films
Oedipus Complex, 11
Oedipus situation, 11–12, 66, 200–201
Ogden, T., 5, 90, 121, 158
Origins of Love and Hate, The (OLH), 3
oscillating transferences, 75
over-and under-symbolisation in cinema, 129. *See also* puzzle films
    aesthetics and ugliness, 131–132
    artistic activity, 130
    id-structure, 130
    principle of optimal synthesis, 130
    sublimation, 131

Padel, J., 5, 12, 31, 63, 68, 83, 153, 160, 171, 179
    two-way process in Padel's model, 65
Palmer, S., 156
Panksepp, J., 193, 194, 202, 211
    diagram, 203
paranoid psychopathological defences, 98
paranoid-schizoid position, 102, 108–109
paternal seduction, 79
personality clusters, 69. *See also* dissociative identity disorder (DID)
personality, problems of, 196
personification, 56–57
phantasy, 59
phenomenon of Rudyman, 211–212
phenomenon of splits, 211–212
phobic psychopathological defence, 98
Pontalis, J. B., 13, 123–124, 136, 171–172
potential powers, theory of, 152
preconscious, 66
    ideal self, 98
primal emotions, 194, 195
primary-process activity, 204
principle of optimal synthesis, 130

progressive slowing of time in dreamtime, 104
projecting bad objects onto others, 109
projection based on memory, 105
psychic change in Fairbairn's model, 175
psychic death, 85
psychic growth, 73
psychoanalysis, xxix
psychoanalytic approach to dreams, 123
psychoanalytic theory, 132
psychoanalytic thinking, 132
psychopathological defences, 98
psychopathology, hysteria to understand, 108
psychotherapeutic approach to act out his delusional role, 100
psychotherapy, guilt as resistance in, 99
punitive super-ego, 113
puzzle films, 119, 142–143
    challenges to Freud's theory, 133
    dissociation, 126, 133
    distortions in time, 134–138
    "embodied affect" in film theory, 143
    examples, 125–128
    Fairbairn and Glover, 133–134
    Jacket, The, 126, 127, 138–142
    mechanism of, 126
    object relations approach to film, 120–125
    Occurrence at Owl Creek Bridge, An, 125, 127
    over-and under-symbolisation in cinema, 129–132
    perspectives in, 128
    psychoanalytic theory, 132
    resolution, 126
    restituitive phantasy, 126
    "state of affairs" approach, 143
    structure of stories depicted, 128–129
    time travel, 128
    trauma, 132
    war neurosis, 133

Rank, O., 5
Rayner, E., 31
reactive tendencies, 188, 189
Read, H., 107, 108, 123, 129, 148
re-enactment of life, 76
Repeated Interactions Generalised (RIGs), 173
repetition compulsion, 15, 110
repression, 52, 53–55, 161–162. *See also* dissociative identity disorder (DID)
repressive desublimation, 212
resolution, 126
restituitive phantasy, 126
Rickman, J., 132
Rivers, W. H. R., 53, 133
Robbins, M., 3
Rubens, R. L., 66, 68, 83, 175, 184, 186, 191
Rudnytsky, P. L., 6
  environment mother, 18–19
Rutherford, A., 143

Scharff, D. E., xxix, 7, 10, 16, 26, 38, 68, 131, 134, 135, 160, 166, 167, 184
schizoid. *See also* dissociative identity disorder (DID)
  breakdown, 109
  factors, 58–59
  position, 30, 58
  split as emotional disorder, 114
  states, 28
Scorsese, 97
secondary-process activity, 204
self and society, 151–153
self-object states, 169
self states, 169
  dreams, 60–61
separation anxiety, 12–14, 87–88
sexual abuse possibility, 78
Shutter Island, the film, 99. *See also* Inception, the film; Memento, the film; moral defence
  alter ego, 100
  disillusion in, 115

ideal object in, 111
imagery of death camp in, 112
memory excision, 112
projection of internalised libidinal bad object, 101
psychotherapeutic approach to act out delusional role, 100
traumatic experiences, 100
unrepressed internalised bad objects, 100
significant others, 111
Skolnick, N. J., 6, 155, 167
Solms, M., 193, 202, 204, 211
space and time, 105–106
Sperling, O. E., 211
splitting, 195–195
  of ego and object, 44
  of ego, 62, 69, 195
  vertical, 91
Starfield, P., 107
"state of affairs" approach, 143. *See also* puzzle films
Steele, K., 124, 134, 135
Steiner, R, 26, 59, 60, 120
Stout, G. F., 189
structural model, Freud's, 60, 61
structural theory, 7
structure generating processes, 68
subconscious dream space sharing, 103, 104–105
sublimation, 131
Summers, F., 7
superego, 55–56, 174
  nuclei, 28
Sutherland, J. D., xxvi, 3, 7, 156, 160, 187
  Fairbairn's Freudian views on aggression, 7–8
Suttie, I.D., xxv, xxvii, 3, 6, 114, 148, 151
Suttie's influence on object relations theory, 3, 21
  aggression, 10–11
  approaches to theory and therapy, 19–21
  Bowlby and, 8
  death instinct, 14–15

ego-ideal, 16
environment mother, 18–19
example, 5–6
and Fairbairn, 6–9
lack of reference to Suttie, 7
libido theory, 9–10
moral defence, 15–16
object relations theory, 7
Oedipus situation, 11–12
separation anxiety, 12–14
social interpretation upon Freudian conceptions, 14
structural theory, 7
transitional techniques, 9, 13, 17–18
Swift, J., 147
symbolisation and cinema, 123, 129–132
dramatic narrative on film, 124
phantasy and desire, 123–124
psychoanalytic approach to dreams, 123
Symington, N., xv
synthesis, principle of optimal, 130

theory of art, 123
theory of dreams, 60
theory of ego-nuclei, 209
theory of erogenous zones, 197, 199
time travel, 128
Tolmacz, R., 6
topographical theory, 65, 67
transference-countertransference of externalised internal object relations, 73
transferences, oscillating, 75
transitional stage in Fairbairn's theory, 32
transitional techniques, 9, 13, 17–18

trauma, 132, 137–138
memory suppression, 108
trauma-induced vertical splitting.
See also dissociative identity disorder (DID)
and duplication of endopsychic structure, 71
of dynamic structures, 70
traumatic experiences, 100
tripartite division of mind, 56

unconditional badness, 111
unconscious phantasy, 120–121, 156.
See also Fairbairn's psychology of dynamic structure
ego-ideal, 160
Fairbairn internalization, 159
and inner reality, 26
internalisation of unsatisfying object, 158–159
internal objects, 157
Susan Isaacs's paper on, 157
University of Edinburgh Library (UEL), 4
unrealistic responses to disillusionment, 112
unrepressed internalised bad objects, 100

vertical split, 91

Wallerstein, R. S., 6
Walsh, M. N., 25
war neurosis, 133
Winnicott, D. W., 114, 147, 154, 168, 209
wish-fulfilling aspects of dreams, 109

Žižek, S., xxiii